Universal Politics

Universal Politics

ILAN KAPOOR AND ZAHI ZALLOUA

OXFORD
UNIVERSITY PRESS

Oxford University Press is a department of the University of Oxford. It furthers
the University's objective of excellence in research, scholarship, and education
by publishing worldwide. Oxford is a registered trade mark of Oxford University
Press in the UK and certain other countries.

Published in the United States of America by Oxford University Press
198 Madison Avenue, New York, NY 10016, United States of America.

© Oxford University Press 2022

Library of Congress Control Number: 2021941276
ISBN 978–0–19–760761–9

DOI: 10.1093/oso/9780197607619.001.0001

1 3 5 7 9 8 6 4 2

Printed by Integrated Books International, United States of America

To Kent and Nicole

Contents

Acknowledgments

Our thanks to the two anonymous reviewers for their helpful comments and questions. We'd also like to thank Angela Chnapko and the Oxford University Press team.

Ilan Kapoor. Immense gratitude to my dear friends for their always warm and invaluable camaraderie: Michael Bach, Nigel Barriffe, Anne-Marie Cwikowski, Leesa Fawcett, Honor Ford-Smith, Liette Gilbert, Shubhra Gururani, Sherdil Hussain, Kajri Jain, Zamil Janmohamed, Alok Johri, Mohamed Khaki, Prabha Khosla, Stefan Kipfer, Jennifer and Kevin Knelman, Terry Maccagno, Patricia Messica, Radhika Mongia, Justin Podur, Usha Rangan, Nicky Short, Vasanthi Srinivasan, Aparna Sundar, Gert ter Voorde, Cyril Thivollet, Geeta Uppal, Karen Wirsig, Paul Yee, and Anna Zalik. I owe to my family so very much: Kent, Anish, Roy, Michele, Sophie, Dev, Alba, Ben, Ishan, and Habiba. A special shout-out to Jodi and Charlie and kids.

Zahi Zalloua. I'm grateful to my brother Mounir for his humor and kindness. For the many fruitful exchanges that have informed my reflections in this book, I want to thank Jake Blevins, Clint Burnham, Jeffrey Di Leo, Peter Hitchcock, Sophia McClennen, Brian O'Keeffe, Paul Allen Miller, Russell Sbriglia, and Robert Tally. At Whitman College, my work has also benefited from rich exchanges with my colleagues. I wish to thank, in particular, Shampa Biswas, Matt Bost, Chetna Chopra, Tarik Elseewi, Gaurav Majumdar, Lydia McDermott, Suzanne Morrissey, Jason Pribilsky, and Lisa Uddin. Vlad Voinich provided crucial research assistance in the early stages of the project. One event at Whitman, in particular, left its mark on this book. In the fall of 2020, I participated in a Gender Studies Research Roundtable on the theme "Decolonizing Activism," organized and chaired by Nicole Simek, where I presented a paper titled "Decolonizing #MeToo." To Nicole, I owe my greatest thanks; her support transcends the realm of the possible. This project was funded in part by a Louis B. Perry Summer Research Grant.

1

Universal Politics

This book claims that there is a negativity at the core of all social articulations that provides the basis for a universal politics. Drawing principally on the work of Slavoj Žižek, our book suggests that the social, as much as the subject, is punctured by an impossibility—an incompletion—which rather than serving as a barrier to politics, lays a foundation for shared struggle. We thus argue for a *negative* universality, rooted not in a positive element (e.g., identity-based politics) but a discordant one, so that under our current global capitalist system, solidarity is to be forged on the basis of social antagonism (i.e., shared experiences of exploitation and marginalization). Such a conception of shared struggle, we believe, avoids the trap of both a neocolonial universalism (e.g., the rights of white men parading as universal rights) and the narrow particularism of identity-based politics. Most importantly, it foregrounds the struggles of the systematically dispossessed and excluded (the permanently unemployed, migrants, refugees, sweatshop laborers, etc.), who stand as symptom of our global capitalist order.

Our book not only explains and illustrates (with the help of case studies) what is meant by "universal politics," but also compares it to other conceptions and critiques of the universal. Accordingly, the present chapter focuses on both explicating it and outlining why there is a pressing need for it today. Chapter 2 compares and contrasts it with four competing contemporary versions of universalism—conservative, liberal, postcolonial, and Marxist. Chapter 3 brings it into dialogue with present-day critics of universalism—those who advocate instead for a decentralized politics (postmodernists, post-Marxists, queer theorists, decolonial pluriversalists, and new materialists). Chapter 4 focuses on what it might look like in the context of such key global sites of struggle as climate change, the refugee crisis, Black Lives Matter, #MeToo, political Islam, the Bolivian state under Morales, the European Union, and Covid-19. The latter case studies are complemented by two others—the Palestinian question and workers' struggles—which serve as important backdrop for chapters 2 and 3. Finally, the conclusion considers

Universal Politics. Ilan Kapoor and Zahi Zalloua, Oxford University Press. © Oxford University Press 2022.
DOI: 10.1093/oso/9780197607619.003.0001

the conditions of (im)possibility for a universal politics—its key political ingredients, but also its gaps, limitations, and failures.

Why a Universal Politics?

Now more than ever, a universal politics is sorely needed and lacking. This is because capitalism appears unstoppable today, spanning every last corner of the globe and integrating everything into its orbit—from animals, people, and plants to ideas, genes, and lifestyles. And the problem, as we will summarize in what follows, is that while global capitalism has been highly successful in accumulating wealth, it has left havoc in its wake—rising inequality, geographic disparity, and environmental devastation: the latter are not simply its minor inconveniences, to be addressed after the fact, but its very hallmark, now threatening human survival, if not capitalist accumulation itself. Added to such troubles, moreover, is that there are diminishing avenues for political contestation. This is the consequence of "postpolitics," whereby state and multilateral institutions alike resort to depoliticized administration, increasingly foreclosing the moment of the political. Thus, the universal politics that we propose is an attempt at countering both the globalization of capital and its accompanying postpolitical accoutrements.

The Debris of Global Capitalism

The basic problem with global capitalism is that inequality is written into it, so that wealth accumulation by the few is premised on the exploitation and immiseration of the many. As Marx wrote in *Capital*, "Accumulation of wealth at one pole" is "at the same time accumulation of misery, agony of toil slavery, ignorance, brutality, mental degradation, at the opposite pole" (1887, 451). This is because of the constitutive inequality of access to property under capitalism, which creates a hierarchical class structure between owners of the means of production (the elite few) and wage-labor (the exploited many). Such exploitation, it must be noted, is the result not of a low wage per se, but the commodification of labor, which ensures the extraction of surplus that enables capital accumulation. Hence the system is exploitative even if labor is "well remunerated" (as it sometimes is today): injustice is the result of the inequality required to sustain the system.

Such injustice is perhaps no more visible these days than in the widespread reliance on sweatshop labor and new forms of slavery: ill-treated sweatshop workers (mostly women, children, and migrants) across Asia, Latin America, and the Caribbean; low-paid, racialized migrant labor in the farming sector in Europe, Canada, and the United States; immigrant workers in the oil-rich states of the Middle East, deprived of basic human rights and freedoms; forced labor in mining and resource extraction in Central Africa (especially Congo); debt/bonded labor in South Asia; and human trafficking and child slavery across Europe, the Middle East, and Asia (involving, for example, forced marriage, begging, prostitution, and domestic servitude). There is also the increasing trend toward the automation of work, which enables capital to do away with such inconveniences as pay rises or unions (because, as they say, robots "don't talk back!"); and the move toward casualization of work (underemployment, insecure and part-time work), allowing corporations to exploit labor through flexibilization. We are reaching a point, in fact, where sweatshops and precarious work are themselves becoming a "privilege," with millions of people no longer able to be absorbed by the global capitalist market. As Žižek puts it, "The coming global economy tends towards a state in which 20% of the workforce can do all the necessary jobs, so that 80% of the people are basically irrelevant and of no use, potentially unemployed" (2018b, 14). The overall result, though, is social inequality on an unprecedented global scale—between those few who profit from such inequality (the 1 percent) and those who succumb to it (the 99 percent), and, increasingly, between those the market includes and those it excludes.

David Harvey (2003) has brought our attention precisely to such forced exclusion during our neoliberal times: he calls "accumulation by dispossession" the process by which the commons has been deregulated and privatized, resulting in the forceful eviction and deprivation of the subaltern (the landless, small farmers, indigenous communities, the urban poor, etc.). Facilitated if not encouraged by the state, accumulation by dispossession implies the conversion of communal/ancestral/public rights into exclusive private property rights, engendering the privatization of public utilities (water, transportation), social welfare (housing, education, healthcare, pensions), public institutions (universities, prisons), biodiversity (e.g., the pillaging of biogenetic materials by pharmaceuticals), and even warfare (e.g., the use of private security firms in combat). In China, for example, the closure and the privatization of state enterprises have created a huge pool of unemployed workers, now deprived of welfare and pensions (Harvey 2005, 155–56).

The enclosure of the natural commons (water, land, forests) as a result of such privatization and commoditization is particularly noteworthy. In many countries (e.g., Mexico, India, Brazil), it has entailed the eviction and displacement of millions of peasants and indigenous communities from communal or ancestral lands, creating a sizable class of pauperized and landless people, as well as notable rebellion (e.g., the Zapatistas in Chiapas, the Naxalites in eastern India, the Kayapo in the Brazilian Amazon). In India, state-led hydroelectric dam construction has displaced some thirty million people since the country's independence, submerging vast arable lands and destroying precious biodiversity (see Whitehead 2010). For the mostly indigenous communities displaced, such dam construction has also meant the devastation of their sociocultural livelihoods and institutions.

That such inequality (and dispossession) is constitutive of capitalism is evidenced by historical data. Thomas Piketty's book *Capital* (2014) documents how inequality has developed over the last two centuries. While not a Marxist, he is highly critical of the argument that the market distributes wealth globally, arguing that capital has consistently produced social inequality. He shows how inequalities of income and wealth steadily increased from the late 1700s to the 1930s, with slow overall declines after the First World War, but increases again after the mid-1970s. In the United States, for example, inequality has "exploded" since the 1980s, with the "upper decile's share increas[ing] from 30–35% of national income in the 1970s to 45–50% in the 2000s—an increase of 15 points of national income" (2014, 294).

Now it is true that extreme poverty worldwide has fallen of late, with millions joining the ranks of the middle class during the last fifty years (especially in China and India); but this has not prevented income inequalities from growing sharply. For example, the 2010–2015 Palma ratio (measuring the difference between the top and bottom income brackets) reveals a growing divide between the richest and poorest in almost all countries of the global South, with South Africa, Haiti, and Central African Republic leading the pack (Barr 2017; Davies and Shorrocks 2018; Kanbur 2019). This is also why, today, China, India, and Brazil can figure among the top ten global economies yet still rank comparatively low in the United Nations Development Programme Human Development Index (90th, 131st, and 79th, respectively, among 188 countries). All three countries have witnessed rapid economic growth in recent years (averaging over 7 percent annually in China between

2012 and 2016, for example), yet Brazil places among the highest globally in terms of income inequality, China among the highest in terms of rural poverty, and India among the highest in terms of infant mortality (UNDP 2016, 199–200, 207–8; Tobin 2011; Yang and Liu 2020). The same is true of such countries as Senegal and Rwanda: although they have stood out as some of the world's fastest-growing economies in the last decade, both countries remain among the most unequal in sub-Saharan Africa, with almost half of their citizens facing shortages of food, clean water, medicine, and health services (Nossiter 2013; Sindayigaya 2015; WID 2019).

Of particular note since the 1990s has been spectacular wealth accumulation in the hands of the few. The emergence of billionaires, multimillionaires, and a highly remunerated corporate bourgeoisie (earning fat-cat salaries, bonuses, and stock options) stands alongside the growing underclass referred to earlier (and to which we will later refer as the "part of no-part"), made up of sweatshop labor, unemployed youth, rural subalterns, the precariat, urban and suburban slum-dwellers, and the like. Piketty points out that, in 1987, there were 140 billionaires on the planet, and in 2013, 1,400 (2014, 433). Currently, the world's richest 1 percent holds as much wealth as the rest of the world combined, with the richest twenty-six people owning as much wealth as the poorest half of the globe (BBC 2016b; Elliott 2019).

Such wealth accumulation by the rich is in large part due to the recent financialization of global markets: it is rapidly rising income inequalities that have allowed global financial elites to use their liquidity to make drastically more "money from money," leaving the liquidity-strapped "99 percent" of the world significantly worse off (Storm 2018). The problem with financialization is that it generates massive wealth/profits without necessarily being reinvested into production. No wonder the global economy has been unable to absorb labor: lack of investment, coupled with state neoliberalization of the economy (including union busting, wage cutbacks, and corporate tax reductions), has simultaneously spelled unemployment/underemployment/dispossession and super-wealth creation. In this sense, not only does capitalism engender socioeconomic inequalities, but the latter themselves become its driving forces.

But in addition to generating inequality, capitalist globalization has generated unevenness. As dependency theory and world-systems analysis have now well established (Frank 1967; Amin 1976; Cardoso and Faletto 1979; Wallerstein 2004), starting around the sixteenth century, the deepening international division of labor produced a world economic system in which "core" (mostly Western) countries have dominated "peripheral" ones (mostly in the Third World). Over time, this system has become more geographically differentiated, with the emergence of "semi-peripheral" countries (e.g., the decline of Portugal and Spain at the turn of the twentieth century, the rise of South Korea, China, Brazil, South Africa, or Saudi Arabia today), as well as "global" cities and hinterlands (i.e., third worlds in the global North and first worlds in the global South).

Of late, this geographic inequality has been increasing. The world's poorest countries' GDPs per capita in 2010 (averaging about $252 each) was less than half of what it was in 1900 (around $545 each). Between 1960 and 2010, the GDP per capita gap between the richest and poorest countries increased by 252 percent (i.e., inequality almost tripled during this period). The same trend emerges regionally: between 1960 and 2010, inequality between the United States and Latin America grew by 206 percent (again, as measured by GDP per capita), with the corresponding figures comparing the United States to the Middle East / North Africa region, sub-Saharan Africa, and South Asia standing at 155 percent, 207 percent, and 196 percent, respectively (Hickel 2017, 2214, 2217; see also Piketty 2014). It is of course this spatial inequality that is at the heart of such contemporary problems as the refugee and immigration crises (e.g., in Europe, the United States, Turkey, Jordan, Uganda), with poverty and dispossession (as well as conflict) acting as push factors, and wealth and economic opportunity as pull factors (see chapter 4).

What such data confirms, then, is not simply that under our global capitalist system wealth and capital accumulation stand alongside poverty, but that—to recall Marx's words already quoted—impoverishment is integral to wealth creation. This explains why poverty has persisted even as market economies have continued to "develop," and why, as evidenced in the preceding discussion, rapid economic growth has resulted not in less but in more inequality across the globe.

To such social and spatial inequality, finally, we must add environmental destruction—another hallmark of global capitalism. Until relatively recently, humans assumed (wrongly, in retrospect) that they could exploit nature without consequence, that life, freedom, and wealth were made possible by the dependability and reliability of nature. But two related developments have put paid to this view. The first is the gradual realization that the degradation of the "natural" environment is almost always accompanied by social strife, negatively affecting especially the most marginalized: dispossession and the loss of lifeworlds of poor, racialized, and indigenous communities around the world resulting from desertification, deforestation, land deg-radation, overfishing, or water and air pollution; threats to island nations and coastal regions as a result of climate change; the rising tide of climate refugees—all are evidence of the inevitable dialectical relationship between humans and nature. And second is the onset of global warming, which per-haps more than any other environmental disaster to date has made the global environmental crisis a palpable one for *all* (not just the most socially mar-ginalized). Not only are life, freedom, and wealth increasingly threatened, but many of us (climate change deniers notwithstanding) appear to have woken up to the fact that "nature" is a socio-historical category, as a result of which we, humans, must confront the results of our own destructive ac-tivities: "The lesson of global warming is that the freedom of humankind is possible only against the background of a stable environment" (Žižek 2018b, 19, 333). The climate crisis is thus not a crisis of morals and values, but a structural one requiring systemic change. Addressing our generalized eco-logical crisis means reconceptualizing nothing less than our global neolib-eral capitalist order (see Klein 2014). Žižek constantly identifies the climate crisis as one of the four antagonisms that are unanswerable by today's global capitalism: "The looming threat of ecological catastrophe; the inappropri-ateness of private property for so-called intellectual property; the socio-ethical implications of new techno-scientific developments, especially in biogenetics; and last, but not least, new forms of social apartheid—new walls and slums" (2009e, 53). Giving critical attention to ecological catastrophe without simultaneously addressing the economic antagonism that produces the included and the excluded can never yield a permanent and viable solu-tion. Unless we confront the exploitive logic of global capitalism, "ecology turns into a problem of sustainable development" (2016d, 105), a problem that only needs to be managed rather than solved.

The monumental problem is that the revolutionary system that is capi-talism seeks to expand relentlessly by turning even critical crisis into market opportunity. Witness, for instance, such examples of green capitalism as "clean" coal, carbon trading, biodiversity offsetting, green consumerism, or "carbon-sucking" trees, all of which are attempts at transforming the eco-logical limits of the system into a source of profit and economic power. Žižek points out, in this connection, that "a capitalist who dedicates him-self unconditionally to the capitalist drive is effectively ready to put every-thing, including the survival of humanity, at stake, not for any 'pathological' gain or goal, but simply for the sake of the reproduction of the system as an end-in-itself" (2010b, 335). As the quip goes, even when jumping off a cliff, the capitalist will bet on who falls to their death first! Thus, responding to such unceasing quest for accumulation and growth, Fredric Jameson famously muses that it is "easier to imagine the end of the world than it is to imagine the end of capitalism" (2003, 76).

So this is why a universal politics is so wanting today: to counter the environmental devastation, and the social and geographic inequalities, wrought by global capitalism; to rethink and rework our global economic system, founded on unrelenting accumulation at any cost; to reinvigorate a commitment to the idea of the commons; and to address the accompanying social apartheid that separates those on the inside from the outside, with the former afforded human rights, welfare, and social and environmental security, and the latter condemned to bare life (although not without resistance, as we shall see later).

Postpolitics

Postpolitics refers to a situation in which "the political—understood as the space of contestation and agonistic engagement—is increasingly colonised by . . . technocratic mechanisms and consensual procedures" that operate within the unquestioned framework of market economics (Wilson and Swyngedouw 2014, 6; see also Žižek 1999, 198–205; Rancière 1999).[1] Broadly speaking, if the world today can be divided into two main camps—authoritarian capitalist (Singapore, China, Vietnam, Russia, Saudi Arabia, Iran, etc.) and capitalist liberal democratic (much of the rest of the global North and South)—then postpolitics is the political setup common to both, which is to say that postpolitics is the contemporary political arrangement of global capitalism. In both camps, socioenvironmental contradictions (inequalities, environmental crisis) are reduced to technocratic and policy problems. Governance is increasingly depoliticized so as not to threaten the smooth flow of capital accumulation and mobility.

In the authoritarian camp, such depoliticization is flagrant: disagreement and protest tend to be quashed, with the state (Communist Party, secret service, police, army, state-organized vigilante groups) often creating a climate of fear and self-censorship. In today's China, for example, it is estimated that thousands of peasant revolts (against corruption, rural poverty) and ethnic rebellions (in Tibet, Inner Mongolia, Xinjian Uyghur Region) are suppressed every year by the state (Platt 2012; Roberts 2020). In Russia, democratic elections happen regularly, but in an atmosphere of press censorship and political intimidation that benefits the Putin regime and its allies. Instead, in China as much as Russia, people sublimate (and are encouraged to sublimate) their desires in the realm of the economy, with the state keeping an overall firm grip (through crony capitalism) but favoring market-friendly behavior (consumerism, entrepreneurialism, corporate investment).

For their part, liberal democracies can be characterized as comparatively more tolerant of dissent, but in increasingly controlled ways. Party politics tend to be "competitive" only in name, with party platforms for the most part indistinguishable, focusing less on substantive issues than on leaders, personalities, soundbites, and media-friendly messaging. Elections have, in this sense, become routinized, marketized, spectacularized: voting is just another consumerist "choice" based on small differences and charismatic appeal. Postpolitics thus progressively forecloses the space of the political, replacing party competition with consensus-based politics, issue-oriented debate with charismatic leadership, and ideological divide with political agreement (especially in relation to the market).

Postpolitics thus ends up reducing the political to "enlightened" policy-making. Socioeconomic decisions are reached through "expert" knowledge and administration, relying on the likes of technocrats, economists, bankers, business executives, corporate lawyers, scientists, pollsters, NGO leaders, social media gurus, and celebrities, who putatively negotiate diverse interests and are able to capture and express popular consensus—to perfect what, more or less, already *is*. The point is not to question the status quo too much, but to make practical and workable policy. Often, such depoliticized decision-making resorts to a moralizing politics—a notable feature of our neoliberal times—as a result of which it is individuals and businesses that are responsibilized: corporate philanthropy and celebrity charity are championed over the welfare state, personalized moral injunctions (such as checking your privilege) substitute for any call to transform the existing structures of privilege and oppression, ethical consumerism and corporate social and environmental responsibility are preferred to state regulation of industry, and NGO and nonprofit do-gooding supplants government programs.

The overwhelming consensus here is on neoliberal capitalism, which is generally accepted as objective fact, providing the primary horizon of meaning. This means that the real object of postpolitics is the depoliticization of the economy, which thereby tends to be "increasingly insulated from even the most limited forms of democratic accountability" (Wilson and Swyngedouw 2014, 9), making a Marxist critique of political economy a relic of the past. When it comes to market capitalism, then, the neoliberal state has gradually relinquished its authority in favor of moral suasion, becoming more of a facilitator than a regulator (Shamir 2008, 6). Its proper role now is to create business-friendly environments, tax-free havens, private-public partnerships, or conformity to World Trade Organization agreements. It duly implements "sound" austerity measures and corporate tax cuts, the latter of which lead to the massive wealth accumulation by the 1 percent discussed earlier. More often than not, political leaders slavishly follow the dictates of international financial institutions and banks (World Bank, International Monetary Fund, European Central Bank, etc.), with even the likes of Greece's Syriza government caving to the pressures of structural adjustment (see chapter 4).

Where state power *has* increased of late is in the domains of security and immigration. Yet these, too, accord with postpolitics, the one enabling greater surveillance of the population (often under the guise of "antiterrorism"), the other allowing stricter control over the movement of people and labor. As Žižek points out (2008c, 102), increasingly we have greater mobility of capital but declining movement of people, with states constructing physical and politico-legal barriers to better and more strictly regulate migration (e.g., "fortress Europe," walls between Israel and Palestine and between the United States and Mexico, gated communities, slum cities). The human dimension of postpolitical globalization is thus greater immobility.

Culture is the one area in which "difference" is tolerated in today's liberal democratic landscape: it is the realm in which the main struggles for recognition have happened during the last few decades, bringing notable victories for gender, LGBT+, disability, and antiracism movements. Yet even these are consistent with the postpolitical—as long as capitalist political economy is generally left unthreatened, cultural politics can proceed, it seems. In fact, corporate capitalism now banks on the proliferation of identities and lifestyles, seeing in them yet another opportunity for commodification ("ethnic chic," gay fashion, "chick lit," Prozac, etc.). Today, even protest movements are corporatized, with cosmetic firms targeting the Women's March, MTV creating a music award for "Most Memorable #OWS (Occupy Wall Street) Performance," and corporate giants like Apple, IBM, Nike, and GE denouncing anti-trans public restroom regulations. That "progressive"

DOMESTICATING IDENTITY POLITICS
→ DEPOLITIZATION

↗ POPULISM
↗ =

identity-based struggles are co-opted and neutered by the corporate sector in this way is a sure sign of their depoliticization—not only do they pose no threat to the system, but they become fodder for new markets.

But of late, such postpolitics appears to be transforming. Liberal democracies around the world have witnessed notable public dissatisfaction and apathy with democratic institutions. The most obvious sign is lower voter turnout at elections, witnessed as much in the United States and Britain as in South Africa, India, and Argentina. As underlined earlier, the competitive party system, as well as identity politics, appears to be stalling if not failing. The same is true of the state, increasingly subjected to laissez-faire economic policymaking and the demands of the corporate sector, all the while growing its presence on questions of security, surveillance, and control. More and more, it seems, our political and economic institutions are beset with scandals (e.g., corruption, money laundering, surveillance overreach), with political leaders out of touch and economic elites untouchable. Outbursts of "fundamentalist" violence are commonplace, often a desperate response to the threats that capitalist globalization wreaks on local cultures and traditions. The overall result is the increasing lack of accountability and responsiveness of our mainstream liberal democratic institutions. Hence the current draw of the political alternative represented by (neo)populist leaders and movements.

Indeed, the recent rise of such political figures as Trump, Orbán, Bolsonaro, Chávez, Duterte, Erdoğan, and Modi appears as the result of the breakdown of political consensus, the rise of antiestablishment rage, mistrust of political and economic elites, and suspicion of the media (yielding to rumor-mongering and alternative and "fake" news). Populist politics— particularly of the right-wing type—is in this sense a kind of backlash or doubling down against the turbulence of our times, promising a return to traditional norms and authority. The populist leader resorts to scapegoating, demagoguery, and authoritarianism as a way of providing greater national unity, stability, and harmony.

The peculiarity of populism, though, is that it responds to real problems— social anxiety and alienation—but displaces them onto the wrong targets— the big bad bureaucrats, refugees, immigrants, terrorists, greedy bankers, foreign infiltrators, biased judges, NGOs, and so on. That is to say, it blames symptoms and individuals rather than broader social and political structures (i.e., social inequality and dispossession, the rule of corporate and political elites, cultural turbulence). It captures well the popular anger and resentment of our times but mystifies the social causes, refusing to confront them directly. For the populist, the reason for our troubles is never really the system but an outsider or intruder who corrupts it (Žižek 2006d, 555; 2008a, 264–333; see also Mouffe 2005a, 64–72). Such a contradiction will of course likely catch up with populist movements/leaders when they are unable to deliver on many of their commitments: Europe's continuing refugee crisis, Trump's relative neglect of Covid-19 and inability to fully build his wall or get Mexico to pay for it, Brazil's deteriorating environmental hazards and Covid-19 debacle, and so on, are early clues of such faltering.

But such successes and failures notwithstanding, the rise of populism today appears as a sign of the further entrenchment of postpolitics in capitalist liberal democracies—a fresh narrowing of the space of the political, a move toward greater authoritarianism. It is as if the turbulence wrought by late global capitalism demands political stability to ensure continued capital mobility and accumulation, something that populism offers seemingly more than latter-day liberalism. In a sense, authoritarian capitalism serves here as the model for the more successful, efficient, and stable political economy, so that the onset of (neo)populism is evidence of an attempt at adapting this model to the bygone liberal democratic landscape. This is not to say that we are all headed toward authoritarian capitalism but that the liberal democratic consensus is floundering, and in this vacuum, authoritarian capitalism provides one possible path forward, implying a consolidation of the postpolitical.

Thus, the "New World Order that is emerging is . . . no longer the Fukuyamist one of global liberal democracy, but that of the peaceful coexistence of different politico-theological ways of life—coexistence, of course, in the context of the smooth functioning of global capitalism" (Žižek 2018b, 53). Here, every country/region will be able to assert its nationalist autonomy ("America first," "Turkey first," "China first," "South Africa first," "Brazil first," etc.), each defending its own particular cultural values, but with a political arrangement (on the authoritarian capitalist-capitalist liberal democratic continuum) that accords well with the advance of global capitalism.

Yet if the turbulence of our times delivers increasingly postpolitical forms of governance, this same turbulence becomes an opportunity for the Left to rethink and rework politics, to find ways of rejuvenating and expanding spaces for disagreement and contestation on a broad and universalizing scale. Indeed, Žižek repeatedly evokes Walter Benjamin's observation that "every fascism is a sign of failed revolution" (2012d, 452). He squarely blames

IT'S NOT 'ABOUT' STRUGGLE TO THE DEATH!

MAXIMALIST UTOPIANISM

CH 2

this failure on the Left and its "palliative damage-control measures within the global capitalist framework" (2000, 321), that is, its inability or refusal to argue for and insist on egalitarian justice and economic equality. Global capitalism has successfully *imposed* its universalism, accompanied by a postpolitics that deftly forecloses the political by particularizing political claims (e.g., identity-based rights) that remain unthreatening to capital. The challenge for the Left, then, is to respond with a politics that does not just settle for making particular demands, but finds ways of universalizing these demands to counter both capitalist globalization and the retreat of the political. In his goal to awaken the Left from the postpolitical slumber, Žižek often turns to the '68 motto *Soyons réalistes, demandons l'impossible!* Against the champions of postpolitics, who prescribe reformist interventions "within the liberal-democratic horizon" (2000, 326) that amount to an ideological dream of a capitalism with a human face, Žižek juxtaposes their phantasmatic, toothless utopia with a more material, radical utopia of "demanding the impossible." Here the Left must appreciate the full force of the demand:

> First, there is "demanding the impossible" in the sense of bombarding the existing system with demands that it cannot meet: open borders, better healthcare, higher wages. . . . Here we are today, in the midst of a hysterical provocation of our masters (technocratic experts). This provocation has to be followed by a key step further: not demanding the impossible from the system but demanding the "impossible" changes of the system itself. (2018a)

A universal politics worthy of its name must demand the impossible changes of global capitalism itself. Let us turn our attention, then, to how such a universal politics can be constructed, that is, to retrieving precisely the agonistic universal dimension that is proper to politics.

Universal Politics

We live in times when the universalist project that is capitalist globalization is matched politically by a skepticism about advancing any alternate universal project; it is squarely this contradiction that this section (and this book!) aims at addressing. Chapter 3, devoted to those who have mostly abandoned universalism in favor of more localized forms of politics, outlines the reasons for such skepticism in more detail, but for the moment let us distinguish broadly between two main forms of universalism, while also summarizing key criticisms associated with each: an abstract universalism (which parades as neutral but ends up dominating particulars) and a universalism based on commonalities (which ends up excluding particulars).

Abstract (or "objective") universalism asserts an a priori category (rooted in, say, nature, humanism, or reason) and applies it to all circumstances. This is a universalism that is indifferent to particulars, "disinterestedly" deploying an assumed or self-evident truth to all specifics ("All men are born equal," "Europeans are civilized," "Reason trumps passion," etc.). The problem, of course, is that such a view masks itself as neutral but is enunciated from a particular position. This is Marx's critique (1992, 398ff.), claiming that bourgeois abstract universalism is impossible because it is always determined by a privileged particular content (e.g., "political equality" during the early British Industrial Revolution concealed that only wealthy landowners had the right to vote). Fanon has a similar take (2008), arguing that European colonialism proclaimed universal values but practiced racial discrimination and socioeconomic exploitation in the colonies. He points out that abstract universalism amounts to, and is used to rationalize, domination of the particular, thus often being associated with (neo)colonialism, violence, and oppression. "All men are born equal" can thus be twisted to condone the exclusion of women, "Europeans are civilized" can legitimize the mistreatment of non-Europeans, and "Reason trumps passion" can countenance the repression of sexual desires or the triumph of ("rational") Western science over ("irrational") indigenous knowledges.

Today, it is liberal human rights discourse that is often seen as the embodiment of abstract universalism. Based on a rational-moral account of the requirements for human flourishing, the discourse famously promulgates universal rights and protections (equality before the law, private property rights, civil and political freedoms and protections like freedom of expression, freedom from torture, anti-discrimination laws, etc.). But again, the problem is that such a conception is a Western liberal one parading as universal: it secretly privileges, for example, individual rights over group ones; civil and political rights and protections over socioeconomic ones; private property rights in the context of patriarchy; and white male property owners over workers, racialized groups, and women. Moreover, in recent decades it has been used to justify neocolonial and military-foreign policy objectives: as is well known, the US invasion of Iraq, and takeover of its oil fields, was justified on the basis of "bringing freedom and democracy" to the country, pointing up anew the extent to which abstract universalism can serve as a facade.

In contrast, universalism-as-commonality unifies a series of particulars deemed to share common content. Universalism here is induced from a list of particular cases (e.g., monotheism as shared by Islam, Judaism, and Christianity). The problem, of course, is that the list is never complete, as (by definition) there will always be an exception that does not fit. The difference that makes the particular particular can never be fully encompassed. Universalism-as-commonality therefore necessarily functions through omission and exclusion. The feminist movement is all too aware of this limitation, since "womanhood" is neither a necessary nor a sufficient attribute for shared feminist struggle (it is always crisscrossed by questions of gender, class, racialization, sexual orientation, disability, etc.; see chapter 4).

In a similar vein, human rights discourse, rather than resorting to abstract universalism, may see it fit to find common cross-cultural characteristics to establish a universal basis for rights. But this appears a Sisyphean task: when the Universal Declaration of Human Rights declares that "all human beings are born free and equal in dignity and rights," it must contend with, say, caste-based Hinduism (relying on the Laws of Manu) that denies social equality, or "fundamentalist" strands of Islam and Christianity that uphold gender inequality or abhor homosexuality. What is noteworthy about this type of universalism is that its founding gesture is most often hidden, as when the United States declares universal suffrage in 1870 but denies the vote to women or Blacks, or the Ugandan state upholds equality before the law but discriminates against LGBT+ people. The exception must be disavowed for such universalism to function in practice.

Both abstract universalism and universalism-as-commonality therefore suffer from a proclivity toward ideological deception, pretending to be neutral or all-encompassing, but practiced in order to privilege and exclude. Both universalisms naturalize and dehistoricize, abstracting from the material, historical, and dynamic fields of power. Indeed, the history of universalist politics, as Marxist, feminist, and postcolonial critics alike have rightly underlined (see chapters 2 and 3), is one rife with a will to power, domination, and oppression.

A Negative Universality

But that is not the end of the story: there is an alternate conceptualization of universalism—a negative universality—that, we believe, averts these problems while enabling a universal political project. We draw on Žižek to argue that not all universals are bad, and in fact that a negative, antagonistic version of universality is oriented toward subaltern emancipation. For Žižek, the globalization of capital cannot be confronted through fragmentation and localized particularisms (which are all too easily blunted, colonized, or co-opted, as mentioned previously); it can only be challenged through a universal politics. And such a politics would not ignore the local/particular but retrieve from it an antagonistic dimension (e.g., the experience of being marginalized under postpolitical global capitalism) that then forms the basis for a shared and universalized struggle, most especially for the subaltern (the "part of no-part").

An important terminological-theoretical note here: while "universalism" and "universality" tend to be used interchangeably, strictly speaking, universalism refers to the state of being universal (i.e., universal*ism* as a consistent essence throughout the universe), while universality is the property of being universal to members of a given class. Since Žižek's notion of a negative universal refers, as we shall see later, to a contextual Real (i.e., it is not an essence, but a negativity that cuts across particulars), the latter term (universality) is the more appropriate one. It is also the term he tends to use (see Žižek 1999, 70ff.). Heretofore then, our deployment of "universality" is intended to highlight a shared deadlock, rather than a common positivity, that links a series of particulars.

Indeed, the fundamental limitation of both abstract universalism and universalism-as-commonality is that they identify the universal with a *positive* content (an a priori or particular essence), which is what ends up imperiling them. This is because, as underlined already, there is always a gap between a positively defined universalism and its particular content: for example, the moment one posits universal tolerance of belief systems, it is contested and contradicted by those belief systems that stand against tolerance: each new application of tolerance "retroactively *redefines*" the very concept of tolerance, bringing out the exclusion, gap, contradiction in the very concept (Žižek 1999, 180; McGowan 2019, 12). An essentialized notion of the universal inevitably requires a particular content that is thereby privileged and exclusionary.

The challenge is to avoid the trap of identifying universality with a
itive content, and so, drawing on Hegel (and Lacan), Žižek's proposal is
to identify it *negatively*, that is, through what is absent rather than present: "Every universality can only present itself 'as such' in a negative way"
(Žižek 2010b, 335). Since, according to Hegel (2010, 360; 1977, 138), every
identity/thought depends on that to which it stands in opposition (e.g.,
positive universalism is meaningful only in relation to an Other, i.e., particularism), contradiction is not to be seen as its limitation or weakness
but its very driving force. The crucial feature, in fact, is that this contradiction is not transcendental to, but emerges from within, the very dynamics
of thought itself: it is consciousness's immanent self-limitation that causes
it to move forward, to try to overcome its incompletion (an impossible
and never-ending task).[2] Thus, antagonism is the "internal condition of
every identity" (Žižek 1989, 6); it is ineradicable and ontological. Hence
what is universal is neither identity nor thought but the antagonism that
structures both: "The Universal 'as such' is the site of an unbearable antagonism, self-contradiction, and (the multitude of) its particular species are
ultimately nothing but so many attempts to obfuscate/reconcile/master
this antagonism" (Žižek 2012d, 782).

The Universal in the Particular

What this means is that, unlike an abstract universalism that privileges a
particular content, a negative universality empties out its particular content, since only through such negation does the universal-as-antagonism
come into view. It is by ridding itself of particularity, by facing the hindrance
that prevents it from actualization, that the abstract universal becomes what
Žižek/Hegel call "concrete universality" (Žižek 1999, 92). So paradoxically,
what makes the universal concrete in this case is not its content but its limitation (or what Žižek, following Lacan, denotes as "the Real," the stumbling
block to any attempt at closure, harmony, or stability). The actualization of
the universal occurs only when it faces its inherent or immanent contradiction: it is concretized because it is "forever prevented from acquiring a figure
that would be adequate to its notion. . . . This is why . . . the Universal genus
is always *one of its own species*: there is universality only in so far as there is a
gap, a hole, in the midst of the particular content of the universality in question" (Žižek 1999, 103).

The same is true when one zeroes in on the particular: the universal is the name of the gap (the Real) that prevents the particular from achieving its self-identity (Butler, Laclau, and Žižek 2000, 217). Here negative universality concurs with universalism-as-commonality in being grounded in the particular but differs from it in doubting and questioning rather than valorizing particular content. So once again, it is the lack/void within the particular that makes it universal. This is only to rehearse the earlier-mentioned point that every identity is always unstable, that is, at odds with itself, unable to be identical with itself, as when the "universal" rights of white male property owners inevitably bump up against the rights of women, racialized groups, workers, and so on. As Žižek states, "The Universal emerges within the Particular when some particular content starts to function as the stand-in for the absent Universal—that is to say, the universal is operative only through the split in the particular" (1999, 176).

Several important political implications follow. First, the crucial step in universalizing a particular position is subjecting it to challenge and debate, rather than glorifying or essentializing it; seeking out its weak spots, exclusions, and contradictions, rather than its proclivities toward harmony, balance, or unity. This is a point brought out well by Frantz Fanon on issues of identity and authenticity: he sees the Negritude movement,[3] for example, as a "blind alley"—a narrow "racism of defense" that is nothing but the "logical antithesis" of white European prejudice against Blacks. Instead, he defends national culture as an always "contested culture" that refuses to be fixed or stabilized, whether by Europeans or Africans themselves (1963, 163–64, 214, 212, 237). Note here that a (negative) universal politics stands pointedly against depoliticization, and in our case, against the depoliticizing tendencies of today's postpolitical capitalism, under which, as we emphasized earlier, debate and scrutiny are being replaced by consensus on questions of culture as much as economy.

Second, because negative universality is (and can only be) taken up from a particular vantage point, it is always partial, partisan, engaged (Žižek 2012d, 285). One's response to the antagonism of one's position never happens neutrally or objectively; it unfolds only by taking sides. Žižek refers to this as a "struggling universality" (2006c, 35), recalling once again Fanon's idea of a fighting or partisan universality (see Sekyi-Otu 1996, 3, 26, 104; 2019, 12).[4] Indeed, for Fanon, native intellectuals are not ones who take shelter in "mummified" tradition, but who reactivate the latter by going through a "fighting phase," thereby constructing a militant and "revolutionary literature": "A national culture . . . should therefore take its place at the very heart of the struggle for freedom. . . . National consciousness, which is not nationalism, is the only thing that will give us an international dimension" (1963, 222–24, 233, 247). Partisan (negative) universality is, in this sense, never predefined or given; it is always struggled for, incomplete, and in-the-making (see Balibar 2002, 146ff.).

The noteworthy feature of such a universality is that it is radically contingent—it can only be articulated from a particular standpoint—yet it does not fall into the postmodern trap of denying universalism or truth. Žižek avers in fact that "*universal Truth is accessible* [but] *only from a partial engaged subject position*" (2006c, 35). In part this is definitional, since any claim to the particular cannot be made without recourse to the universal. As Hegel famously notes, the master *needs* the slave-as-Other in order to be recognized as master (i.e., the very claim to masterhood is unintelligible without a shared universal language). In the same vein, Balibar (2002, 146ff.) points out that a racist anti-universalism (e.g., "Whites are superior to Blacks") must invoke a universal benchmark (the notion of what it is to be human) to enable the comparison between white and Black in the first place. Particularity needs an Other (and a shared language) to distinguish itself as unique, thus always proclaiming its particularity from a universal standpoint.

But partly, the universal truth-dimension of every particular stems from the antagonism (the Real) at its very heart. Truth emerges from both the specific configuration that makes particularity particular and the universality of the antagonism to which such particularity responds. This is to say that truth is both contingent *and* universal. Every situation may well articulate a particular truth, but the emergence of that truth arises due to the universal-as-Real that besets all situations (see Butler, Laclau, and Žižek 2000, 315).

It is worth noting in this regard that analysts such as Lois McNay (2000, 20, 126–29) and Judith Butler (1993, 202, 207; Butler, Laclau, and Žižek 2000, 12–13, 29–30) have accused Lacanians (and Žižek in particular) of elevating the Real-as-antagonism to an ahistorical category. According to them, the Real lacks social and historical specificity and can thus only be understood as external to history. But what they miss, as implied earlier, is the distinction between the Real as transcendent (standing outside history), which Lacanians oppose, and the Real as internally transcendent (standing at the limit of any given historical formation), which Lacanians endorse. This is to say that the Lacanian Real is specific to every discursive formation, marking its impossibility in distinctive ways. The Real is therefore a contextualized antagonism: it is not some unchanging substance, but is immanent to every sociohistorical order, reflecting any such order's inability to fully constitute itself. As Eisenstein and McGowan put it (2012, 69), "There are no transcendent principles that every society shares, but there is a constitutive failure that marks every society." In the same vein, Žižek declares: "What all epochs share is not some trans-epochal constant feature; it is, rather, that they are all answers to the same deadlock" (Žižek and Daly 2004, 76).

Finally, and most importantly for our purposes, it is the Real-as-antagonism at the hub of every particular that enables the possibility of shared struggle. When each particular (e.g., an identity-based movement, worker's struggle, or antiglobalization protest) discovers that the deadlock that stymies it is also the deadlock that stymies others, then their common predicament becomes the basis for political solidarity. What each particular shares is not a positive content (e.g., an identity, which can end up dividing people across class, gender, North-South, or racial lines), but an inability to complete itself (as a result of common patterns of socioeconomic marginalization, exploitation, etc.): "A particular demand . . . starts to function as a metaphoric condensation of the global [universal] opposition against Them, those in power, so that the protest is no longer just about that demand, but about the universal dimension that resonates in that particular demand. . . . What post-politics tends to prevent is precisely this metaphoric universalisation of particular demands" (Žižek 1999, 204). Žižek's words resonate here again with Fanon's, who writes that "there is no common destiny between the national cultures of Senegal and Guinea; there *is* a common destiny between the Senegalese and Guinean nations which are both dominated by the same French colonialism. . . . There will never be such a thing as black culture" (1963, 234).

Negative universality therefore avoids the trap of both a narrow or ghettoized particularism and a neocolonial universalism. It neither pretends to transcend the particular nor imposes a positive universalized norm. Rather, it works in and through the particular and the universal negatively to bring out the antagonistic element(s) in both. And while each particular responds idiosyncratically to the Real-as-antagonism, this same negativity becomes the basis for a shared horizon of meaning and struggle. Žižek explains it this way: "[The universal is about] an antagonistic struggle which, rather than taking place between particular communities, splits each community from within, so that the 'trans-cultural' link between communities is one of a shared struggle" (2010b, 53).

Politics, the Real Neighbor, and Solidarity

Politics, in this view of the world, is to be understood as an abyssal act, a kind of "short circuit" between the universal and the particular (Žižek 1999, 188). In fact, as McGowan tells us (2018, 214), without the universal as site of antagonism, "There is no politics": it is because of the gap in the social—the fact that it is always incomplete, contradictory, contested—that political struggle becomes possible. Politics here is an active response to a deadlock, a retort to the always-already fissured nature of the social. Thus, queer or gender politics happens, not because the political is "naturally" inscribed in social identity, but because the out-of-jointedness of each position necessitates an active intervention. The bar of impossibility (the universal) of a subject position (the particular) is what helps initiate and sustain politics.

Such a viewpoint stands in sharp contrast to current-day postpolitics, which, as we have seen, is an attempt at covering up social antagonism through agreement and consensus. To be sure, Rancière distinguishes between *la police*—mainstream institutions that defend and reproduce socioeconomic hierarchy—and *la politique*—an agonistic politics aimed at confronting the inegalitarian and authoritarian logic of *la police* (1999, 21–42; see also Mouffe 2005b, 9). What activates the latter for him (as for Žižek) are the contradictions wrought by social injustice, opening up a political space from which to confront *la police* with its own contingency.

Žižek supplements such an agonistic conception of (universal) politics with a notion of the "Real neighbor," which provides a model for thinking not just the political but also solidarity. In contradistinction to the common Christian injunction to "love thy neighbor," he retrieves the Jewish biblical view of the neighbor as "inert, impenetrable, enigmatic" (2010a, 140): here the Other is not unquestionably good, your *semblable*, to be cherished without reservation, but on the contrary, the embodiment of the Real, a "traumatic Thing," bearer of an impenetrable monstrousness. Ultimately, such a position reflects one's inability to relate to the intrusive excess/otherness of one's *own* enjoyment,[5] so that the fundamental antagonism lies not so much between me and you, but within me, in "my own impenetrability to myself" (Žižek 2010a, 138, 140, 162).

This means that one's neighbor, like one's own self, is opaque and mysterious, impossible to master or integrate into one's interpretive frame. Implicit here is a rejection of the notion that one can (or should) "know" and "understand" one's neighbors, thereby reducing them to sameness (i.e., to a mirror

SOLIDARITY

image of the self), which may in turn yield to essentializing or controlling them under the pretense of beneficence and care. "Loving thy neighbor" is reconceptualized here as an agonistic rather than a positive admonition: we should extend an ethico-political obligation to others precisely because they are *not* like us. But the idea is not to go too far to the opposite side either—to conceive of the neighbor as totally unknowable, beyond symbolic mediation. The latter discourse of radical alterity too easily morphs into a "clash of civilizations," lending itself to multiculturalist notions of tolerance (of the incommensurable Other), under which others are countenanced, but only as long as they are kept at a distance, apart from "us," ghettoized. No, loving my (Real) neighbors is encountering them neither as the same nor as totally different but as the traumatic Other that inheres in *both* of us. That is, one's neighbor's universality is based not on shared humanity, but in the acknowledgment of the *in*human as the condition for universality.

Political solidarity—forging political relationships with one's neighbors—thus requires learning to live, love, and struggle together with antagonism. One extends solidarity with one's neighbor by facing the inhuman core that remains a stranger to both of us, as well as the social injustice that affects us all. "This mutual recognition of limitation . . . opens up a space of sociality that is the solidarity of the vulnerable" (Žižek 2010a, 139; see also McGowan 2018, 200–201). What political subjects have in common, then, is not a positive but a negative commonality, a cut that blocks the completion of the social as much as the subject.

The notable feature of such agonistic solidarity is that it allows for the creation of political alliances without forcing sameness. Indeed, one of the main vulnerabilities of political movements and transnational networks has been the risk of stifling difference by imposing a single vision/tactic or ignoring and excluding voices (along class, gender, disability, sexual, racial, and North-South lines), particularly the voices of the most marginalized. Coalitional identity politics, for example, often stumbles not only because it becomes difficult to forge alliances with those who are different from "us" (finding common ground between women, queers, and disabled people) but also because of the neglect of differences *among* us (i.e., not all "women" or "queers" or "disabled people" are the same). Agonistic solidarity averts these problems by focusing not on positive but on negative commonality: group members share their common antagonisms without surrendering their particularities; their political unity (within and without) is forged without smothering diversity or disagreement. The challenge, of course, lies in remaining true to the spirit of such political agonism: working together while also working *through* internal debate and dissent. As Edward Said often used to repeat, "never solidarity without criticism" (1996, 31). In other words, there is no truly loving thy neighbors without a traumatic fall: such love is challenging if not grisly, requiring that you accept your neighbors—or indeed your close friends and lovers—with all their shortcomings, imperfections, and disagreements, which is to say that you face the gulf that inheres in not just them but you, too.

The Part of No-Part
(THE ABJECT, THE EXCLUDED)

The final significant feature of a negative universal politics is its commitment to, and orientation toward, the "part of no-part." This is because any positive universalism has a symptom, an element that must remain an exception for the very constitution of that universalism. And indeed, as underlined earlier, the universalism that is global capitalism entails a notable symptom/exclusion: the dispossessed and marginalized (slum dwellers, rural subalterns, refugees, indigenous communities, the homeless, the precariat, the permanently unemployed, the gendered, disabled, and racialized poor, etc.)— whom Rancière famously refers to as the "part of no-part" (2010, 6, 33; 1999, 9, 11, 14, 30).[6] They are symptomatic of capitalism's founding gesture—social and spatial inequality—and although excluded from the system, they are its ultimate support. It is their constitutive exceptionalism that makes them the measure of true universality in our global capitalist times: "One pathetically asserts (and identifies with) *the point of inherent exception/exclusion, the 'abject,' of the concrete positive order, as the only point of true universality*" (Žižek 1997a, 50).

The fact that the part of no-part belongs to the system but has no proper place in it reveals the truth—the injustice—of the system. The excluded are precisely those who must be negated for capitalism to function "normally." And it is not simply that they are the most exploited or occupy the lowest social position in the system that makes them universal, but that they have *no* place: they embody the "living contradiction—that is, [they give] body to the fundamental imbalance and inconsistency of the . . . social Whole" (Žižek 1999, 225). The truth of the system appears precisely where one assumes it wouldn't—not in the enormous wealth created by the system (that's what it would have us believe), but at its moments of abjection, exposing the inherent socioeconomic and environmental contradictions of global capitalism.

The paradoxical feature here is that the truth of global capitalism is perceived from the *partial* standpoint of the excluded / part of no-part. But this should come as no surprise, since as emphasized earlier, the truth is always and necessarily contingent, one-sided, partisan. The inequity of the system is revealed by the element that the system prevents from actualizing; that is why the excluded stand for universality. To be sure, Žižek refers to them as the "singular universal" (1999, 188, 232), denoting not just their status as singular exception in the system, but also their emancipatory potential. Because they are a gap in—an excess to—the system, they represent an irritant, if not a possible threat, to business as usual. Their out-of-jointedness and unpredictability annoys, unsettles, menaces. Moreover, because they are outcasts, when they present themselves as exemplars of the universal, they can do so credibly since, unlike all other groups, they have no stake in the system. Their exceptional particularity enables them, paradoxically, to embrace universality, standing for not exclusive but universal interests.

The political demands of the excluded are expressed most often in terms of what Balibar refers to as *égaliberté* (2014)—their unconditional claim to equality-freedom, recognized as legitimate and universal because it represents not their particular interest but the interests of all. Their call for *égaliberté* points accordingly to what is absent in the system (i.e., ignored, excluded, lacking, unsaid, unsayable) as a consequence of social domination. Thus, when Canadian indigenous groups lay a claim to equality and self-determination, for example, they are underscoring what is missing in the system (i.e., the failure of the Canadian state to live up to its land/ treaty obligations or provide indigenous communities with socioeconomic security). They are demanding not privilege but equality-freedom; if anything, they are calling out the privileges of white settlers, which stand in stark contrast to the systematic colonialism and pauperization faced by indigenous communities. Their claims are in this sense a threat to the establishment, undermining and delegitimizing it. *Egaliberté* "remains an unconditional excess, setting in motion permanent insurrection against the existing order, and can thus never be 'gentrified,' included in the existing order" (Žižek 1997a, 40). *Egaliberté*, in short, operationalizes well a negative universal politics, revealing the truth of the system from the contingent yet universal-antagonistic position of the part of no-part, while making demands that necessitate nothing less than an overhaul of this very system.

Conclusion

Drawing on Žižek, we have argued for a universal politics, which steers clear of neocolonial universalist forms that parade as neutral while advancing Western interests (e.g., the rights of Westerners as universal rights), opting instead for a universality that centers on negativity and contradiction. Here the universal is the result of shared antagonisms rather than identities: for example, workers, women, or LGBT+ people around the world may respond in unique ways to the traumatic inequalities wrought by global capitalism, but what they have in common is not their particular identities as workers, women, or queers—in fact, these are what often divide them across cultures—but precisely their shared trauma. The universal is thus not about finding a common positive element but a shared excluded element so that, under our current global capitalist system, solidarity around the world is to be forged on the basis of shared experiences of exploitation and marginalization. This means that the universal is firmly rooted in the particular, but emerges as a result of that which impedes and limits each particular (the Real), making possible a shared horizon of meaning and struggle. It also means that political solidarity is constructed both vertically and horizontally: people come together not only because they face common patterns of exclusion but also (and more importantly) because of the existential gulf that inheres in everyone—in me as much as my neighbor. The resultant politics of the Real is therefore radical and thoroughgoing—particular as much as universal, contextual as much as partisan, inside as much as outside, personal as much as political.

A negative universal politics is consequently well equipped to take on our postpolitical capitalist order. Rather than shying away from a universal political project, thereby letting the powers-that-be off the hook, it decidedly affirms the possibility of broad-based political solidarity. Its agonistic politics stands against the postpolitical capitalist tendency to cover over the Real, that is, to rationalize capitalist political economy through agreement, consensus, and, increasingly, authoritarian rule. It aims instead at exposing and struggling against the antagonisms of our times—the environmental crises and socioeconomic and spatial inequalities inherent to the system. And it identifies most with the part of no-part—those who are excluded by the system, revealing the truth about the system, but also posing a potential threat to it.

No Puppurism

It is important, in closing, to qualify the scale and scope of the universal politics implied here: while the overall objective is surely a radical rethinking and reworking of the system, this does not necessarily mean a single or complete revolutionary assault. The universal politics of the Real is anchored in the particular, after all, requiring political subjects to first face up to their own contextualized antagonisms, which may or may not form the basis of a broader coalitional politics. A successful universal politics, if it is to happen at all, will thus likely need to take place in stages, at multiple political levels (local, national, regional, transnational), and over a period of time.[7] Much stands in the way of such a process of universalization, as chapters 3 and 4 will underline, with the failure to adequately engage in agonistic politics more than a distinct possibility. To be sure, loving one's neighbors in spite of their faults—constructing solidarity despite difference—is a monumental task, even if it has been done, at least to a small degree, by the likes of the Hong Kong umbrella movement, the 2018–19 Sudanese revolution, and the burgeoning climate change movement (see chapter 4). And this is not to even speak of the "external" obstacles faced by oppositional movements in the form of state or market repression, infiltration, and co-optation.

THERE ARE MANY INTERESTING INSIGHTS HERE THAT ARE COMPATIBLE W/ PCF, ESPECIALLY AFTER THE QUALIFICATIONS MADE ON THIS VERY PAGE. BUT THE AUTHORS ARE WRONG TO THINK THAT THE MOST EXCLUDED ARE THOSE W/ THE MOST POTENTIAL FOR EMANCIPATION, THIS IS A RESULT OF PHILOSOPHICAL THEORETICISM THAT IS UNINFORMED BY THE HISTORY OF SOCIAL MOVEMENTS: THEY NEED A MINIMUM OF RESOURCES TO MOBILIZE, & WILL IT IS NOT THE MOST EXCLUDED THAT DO MOBILIZE. STILL, THERE ARE GOOD INSIGHTS ON SOLIDARITY BASED NOT ON SAMENESS BUT ON BEING EXCLUDED — HENCE NEGATIVE UNIVERSAL POLITICS.

2

Universalisms Compared

As suggested in the previous chapter, the appeal to universalism can take many forms. The concept has a generative power reflected by the significantly wide political spectrum of those who embrace it—Hegelian-Lacanian intellectual Žižek of course, but as this chapter will elaborate, also champion of republican secularism Alain Finkielkraut, democratic theorist Seyla Benhabib, Marxist Étienne Balibar, and postcolonial critic Edward Said. The eclecticism of this list makes abundantly clear the different political platforms that universalist thought can underpin. For that reason, it is preferable to speak of universalisms in the plural rather than the singular. One common defining feature of these universalisms that we might cite—especially in the context of ethical and political philosophy—is their historical reliance on Enlightenment human rights discourse. And yet this reliance is by no means unchallenged or unqualified.

Is Western rights discourse a priori vulnerable to the charge of Eurocentrism? Can the language of universal rights only be spoken in one voice? Or can we think outside a disavowed provincialism and fashion a universalism that would confront the ideological trappings of human rights discourse without simply jettisoning its emancipatory political potential? Moreover, do all forms of universalism obliterate the differences of others? If identity politics, along with the push for diversity and multiculturalism, emerges as a justifiable, though ultimately limited, corrective to an arrogant, masterful, and violent universalism—one that translates or assimilates difference, be it racial, sexual, or cultural, into the already known—can competing universalisms offer a genuine alternative to the short-term political values of identitarian thought and rootedness, *while also* providing a more effective critique of *that* very universalism, the "blithe universalism" of Europe, as Edward Said called it in *Culture and Imperialism* (1994, 277)?

What all universalisms have in common is a commitment to the view that the proper vocation of philosophy is to theorize the universal, to distinguish the essential from the contingent, the ontological from the ontic, and so on. A universal politics worthy of its name, however, cannot simply rely on the

Universal Politics. Ilan Kapoor and Zahi Zalloua, Oxford University Press. © Oxford University Press 2022.
DOI: 10.1093/oso/9780197607619.003.0002

distinction between abstract universalism and concrete particularism and affirm the former over the latter, as chapter 1 underlined. A universal politics dialecticizes the opposition, producing something new, or what Žižek, after Hegel, names the birth of the "concrete universal."

Who or what becomes a concrete universal is, to be sure, a contested matter. To evaluate models of universalism vying to define what constitutes universality itself, we will turn here to the Palestinian question—the question of what to do with a people who resist their systematic dispossession, who insist that they've been wronged from the time of the Balfour Declaration to the latest Gaza war—as a case study for thinking universal politics. Balibar famously characterized the plight of the Palestinian people as a "Universal Cause" (2004). The Palestinian question or cause is not merely a local matter, a regional dispute. It touches all of us, Balibar argues; it compels all to imagine and invent the conditions for justice and equality in a postcolonial era, to rethink citizenship on a global scale. Said's postcolonialism frames the universalism of the Palestinian question as a matter of global democracy and secular humanism. Humanism demands an ethico-political solution to the plight. Needless to say, not all concur with this assessment. Finkielkraut and Benhabib object to a model of the universal that would unfairly single out Israel for its abuses, failing to appreciate the stakes in developing global democracy. What the Israeli-Palestinian conflict brings to light for Benhabib are the sober complexities of mediating between conflicting rights and demands. For Finkielkraut, the matter is far clearer: Europe must sustain the division between the friends of civilization (of which Israel is one) and its enemies (Palestinians and their fundamentalist and leftist supporters).

This chapter puts Žižek's vision of universality, and its corollary empty subject, in critical dialogue with the preceding competing versions of universalism. With the Palestinian question serving as a testing ground for thinking universal politics, we will explore the ways Said's exilic cosmopolitanism, Finkielkraut's republicanism, Benhabib's democratic subject, and Balibar's insurrectional politics converge with and diverge from Žižek's politico-hermeneutic framework.

Said's New Humanist Universalism

Throughout his writings, Said exerts significant interpretive pressure on European universalism, and yet his long attachment to the tradition of humanism complicates a straightforward disentanglement from Western modernity. Said's postcolonial universalism straddles the historically specific demands of anti-colonial studies and the timeless aspirations of humanism. In his preface to the twenty-fifth anniversary edition of *Orientalism*, Said describes humanism as "the only—I would go so far as saying the final—resistance we have against the inhuman practices and injustices that disfigure human history" (2003, xxix). To be a humanist is to be "able to use one's mind historically and rationally for the purposes of reflective understanding" (xxiii). Saidian humanism is characterized by indocility, a will to contest the status quo, the "received ideas and approved authority" we inherit.

This new humanism declines the ideological appeal to rootedness: "To leave the historical world for the metaphysics of essences like negritude . . . is to abandon history for essentializations that have the power to turn human beings against each other" (Said 1994, 228–29). Orientalism, in this respect, leaves history behind, reifying the "Oriental" as a "subject race" (Said 2003, 34). Said appreciated, for example, the ways a universalist orientation, an un-flinching commitment to the "wretched of the earth," always supplemented Fanon's solidarity with and attentiveness to Black bodies. This was true even when meditating on one's own trauma or the trauma of *a* people. Against the myopic impulse to fetishize one's suffering, to ossify the particular, Said follows Fanon in reorienting his discussion toward the universalist plight of the dispossessed, those who *do not count*, the part of no-part:

> It is inadequate only to affirm that a people was dispossessed, oppressed or slaughtered, denied its rights and its political existence, without at the same time doing what Fanon did during the Algerian war, affiliating those horrors with the similar afflictions of other people. This does not at all mean a loss in historical specificity, but rather it guards against the possibility that a lesson learnt about oppression in one place will be forgotten or violated in another place or time. (1996, 44)

What he values in Fanon is precisely a refusal to fetishize one's own identity.

Said practices what he preaches when it comes to the Palestinian question, infusing it with a universalist sensibility, with a humanism, a being-with, that is not exhausted in filiation (relation that "belongs to the realms of nature and 'life'") but also insists on affiliation (relation that "belongs exclusively to culture and society") (1983, 20). This universal humanism is not grounded in "sovereignty as an end in itself" (2001, 452); rather, it fosters a view of sovereignty "as a step toward a more generous idea of coexistence" (2001, 452), foregrounding a relationality at odds with a nationalism myopically defined, a nationalism aligned exclusively with a particularist identity (one nation, one people).

A new humanism functions as an antidote to tribalism and the cult of monolithic differences. Rather than elevating his own Palestinian difference over his Jewish counterpart, Said playfully identifies with the signifier Jew, embracing an exilic cosmopolitan mode, designating himself as a "Jewish-Palestinian":

> Of course. I'm the last Jewish intellectual. You don't know anyone else. All your other Jewish intellectuals are now suburban squires. From Amos Oz to all these people here in America. So I'm the last one. The only true follower of Adorno. Let me put it this way: I'm a Jewish-Palestinian. (2001, 458)

As with Fanon, it is Adorno's anti-identitarianism, his refusal to subscribe to an ideology of difference, that appeals to Said. This trope of exile clashes with Eurocentric humanism. Saidian humanism is marked by its sense of vulnerability and exposure; the true humanist is in exile; he or she does not flourish at home, in the comforts of the nation-state, but away and at an ironic distance from the organically given. Said's new universalist humanism draws its intellectual inspiration from this disappearing Jewish tradition. Likewise, Žižek, on numerous occasions, praises the model of universality embodied in the figure of the diasporic or cosmopolitan Jew who always preserves and nurtures a critical separation between self and community. Žižek sees this figure of the Jew as making full use of what Kant called the "public use of reason." In "What Is Enlightenment?," Kant distinguished between two uses of reason: in the domain of the "private use of reason," individuals in their official capacity must obey orders; but in the domain of the "public use of reason," individuals (as would-be-philosophers) express their thoughts without compromise, speaking as "*a scholar . . . before the entire public of the reading world*" (1996, 60). As Žižek observes, the public use of reason, "in a kind of short-circuit, by-passing the mediation of the particular, directly participates in the universal," illustrates and enacts the individual as cosmopolitan, making possible his or her break (the Real) with the "communal-institutional order of one's particular identification" (2008c, 143). The pursuit of concrete universality—confronting particularity with its own negativity/

RESHAPING THE SHAPE OF ISRAEL

limitation, rather than a retreat into ideological difference—is thus the genuine alternative to abstract universalism.

Whereas individuals are perpetually interpellated by the big Other (the order of laws and rules) as particular members of a community, (some) Jews have always resisted this ideological gesture, according to Žižek:

> The privileged role of Jews in the establishment of the sphere of the "public use of reason" hinges on their subtraction from every state power. Theirs is this position of the "part of no-part" in every organic nation-state community, and it is this position, not the abstract-universal nature of their monotheism, that makes them the immediate embodiment of universality. No wonder, then, that, with the establishment of the Jewish nation-state, a new figure of the Jew emerged: a Jew resisting identification with the State of Israel, refusing to accept the State of Israel as his true home, a Jew who "subtracts" himself from this State, and who includes the State of Israel among the states towards which he insists on maintaining a distance, to live in their interstices. (2013d, 6)[1]

This is the gift of the public use of reason: "You can be a human immediately, without first being German, French, English, etc. This legacy of Kant is more relevant today than ever" (Žižek 2009d, 72). Said would agree. As the part of no-part, the cosmopolitan Jew stands for "the empty principle of universality" (Žižek 1998, 988). By claiming the epithet of Jewish-Palestinian, Said inscribes himself in this long and rich universalist tradition.

However, this type of elevation of Jewish cosmopolitanism has been met with ire by Finkielkraut, who singles out Said for his policing and (mis)appropriation of Jewishness, considering it anti-Semitic since it purports to lecture Jews about what constitutes a real Jew:

> These are strange times for real Jews. Not long ago, they were on the lookout, ready to strike down anti-Semitism wherever it dared rear its head. They were determined never again to succumb to hatred, and to clip the wings of anyone who spoke of them as "dirty Jews." What they weren't expecting—and what makes it all the more disconcerting—was to be faced with a grievance that is in its form moral and not brutish, virtuous and not vile, an altruistic grievance, sure of its legitimacy, full of kindness, and steeped in concern. While they are used to hearing themselves denounced

as Jewish traitors, they did not expect to be denounced as traitors to their
Jewishness. (2005, 26)

On Finkielkraut's reading, Said's preference for Adornian Jewish (non)iden-
tity has the effect of policing Jews, distinguishing good Jews from bad ones.
The old form of anti-Semitism is now supplemented by a new form to the
extent that this anti-Semitism is couched in the language of antiracism.
Said's new universalist humanism, along with this Jewish cosmopolitanism
(praised and reviled by Jews and non-Jews alike), is effectively bad for Jews.

But there is something anti-Semitic underpinning the very charge of anti-
Semitism. Such a claim assumes all Jews identify with the State of Israel: if
you are critical of Israeli policies, you are critical of Jews, so goes the argument. Consequently, Jews like Judith Butler and Israeli filmmaker Udi Aloni
are repeatedly labeled self-hating Jews or traitors of their race, and so on. But,
as Joseph Massad astutely points out, "*It is Israel's claims that it represents and
speaks for all Jews that are the most anti-Semitic claims of all*" (2013). Jews
of the Diaspora—who stubbornly defetishize the nation-state, not heeding
its endless call to be or stand with the Jewish state—are Zionism's recurring
targets. Žižek coins the saying "Zionist anti-Semitism" (2013d, 6) to capture
this hatred for universality, for a universality at odds with the idea/l of Israel
or any other expression of tribalism.

Challenging the ideological core of the symbolic order is the business of
universal politics. In *Freud and the Non-European*, Said pursues such a politics by further troubling Jewish investments in the nation-state of Israel,
repeating Freud's reading of Moses, "the founder of Jewish identity," as "a
non-European Egyptian" (2014, 54). Drawing on Freud's provocative hypothesis that the exemplary patriarch of Judaism was an Egyptian, Said laments
Israel's missed opportunity in 1948 to imagine Jewish and Arab identity as *not*
mutually exclusive categories. Zionism's uncompromising claims of Jewish
exceptionalism successfully suppressed this promising trace, a genealogy
that would have made one's perceived enemy (the Arab Palestinian) constitutive of one's being (the Jewish Israeli). Freud's/Said's Moses incarnates *an
identity that is more than one*. He is a scandal to Zionism and its preaching of
Jewish identity as "one, and only one, Identity" (Said 2014, 54). Said's new humanism seeks to recover this Freudian mode of thinking identity:

The strength of this thought is, I believe, that it can be articulated in
and speak to other besieged identities as well—not through dispensing

palliatives such as tolerance and compassion but, rather, by attending to it as a troubling, disabling, destabilizing secular wound—the essence of the cosmopolitan, from which there can be no recovery, no state of resolved or Stoic calm, and no utopian reconciliation even within itself. (2014, 54)

Never identical to itself, pure, or exclusive, humanist identity is first and foremost a besieged identity. Said frames humanist identity as always already under assault from within and without.

Judith Butler correctly notes the poststructuralist or postmodern overtones of Said's account of humanist identity. The irony is of course not lost on Butler (2012, 30–31). The longtime defender of humanism introduces a view of identity that resonates more with the anti-humanism of the postmoderns than with the humanists of Western modernity. Still, we want to take Said's aberration, these incongruous echoes, one step further. Thinking Said with Žižek, and vice versa, allows us to view the subject of humanism in a new light and disclose more fully its emancipatory potential. On a first read, Said and Žižek stand apart when it comes to the question of subjectivity. As we mentioned earlier, Said is invested in the agency of the subject, in his or her ability to combat social injustice, to contest authority's power, whereas Žižek seemingly deviates from the Saidian path of universal humanism, opting instead to desubstantialize its political subject. Žižek's universal subject is neither the timeless humanist of Western civilization nor the new historically marked humanist, or the humanist à venir, of Saidian postcolonialism. And yet Said's Moses enables us to recast subjectivity in relation to the neighbor as theorized by Žižek, shifting from the agentic subject of humanism to the inhuman other of humanism.

Whereas Zionists see in Moses their ultimate *semblable*, the authorized and authoritative figure of Judaism, Said's Moses is arguably the incarnation of the "real neighbor" (discussed in chapter 1). In the former instance, Moses's conferred imaginary and symbolic status coincides with Zionist hegemony; in the latter, Moses as Real discloses a gap in that same order, "undermin[ing] any doctrinal attempt that might be made to put Jewish identity on a sound foundational basis, whether religious or secular" (Said 2014, 45). Illegitimate in the eyes of Zionists who view Jewishness as an organic community, the Palestinians dwell in a state of bare life, and their position is analogous to that of an Egyptian Moses. The Palestinian under Occupation is a being for whom relationality and *psychic identification* are categorically unavailable (not unlike an Egyptian Moses who remains unreadable and unavowable for

NEW TESTAMENT?

Zionism). This is where the biblical injunction "Love thy neighbor" takes on its full political relevance. For Žižek, the Palestinian as neighbor interpellates the Jewish Israeli ethically, politically. The refuseniks, Israeli soldiers who decline their compulsory military service in the Occupied Territories, admirably respond to this injunction:

> What the *refuseniks* have achieved is the passage from *Homo sacer* to "neighbour": they treat Palestinians not as "equal full citizens," but as *neighbours* in the strict Judeo-Christian sense. And, in fact, that is the difficult ethical test for Israelis today: "Love thy neighbour!" means "Love the Palestinian!" (who is their neighbour *par excellence*), or it means nothing at all. (Žižek 2002b, 116)

The refuseniks come to realize that Jewish identity is never whole, immune from the outside. We might say that via their exposure to Palestinian bodies the refuseniks discover themselves as neighbors (Žižek 2010b, 120), finding themselves acting in ways that are contrary to their dominant formation, their inculcation of Jewish privilege, and inscription in the Zionist order of things. The "Palestinian question" thus enables a *questioning* of Jewish identity, functioning as the Real to a narrow Jewish particularism, rattling it, thereby opening it up to (negative) universal horizons.

EMPTY SUBJECTS

With the Palestinians, it is their potential elevation to the status of a part of no-part that discloses and highlights the emptiness of their subjectivity. And to be clear, what makes one an empty subject is not some process of abstraction, and thus a necessary diminishing of the subject; as Žižek insists, the "emptiness is constitutive of the subject" (2016f, 43). This distinction is crucial: the subject is not first whole and then subsequently problematized or hollowed out. The subject is "what remains after we subtract all 'human' content. It is as a reject that this subject is universal" (Žižek 2016f, 27). For Žižek, it is precisely by avowing and accentuating the gap separating the subject from the human(ist) that the Palestinian as reject can come to stand for "the empty principle of universality" (1998, 998). In their initial request for social justice, to be listened to, Palestinians reframe the "universal dimension itself" (who stands for the bearer of rights) and affirm a "new universality" (Žižek 2014b, 184): the struggle for justice *for all*. The Palestinian question moves the struggle outside the realm of obligatory morality—where demands take the form of more psychic/imaginary identification with the Palestinians, injunctions to recognize that they are like us (Westerns, rational, caring beings, and so on)—into the necessity of politics: not we *ought* to do—but we "cannot do otherwise" (Žižek 2006c, 334).

But, here as well, a Žižekian orientation would insist that the Palestinian question is never only a matter of domination resolvable, in principle, at the ethical/legal register (by upholding the international human rights of the Palestinians, for example, or by triggering an unlikely mass civil rights movement in Israel for Palestinians). More tolerance—the humanist or liberal answer to most problems—is not enough. Žižek agrees with Fredric Jameson that the struggle against domination is "an essentially moral or ethical one which leads to punctual revolts and acts of resistance rather than to the transformation of the mode of production as such" (Jameson 2011, 150; qtd. Žižek 2012d, 1003). Humanism as an antidote to the biopolitical notion of domination—that which makes life not worth living—only operates at the level of superstructure. The struggle is resolvable in principle at that level: more rights, more recognition, and so on. Yet if the Palestinian fight against neo-imperialism is undertaken exclusively in the name of true democracy, the economy itself is never thematized as a site of struggle. As a result, Žižek notes, "Only in capitalism is exploitation 'naturalized,' inscribed into the functioning of the economy" (2012d, 1004). To see the Palestinian struggle *only* as a socio-legal matter would be then to reduce the Palestinian question to a humanist struggle against domination—and not one against exploitation; it is to continue operating within the humanist precinct (Warren 2018, 4)—be it new or old. On this point, there is thus considerable daylight between Žižek and Said. A critique of domination/postpolitics (a critique of coloniality or Eurocentrism in the name of subaltern difference, for instance) does not exhaust a universal politics. At best, it provides a *necessary* engagement with the injustices of the world, giving voice to the historically marginalized and excluded. At worst, it obfuscates the primacy of the economic system, namely global capitalism. A critique of domination does little to undermine the ideal of capitalism with a human face. Worse, as we emphasized in the previous chapter, it functions to legitimize a reformed capitalism, more democratic, more tolerant, and so on. Such a mode of critique problematically reduces the struggle for justice to what Žižek describes as a form of "pure politics" (2006c, 55). The way to avoid the uncritical path of pure politics (indistinguishable here from postpolitics) is for politics to take a collective form. The wager of a universal politics is that only if/when Palestinians and refuseniks or leftist Israelis (those who disidentify with the State of Israel) join in shared struggle (against Zionism, neocolonialism,

...damentalism, global capitalism)—that is, when each side confronts (separately and together) the Real from *within* and *without*—can the Palestinian question be adequately addressed. Solidarity of the excluded is what a hegemonic state always fears the most, because what they call for can never be fully remedied by the system without its radical transformation.

Balibar's Insurrectional Universalism

Unlike Said, who works within a postcolonial hermeneutics, Balibar operates within a post-Althusserian Marxist framework. In this respect, we might expect Balibar to be more alert to the trappings of *domination critique*; he is also far less ambivalent about the legacy of universalism. It is the aim of philosophy "to speak the universal [*de dire l'universel*]" (Balibar 2020, 19). Indeed, Balibar shares with Žižek a deep investment in the emancipatory powers of the universal. Like Žižek, Balibar builds on the postcolonial critique of human rights (which views the project of human rights as a racist one), envisaging a revival of rights discourse's universalist potential rather than giving up on the transformative potential of this discourse. He acknowledges the violence intrinsic to the universal, noting that "the universal does not bring people together, it divides them" (Balibar 2017b; cf. Balibar 2020). The division that the universal introduces, however, is not in itself good or bad, something either to pursue or avoid. What matters is who is doing it and for what purpose.

If Said militates for a rational subject engaged in the labor of secular criticism, Balibar reconceptualizes the subject as *citizen*, giving the latter an international and insurrectional aspect. For Balibar, the citizen is a creation or invention of the Enlightenment, of the French Revolution, which initiated a rupture with sovereign authority, "put[ting] an end (in principle) to the subjection of the subject" (1991, 38–39). One's identity as a democratic citizen is constituted as a "dialectic" between rights and duties, between freedom and equality. To be an active citizen, Balibar adds, is to practice the art of rebellion, to divide for the purpose of inclusion:

> The active citizen is not, on this account, she who, by her obedience, sanctions the legal order or the system of institutions upon which she has directly or indirectly conferred legitimacy by an explicit or tacit contract, materialized in her participation in representative procedures that result in

the delegation of power. She is essentially the rebel, the one who says *no*, or at least has the possibility of doing so. (2014, 283–84)

To be an active citizen is to be fully committed to the ideal of *égaliberté*, equality-freedom, which, as chapter 1 stressed, is an unconditional and uncompromising demand: "Equaliberty is an all-or-nothing" (Balibar 2002, 165).

What makes the Palestinian cause universal for Balibar, to return to this key example, is precisely its ability to speak to us as *citizens*, as social beings for whom the plight of others (understood as strangers or neighbors in Žižek's register) does not cease to be heard simply because it does not emanate from a familiar national setting. The very conditions of this call's articulation make of the Palestinian question "a test for the recognition of right, and the implementation of international law" (Balibar 2004). We can hear in the Palestinian call for recognition—in the rallying cry that their lives matter, that they should be counted in the Zionist order of things—"the right to demand human behavior from the other [*exiger de l'autre un comportement humain*]," as Fanon would put it (2008, 204).

For Balibar, responding to the Palestinian question necessarily takes us into the politics of recognition, into the realm of human rights discourse and the defense of *the right to belong* (Arendt 1958, 296–97). Though human rights can be deployed to serve a politics of "constitution," legitimizing the status quo—in the Zionist order of things, the universal rights of Jews are predicated on the governmentality of Palestinian bodies, on their "unequal access to citizenship" (Balibar 2020, 98), that is, on the denial of Palestinian rights—a politics of "insurrection"—a progressive or emancipatory use of human rights, the labor of active citizenship—can also fuel the universality of the Palestinian cause (Balibar 2014, 3). As it is for Said, a universalist attitude here is about extending rights to everyone (Said 2000, 433), with the effect of unsettling Western control over who belongs to humanity (the elect) and who is excluded (the damned) from its protection.

Insurrectional universalism is an antidote to Eurocentric violence, to its indifference, to its violence as indifference. Insurrection aims at pluralizing the universal, shifting the boundaries that determine the human, the value of the human as stranger (Said's non-European other). It cosmopolitanizes identity without, at the same time, getting rid of identity altogether. For Balibar, the concept of the nation, and national identity, is at the heart of the violence that insurrection combats—whence the relevance of Palestine. If, following Arendt, human rights are contingent on civil rights (because without the latter, the former evaporates), the challenge is to expand the ways we understand the creation of rights beyond the whims of political institutions. Balibar borrows from Arendt the formulation of the "right to have rights" (Benhabib will also draw on this idea). Balibar interprets the "right to have rights" as a "universal right to politics" (2002, 6): to be a citizen is to have the right to have rights, and an active citizen exercises her right to politics when she politicizes human rights, when she challenges her political institutions, questioning the state's authority over and determination of citizenship—performing, as it were, a skeptical enactment of universalism. To be an active citizen is to invent new forms of citizenship—competing versions of citizenship ideologically decoupled from the nation-state. "Diasporic citizenship" is such an invention:

> What I have in mind is not a "global citizenship" or "citizenship of the world," as if it could be considered a single constituency, but rather a "citizenship in the world," or an increasing amount of civic rights and practices *in the world* as it is, the complex system of spaces and movements forming the reality of what we call "the world," for which we are trying to invent a civilization. (Balibar 2011, 224)

The nation-state system cannot be the only framework for conferring rights, for providing redress and protection against abuse. Those who desperately need protection—the stateless, the *homines sacri* of the world (e.g., the Palestinians)—are sidelined and overshadowed by the existing dominant powers (e.g., the Israelis). The Israeli-Palestinian "conflict" is precisely not a conflict in the proper sense of the term. A conflict is a dispute among equals. This is surely not the case here; indeed, dissymmetry is what characterizes the relation between Israelis and Palestinians.

What does insurrectional universalism look like for Occupied Palestine? How does it intervene in the "conflict"? It does so by preaching the ethico-political ideal of *égaliberté*. This demand does not respect territorial boundaries, borders, or walls. Its universalist appeal complicates national identity, introducing its own form of necessary violence, inducing "identitarian malaise" (Balibar 2017b) in Zionism's chauvinistic ideology. Insurrectional universalism fights against Zionist "ultrasubjective violence,"[2] a type of violence that transforms Palestinians into a fundamental threat or disease, an enemy

Zionism

from without (Occupied Territories) and within (Israel proper) who must be exterminated.

To be an active citizen in Israel on this model is to counter the rewards of Jewish privilege, and to take up the universal cause of the Palestinians (or if you're a Jewish citizen living outside Israel, it is to decline its myopic call for loyalty—and disidentify with the State of Israel): "A universal cause is not only the cause of victims, the oppressed, it is a cause coinciding with the long-term interest of the oppressors themselves, morally and materially" (Balibar 2004). Israelis must decide: do they want to dwell in a Jewish state or a democratic state? The two are mutually exclusive. Like Žižek, Balibar credits the refuseniks for their bold resistance from within, for helping to create a space for *invention*—a way out of the impasse (there is only nonreciprocal recognition), a way for thinking justice outside the confines of the nation-state. From the vantage point of the nation-state, the claims of Israelis and Palestinians are strictly speaking incommensurable and irresolvable. There is no solution to the problem; "Something has to be *invented* and that's why Palestine is so important" (Enns 2005, 390). Israel serves as a warning. It illustrates many of the dangers of the nation-state, such as its capacity to segregate its populations along racial lines, sacrificing political equality in favor of an apartheid regime. Under an apartheid logic, citizenship suffers, and political agency from both camps diminishes. Insurrectional universalism makes rights serve the noble cause of equality. It undertakes the political task of "recreat[ing] the figure of the citizen, or the conditions of democratic politics in Israel and Palestine" (Balibar 2004).

While leaving open how this recreation might take place, and thus refusing to define the solution to the conflict—a one-state solution (binationalism)[3] or a two-state solution—Balibar does make it clear that a retreat into or repetition of the nation-state logic would be detrimental to both parties. Balibar is far more sympathetic to a Euro-Mediterranean "space for cooperation and negotiation" (Balibar and Lévy-Leblond 2006, 7–8). In this space, the peoples of the region would be motivated to come together and participate in cultural and economic exchange:

> Such a space is by definition heterogeneous: it is multicultural, multiconfessional, politically diverse and torn between conflicting economic and demographic interests. It does not provide a guarantee of peace. But it does provide the only antidote imaginable to the logic of the current situation, and the only thing that can force fundamentalism, post-colonial

racism, anti-Semitism and Islamophobia into retreat . . . , allow Israel to
abandon its exclusive dependence on the US . . . and allow the Palestinians
to escape an over-restricted and exclusive relationship with the Arab world.
(Balibar and Lévy-Leblond 2006, 8)

Žižek shares Balibar's cosmopolitan push to move beyond the nation-
state. A Euro-Mediterranean space would indeed be quite hospitable to
the Palestinian cause. Žižek, though, is less hesitant in his determination
of the preferable solution to the conflict, since the question itself has been
resolved. According to Žižek, Israel's settlement policies have changed
the facts on the ground, make it impossible to create and sustain a con-
tiguous, independent Palestinian state. There is only a one-state solution.
But the question now is what kind of one-state solution it is going to be
(Munayyer 2019).

Balibar's insurrectional universalism—the imperative of *égaliberté*, the
rallying cry of active citizens—must be put into the service of binationalism,
a just vision of the one-state solution. Žižek, however, sees this Balibarian
line of critique as "more Jacobin than Marxist," as yet another instance of
"pure politics" (2006c, 55–56). While he fully endorses the revolutionary
force of *égaliberté* (what the parts of no-part are constantly pleading), its deployment in the Palestinian struggle for recognition would invariably signal
a degradation of the economic sphere:

> Within this horizon, there is simply no place for the Marxian "critique of
> political economy": the structure of the universe of commodities and cap-
> ital in Marx's *Capital* is not just that of a limited empirical sphere, but a kind
> of socio-transcendental *a priori*, the matrix which generates the totality of
> social and political relations. (2006c, 55–56)

An insurrectional universalism results in the disappearance of the economy
as fundamental site of Palestinian struggle (which is ironic, given Balibar's
Marxist orientation). The economy as such is deprived of any ontological
value; for Balibar, its status appears merely ontic. A universal politics would
need to vigorously supplement the pure egalitarian democratic logic, that is,
the citizen's struggle against domination (in this case, Zionist domination of
Palestinian lives) with a struggle against exploitation, for there is an obvious
economic disincentive to curtailing Israel's Occupation and necropolitics, its
regulation of Palestinian death and maiming.

If Balibar promotes a universal that divides in order to include, instituting a cosmopolitan spirit in the existing nationalist community, Žižek urges a *deeper* division, one that touches the Real, that introduces a genuine gap in the social order. Žižek draws on the message of Christ: "If anyone comes to me and does not hate his father and his mother, his wife and children, his brothers and sisters, yes, even his own life, he cannot be my disciple" (Luke 14.26). What is at stake in Christ's message, for Žižek, is a rejection of the given, a break with biological and social ties, a disruption of our very being:

> Family relations stand metaphorically for the entire socio-symbolic network, for any particular ethnic "substance" that determines our place in the global order of things. The "hatred" enjoined by Christ is therefore not a kind of pseudo-dialectical opposite to love, but a direct expression of what St. Paul, in I *Corinthians* 13, described as *agape*, the key intermediary term between faith and hope: it is love itself that enjoins us to "unplug" from the organic community into which we were born, or, as Paul put it: for a Christian, there are neither men nor women, neither Jews nor Greeks. (Žižek 2011, 105–6)

For Badiou, this Pauline sensibility, in the context of Occupied Palestine, opens to a binational solution:

> The legitimate solution to the Middle East conflict is not the dreadful institution of two barbed-wire states. The solution is the creation of a secular and democratic Palestine, *one subtracted from all predicates*, and which, in the school of Paul—who declared that, *in view of the universal*, "there is no longer Jew nor Greek" and that "circumcision is nothing, and uncircumcision is nothing"—would show that it is perfectly possible to create a place in these lands where, from a political point of view and regardless of the apolitical continuity of customs, *there is "neither Arab nor Jew."* (2006, 164, emphasis added)

For Badiou and Žižek, Saint Paul is not so much an "example of universality" as an "example of a *theory* of universality" (Badiou and Finkielkraut 2014, 48; see also Zalloua 2017, 89).

Is the Pauline claim that *there is neither Palestinian nor Israeli* sufficient in framing an emancipatory project? Yes and no. It does counter the ethnic substance nurtured by Zionist settler colonialism, the violence of (one version of) Jewish universalism, which makes Palestinian exclusion constitutive of Zionist belonging—the chosen Jewish community. But a universal politics, while fully agreeing with this cosmopolitan critique of Zionism, takes a further step, incorporating more fully the economic sphere in its critique. While some Zionists clearly fantasize about a Greater Israel free of Palestinians (deploying an eliminative logic, annexing all of Palestinian land, and thus actualizing the myth of *terra nullius*), others, invested in the Israeli arms industry, prefer to keep Palestinians alive, or rather dwelling in one of the global order's "*death-worlds*," "new and unique forms of social existence in which vast populations are subjected to conditions of life conferring upon them the status of *living dead*" (Mbembe 2003, 40). The Gaza wars serve as a profitable laboratory, a global showcase for Israeli military superiority, earning the state large profits in arms sales worldwide. To raise the Palestinian question must entail confronting global capitalism: combating both the naturalized reality of Israel's military-industrial complex and the neoliberalization of Palestine/Israel goes to the heart of a *universalist* struggle. Binationalism as an exclusive struggle against (postpolitical) domination risks ignoring the flow of capital; the violence of capitalism that subtends the social realities of Israelis and Palestinians alike. To raise the Palestinian question is thus to ask: Who benefits from Occupied Palestine? Which Palestinian future is less hospitable to *business* as usual, to reproducing what Toufic Haddad dubs "Palestine Ltd." (2016)?

Palestinians' struggle against exploitation is first and foremost what makes them candidates for the part of no-part. Justice is *not* to be found in the superstructural recognition of Palestinian equality but in the reconfiguration of their positionality within Palestine/Israel's economic structure. A Palestine free from Occupation may yet remain oppressed by the pervasive presence of neoliberalism. Binationalism cannot limit itself to revolutionizing the political and social spheres; in its challenge to Israel's apartheid logic, binationalism must also divide from within, taking on Palestine's elites and the widespread adoption of neoliberalism by the Palestinian Authority (PA).[4] Settler colonialism and neoliberalism both engage in what David Harvey describes as "accumulation by dispossession" (2003) (see chapter 1). If settler colonialism's dispossession is brutally apparent in Israel's ever-increasing illegal settlements and transfer of the land's indigenous population, global capitalism with a Palestinian face freezes or normalizes this debilitating reality. Transnational capitalists champion privatization and global elite investment priorities, or land development taking the form of "neoliberal urbanism," which, as Sami Tayeb points out, "ultimately does little to address Palestinians' most immediate and salient social issues—unemployment, poverty, food and water insecurity—or their struggle for liberation from Israeli occupation" (2019, 25).

If Occupied Palestine is to serve as an "authentic evental site in today's society" (Žižek 2008b, 40–41), binationalism must take the form of a *political act*: "The political act (intervention) proper is not simply something that works well within the framework of the existing relations, but something that changes the very framework that determines how things work" (Žižek 1999, 199). As much an invention as an intervention, binationalism must partake in what chapter 1 referred to as "the art of the impossible"; it has to alter "the very parameters of what is considered 'possible' in the existing constellation" (Žižek 1999, 199). With this in mind, to truly address the Palestinian cause as a universal one, we must insist on binationalism as a struggle against exploitation: against the growing division between the haves (the privileged few: the leaders of the PA, their associates, and the national bourgeoisie) and the have-nots (the many Palestinians reduced to cheap labor); against the Gaza blockade, the "de-development" of its economy, the forced availability of Palestinians to be killed or maimed for military profit (masquerading as a security matter).

Mari Ruti faults Žižek for falling prey to a kind of economism ("the economic foundations of society as the only determining structure" [Hall 1986, 10]):

> Žižek unfortunately lapses into the conventional Marxist notion that only the proletariat can truly represent such a "part of no-part." Even if we use economic exploitation as the criterion of universality—as Žižek does—this "part of no-part" could be defined more inclusively, say, by acknowledging that racism, sexism, homophobia, transphobia, and other social inequalities can keep individuals underpaid and even prevent them from participating in the work force. (Ruti 2018, 37)

But Ruti's account distorts Žižek's actual position. While Žižek does give primacy to the political economy, there are no lapses into classic Marxism here. Quite the contrary: Žižek is explicit in his rejection of the identification of the proletariat with the working class.[5] Against the view of "a 'predestined' revolutionary subject" (Žižek 2008a, 289) as in the days of Marx, Žižek subscribes to what he calls the "proletarian position" (2013d, 56–61); what we have now are "different *proletarian positions*. It means those people who are deprived of their substance, like ecological victims, psychological victims, and, especially, excluded victims of racism, and so on" (Žižek 2013d, 102). As candidates for the part of no-part, the Palestinians occupy a proletarian position; they are representatives of "substanceless subjectivity" (Žižek 1993, 10), structurally marginalized by Israel's apartheid logic and materially excluded from participating in the global economy.

For Balibar, this would make Palestinians "remainders" of Jewish universalism and its definition of humanity: "Universal Mankind is *not* total Mankind, or the whole of Mankind—in Lacanian jargon it is *pas tout* or 'not all,' or it leaves a place for the *remainder*, which is the exact antonym of the place of transcendental equality, and only the correlation of both constitutes 'the world'" (2017, 936). But as Žižek notes in a different context, Balibar's use of the "not all" actually distorts Lacan's usage: "He condenses (or, rather, just confuses) the two sides of Lacan's formulas of sexuation, and simply reads exception as non-All: the totality of subsumption is non-All since there are exceptions that resist being subsumed" (Žižek 2020g, 44). For Lacan, the exception aligns with the masculine logic of sexuation, where it is the sovereign exception that proves the universal rule of castration, whereas the non-all is identified with the feminine. And to be clear, "masculine" and "feminine" do not denote anatomical differences, but designate a subject's relation to the phallus. Simply put, "masculine" and "feminine" refer to competing logics and structures of enjoyment.

Lacan lays out four formulas of sexuation (1998b, 78). On the masculine side, there are two: (1) there is at least one X that says no to the phallic function, and (2) all Xs are subject to the phallic function. And on the feminine side, there are two more: (1) there is no X that says no to the phallic function, and 2) not all Xs are subject to the phallic function. Unlike the masculine side, there is no claim of universality rooted in exception here, intimating that woman (unlike Man) does not constitute a totality.[6] If there is no exception that stands outside the system, then the system *as such* is never whole or complete. And because there is nothing of woman *outside* the Law (no constitutive exception), woman is also non-all (*pas-tout*), *inside* of the social system.

The feminine logic of the non-all informs the universality of the proletarian position, putting it at odds with the masculine universalism of humanity (as embodied in Israel's claim to Jewish universalism). The Palestinians, as the parts of no-part, are not the remainders of a Zionist-sanctioned humanity; rather, they disclose the non-all of the Zionist order of things. They affirm that humanity is non-all—opening a space for thinking who or what might also count in Israel's "democratic" community.

The struggle of Palestinians is dual. A proletarian position is always more than a struggle against domination, and its struggle against exploitation is never an expression of economism. The politics of recognition, no matter how subversive and insurrectionist, never touches the Real, does not adequately tackle the economic realities of Occupied Palestine, and thus fails to unsettle the "balance of the Whole" (Žižek 2006c, 103), to yield sustainable changes and emancipatory transformations.

Finkielkraut's Republican Universalism

Not unlike Žižek, though for significantly different reasons, Finkielkraut is hostile to a politics of recognition. His stance is decisively anti-relativist and anti-communitarian (a rejection of French-style identity politics). Indeed, Finkielkraut rejects postmodernism's abandonment of truth, its obsessions with aporia, its deconstruction of the distinction between high and low culture; and he has no patience with multiculturalist discourse and its political correctness. Similarly, to the chagrin of the cultural Left, Žižek and Finkielkraut both praise the European Enlightenment. In their eyes, the champions of diversity—postmoderns and multiculturalists—are part of the problem rather than its solution. Žižek and Finkielkraut both affirm the positive legacy of Europe and thus often receive accusations of racism or proto-fascism:

> The absence of thought [*la non-pensée*] has of course always coexisted with the life of the mind, but this is the first time in European history that the two share same the name (*culture*) and enjoy the same status. Those who believe in "high" culture and dare make the distinction are called racists or reactionaries. (Finkielkraut 1995, 117)

> When one says Eurocentrism, every self-respecting postmodern leftist intellectual has as violent a reaction as Joseph Goebbels had to culture—to reach for a gun, hurling accusations of proto-fascist Eurocentrist cultural imperialism. (Žižek 1998, 988)

The similarities of their defensive stance might explain why Žižek feels some affinity with Finkielkraut:

> I'm friends with him because I like conservatives, but not reactionaries. Marx says that pessimist conservatives are sometimes better than liberals, because the former acknowledge the existence of antagonisms. The problem with Finkielkraut is that he believes one can defend oneself in the name of an identity, while I'm more pessimistic. (Maggiori and Vécrin 2015)

While opting to put Finkielkraut on the side of conservatives rather than on the side of reactionaries is a questionable move,[7] Žižek's comment also helps point up the divergences between their positions on universality. At the heart of Finkielkraut's universalism—a commitment to France's particular republican model of secularism as freedom *from* religion (in contrast to, for example, US liberalism, which emphasizes freedom *of* religion), that is, from any outward signs of investment in religious or cultural values other than those of the Enlightenment—lies an attachment to identity.

This investment in identity spills beyond France and its republican legacy, framing if not overdetermining Finkielkraut's confrontation with the Palestinian question. To start, Finkielkraut extends the coveted European identity to Jewish Israelis: Israel is fundamentally European; its struggle is Europe's. This excuses Israeli exceptionalism. How philosophers and public intellectuals react to the current global mistreatment of Israel (by Islamofascists and their leftist sympathizers) is a referendum about the futurity of Europe: is it a future that learns from its European past (the Shoah) in order to fully realize the promises of the Enlightenment? Or is it a future that obsesses about Europe's historical wrongs (shamefully complying with its non-European others)?

The path Finkielkraut takes to this paradoxical defense of universalism (via the view of Jews as the ultimate, transcendent victims of history) begins with a critique of what he perceives as Europe's misguided turn to particularism, to the cult of diversity, which he equates with a turn away from universalism. In response to calls for recognition and justice in the aftermath of European colonialism and in the face of ongoing discrimination and racism against minority populations, France's cultural Left has developed a progressive antiracism that Finkielkraut deems anti-Semitic and misguided in its multicultural erosion of French secularism. Acquiescing to minority outrage, France's postmodern philosophers and multiculturalists have,

according to him, betrayed the nation's republican ideals and its commitment to the Enlightenment, to its investment in universality and the well-
being of humanity.

Finkielkraut's *The Defeat of the Mind* is in many ways an update of Julien
Benda's *La trahison des clercs* (*The Treason of the Intellectuals*). Like Benda,
Finkielkraut bemoans his contemporaries' failure to live up to the ideals of
the Enlightenment and nostalgically longs for the days of the Dreyfusards,
where intellectuals took a stance in the name of republican universalism.
Now, the cognitive and affective attachment to humanity and universality has been replaced. Finkielkraut traces the path of this betrayal back
to Johann Gottfried Herder—the great betrayer of the Enlightenment.
Against the Enlightenment's cherished values of truth, beauty, and the good
(timeless philosophical ideas since the days of Plato), Herder argued that
"there was no absolute . . . only regional values and contingent principles"
(Finkielkraut 1995, 7). There is no universal reason; each culture or nation
practices and cultivates its own form of reason. Herder, Finkielkraut argues,
planted the dangerous idea of national consciousness (*Volkgeist*), according
to which who you are is no longer defined abstractly in terms of your humanity but rather in relation to culture, the local, the place of your birth,
and so on. Freedom—the affirmation of autonomy—is no longer sought
in the Enlightenment imperative of setting oneself "free of all definitive
ties [race, class, gender, nation, etc.]" (Finkielkraut 1995, 12). An obsession with *Volkgeist* fosters a myopic and narcissistic vision of oneself. The
new intellectual norm consists of "repudiating universalism and glorifying
particularisms, focusing on those qualities that made one people different
from another" (Finkielkraut 1995, 5). Consequently, the ethico-political impulse for cosmopolitanism gives ways to the comfort of rootedness and identity politics. Without transcendence, without a taste for the universal, even
fanaticism changes form: "In a world deserted by transcendence, fanatics no
longer evoke the name of God to justify barbaric customs; they call upon
identity politics instead" (Finkielkraut 1995, 106).

In the age of postmodern multiculturalism, the traitorous intellectuals no
longer worship their nation at the expense of humanity and justice (as the
anti-Dreyfusards did during the Dreyfus affair); rather, their misplaced critique is made "in the name of the Other," in the name of Europe's excluded
others. They celebrate the virtues of diversity and relativism, believing that
they are correcting Europe's previous colonial wrongs, countering its ongoing
racism, when they are in fact evacuating the basis for genuine critique—a

commitment to truth and transcendental ideals. The most serious consequence of this turn, Finkielkraut believes, is that it has spawned a new
version of anti-Semitism by championing the Palestinian cause as a global
struggle against neo-imperialism (Said and Balibar as two prime examples).
Against the alignment of the Left with Third World anti-colonialism and radical Islam's rejection of Western values, Finkielkraut decries the Left's isolation of Israel, its shaming Israel for its wrongdoings.[8] This misplaced leftist
critique, he argues, is doubly bad: the growing anti-Zionist discourse in
Europe is bad for Jews because it puts them further at risk by stoking the
fire of anti-Semitism, and it is ultimately bad for Europe because it puts the
European project of civilization at risk by introducing daylight between the
West and Israel. To question the legitimacy of Israel is to question the legitimacy of Europe, since Israel as such embodies Europe's heritage. Or to
put it slightly differently, to profess anti-Zionism is to stand against the universality of the European ethos. Manifestations of *Judeophobia* in France are
also manifestations of *Francophobia*.

According to this view, the new anti-Semitism that is arising in Europe is
not fueled by neo-Nazis but paradoxically by leftist antiracists. At the origins
of the transmutation of antiracism into anti-Semitism lies a "Jewish 'narrative envy'" (Stam and Shohat 2012, 167), a desire to substitute slavery, colonialism, and other more recent trauma against non-Europeans for the Shoah
endured by Jews. Finkielkraut traces the de-universalization of the Jew to the
postmodern move or decision to identify with otherness. This is the cultural
Left's major failure; it leads to an overcorrection (if a correction were needed)
to the trauma of the Shoah. Rather than attending to the shame arising from
Europe's mistreatment of Jews, the postmodern subject seeks redemption;
now hungering for otherness, this subject seeks to defend the victims of
Western civilization.

The slogan "We are all German Jews" reflects this new postmodern, post-
Holocaust ethos. During the May '68 protests, French students deployed this
slogan as a rhetorical mode of protest, expressing solidarity with one of the
movement's leaders Daniel Cohn-Bendit, who had been described by the
French government as a "German Jew." Standing with Cohn-Bendit, after
he had been refused re-entry into France because of his participation in a
demonstration in Berlin, the French students' performance of solidarity puz-
zled the young Finkielkraut, himself a child of Polish Holocaust survivors. In
The Imaginary Jew, Finkielkraut recounts his ambivalence about this scene.
On the one hand, identifying with—rather than persecuting—Jewishness

was a definite sign of progress. France had come a long way from the Vichy regime's collaboration with the Nazis to a culture in which French students readily joined forces with Jews. On the other hand, Finkielkraut could not deny his uneasiness about the progressive students' effortless appropriation of Jewish identity. He wryly notes, "Jewish identity was no longer for Jews alone" (1994, 17).

As Finkielkraut underscores, the generalizability of Jewish oppression was merely the start of a larger tendency to forget the actual victims of history. The figuration of the Jew—"We are all German Jews"—made it clear that the signifier "Jew" is available to all. This cross-cultural iterability of Jewish victimization marked a turn away from real Jews to an ethical imposture. Because from the postmodern standpoint "Every child of the postwar era could change places with the outsider and wear a yellow star" (Finkielkraut 1994, 17), the universalization of the Jew meant the loss of the universality of the Jew. The Jew now functions as an idea or figure for radical oppression. He or she can no longer claim exclusive right to the status of absolute victim. But for Finkielkraut, the use and (mostly) abuse of the signifier "Jew" meant a desacralization of the Shoah, to a "sudden democratization" (1994, 35) of the victim. "We are all German Jews" gives way to an even bigger moral collapse in judgment: *Shoah for all.* The Jews of Auschwitz are replaced by new victims of colonialism: "Colonized peoples fighting for their independence, Black Power, the Third World reconquering its dignity: these were, for them, the new Jews of history" (1994, 34).

However, Finkielkraut strongly dismisses such any analogy:

> Europe did not lose its innocence in Auschwitz. Its criminal record is heavier and larger than that. It has committed, says the voice, other atrocities. The Jews are not the only victims of European hubris, far from it. Before Hitler and the conquest of *Lebensraum*, there was the colonial conquest and before colonialism, the slave trade. It is time to make room for these other tragedies now that many of their descendants live on our soil. (2010)

Indeed, Aimé Césaire makes this kind of argument, irritating the white French sensibility of Finkielkraut. In *Discourse on Colonialism*, Césaire offers an anti-colonial rebuke to the Western outrage over the Holocaust, exposing the subject of the outrage as "the very distinguished, the very humanistic, the very Christian bourgeois":

What he cannot forgive Hitler for is not the *crime* in itself, *the crime against man*, it is not *the humiliation of man as such*, it is the crime against the white man, the humiliation of the white man, and the fact that he applied to Europe colonialist procedures which until then had been reserved exclusively for the Arabs of Algeria, the coolies of India, and the blacks of Africa. (2000, 36)

Similarly, Frantz Fanon qualifies the rhetoric of the Shoah's unprecedentedness. Unlike the Shoah, racial slavery marked an ontological division in the human as such: "[Jews] have been hunted, exterminated, and cremated, but these are just minor episodes in the family history. The Jew is not liked as soon as he has been detected. But with me things take on a *new* face" (2008, 95).

Finkielkraut will hear none of that. Israeli exceptionalism underpinned more precisely by a vision of Jews as the ultimate, singular, and transcendent figure of the victim. He downgrades the moral catastrophe of colonialism; it was never a "crime against humanity," since to colonize is *not* to exterminate (Finkielkraut 2010). Adding insult to injury, we are reminded of colonialism's redeeming qualities; indeed, we should not forget about France's *mission civilisatrice*. The infiltration of multiculturalism and postmodernism in France's educational institution has led to an impoverished understanding of colonialism as all bad. "We no longer teach that the colonial project also sought to educate, to bring civilization to savages," laments Finkielkraut (2013a, 23).

To sum up Finkielkraut's position: if Europe is understandably haunted by its tragic past, its hypervigilance about racism has in fact backfired. The democratization of victimhood erodes the republican project by smuggling racial and ethnic differences back in to the unmarked and neutral space of the nation-state. At home, Finkielkraut bemoans and fears the "ethno-religious" rebellion of the formerly colonized, the ongoing Islamization of *la douce France*. The situation is dire. "France is in the process of transforming into a post-national and multicultural society," Finkielkraut (2013b) expresses in an interview with *Der Spiegel*. France as a republican project is faltering. Universalism is in retreat.

Finkielkraut's critique of victimhood undeniably resonates with Žižek, for whom the appeal to the rhetoric of victimization has effectively depoliticized the Left. Wronged differences must now be recognized and subsequently tolerated. The multicultural Left takes up the cause of the marginalized (the non-Europeans) at tremendous cost. It forecloses revolutionary struggle. The call for tolerance—the putative remedy for wronged differences—obfuscates the antagonism that cuts across capitalist societies:

> The formula of revolutionary solidarity is not "let us tolerate our differences," it is not a pact of civilizations, but a pact of struggles which cut across civilizations, a pact between what, in each civilization, undermines its identity from within, fights against its oppressive kernel. What unites us is the same struggle. A better formula would thus be: in spite of our differences, we can identify the basic antagonism or antagonistic struggle, in which we are both caught; so let us share our intolerance, and join forces in the same struggle. (Žižek 2008c, 157)

Here Žižek could not stand further apart from Finkielkraut's republican universalism and its aversion to the neighbor. Whereas the latter gives substance to the universal (as embodied by the values of the republican model), the former desubstantializes the universal by foregrounding the ontological antagonism—that is, "the inescapability of antagonism" (McGowan 2013, 48)—that runs through the subject and the community:

> The question is whether every ethical universality [such as the one espoused by Finkielkraut] is necessarily based on the exclusion of the abyss of the neighbor, or whether, to the contrary, there might be a universality which does *not* exclude the neighbor. Our answer affirms the latter: namely, the universality grounded in the "part-of-no-part," the singular universality exemplified in those who lack a determined place in the social totality, who are "out of place" in it and as such directly stand for the universal dimension. (Žižek 2010b, 124)

Žižek privileges "excess [as] the site of universality," attending to "those who are without their proper place within the social Whole," like the Palestinians, "that stand for the universal dimension of the society which generates them" (2013c, 189). The part of no-part is the legacy of universality that Finkielkraut and other public intellectuals are in fact betraying. Finkielkraut's choice between a fetishized, nostalgic idea of France/Europe/Israel (i.e., an abstract universalism) or the proliferation of identity politics must accordingly be thoroughly rejected. It is an ideological lie that works to compound the problem rather than address it. The "treason of the intellectuals" lies not only in the rejection of the universal but in the promotion of a reactionary version of itself. A universal politics worthy of its name is never engaged in the *preservation* of a way of life (no matter whose) but in the incessant probing of its antagonistic (ontological/cultural) roots. The exilic Palestinian, the cosmopolitan Jew, the idea of binationalism (conceived as much as a struggle against exploitation as it is one against domination), all work to advance such a universal politics.

Benhabib's Interactive Universalism

Like Finkielkraut, Benhabib expresses reservations about the elevation of the Palestinian question as a universal cause and is also distraught by Left's one-sided critique of Israel. Here, the liberal democrat, alert to the challenges to transnational law posed by the "clash" of rights, hesitates to advocate decoupling the Israeli state from the Jewish nation in the case of Israel (though also cognizant of the need "to think beyond the murderous politics of nation-states" [Landes 2017]), arguing that a less aggressive critique, or thematization of the problem, will better advance the cause of universal rights. "I do not believe," she affirms, "that we will get very far by repeating the formula that 'Zionism is a form of settler colonialism'" (Benhabib 2018a, 82).

Echoing Finkielkraut, Benhabib also sees universalism under attack, and yet she avoids Finkielkraut's quick and simplistic framing of the problem as a "clash of civilizations." Her universalism never takes the form of "French universalism, love it or leave it!" Benhabib favors a liberal democratic mode, one that acknowledges "the clash of two rights, of two moral principles with equal claim upon our allegiance facing each other in struggle" (2018, 96). We can ascertain their differences by considering their diverging reactions to France's *affaire du foulard* (headscarf affair), the public debates ignited in the fall of 1989 when three Muslim girls at the Gabriel Havez Middle School in the town of Creil near Paris were sent home after declining to remove their headscarves in school. Eugène Chénière, the headmaster, justified his decision "on the grounds that the scarves infringed on 'the *laïcité* [secularism] and neutrality of the public school'" (Bowen 2007, 83). Finkielkraut applauds the decision to ban the Muslim hijab in schools as a valiant effort to protect the universal values of *laïcité*:

Back in 1989, on the 200th anniversary of the revolution, I signed a peti-
tion against the Islamic headscarf. For me it had to do with the notion of
secularism, which is running into criticism around the world these days.
France believed at the time that this was a model for the world, and is today
reminded of its distinctiveness. It is no longer a question of exporting our
model. We have to remain modest, yet steadfast. (Finkielkraut 2013b)

The open letter signed by Finkielkraut (along with other renowned French
intellectuals, including André Glucksmann, Pierre-André Taguieff, and
Elisabeth Roudinesco) had the provocative title "Profs, ne capitulons pas!"
("Teachers, Let's Not Capitulate!"). The inference is straightforward: to capitulate to the Muslim threat is analogous to Europe's capitulation to the
demands of Nazism.

But Benhabib sees the intervention of the Muslim schoolgirls not as
a simple transgression of *laïcité*, nor a threat to France's character as a
beacon of universalism. Rather, the contestation of *laïcité* presupposes the
values of *laïcité*; the critique of *laïcité* is rendered possible by *laïcité* itself.
If Finkielkraut places the Muslim schoolgirls outside France's secular law,
Benhabib inscribes them within that very discourse of *laïcité*:

> Ironically, it was the very egalitarian norms of the French public educa-
> tional system which brought these girls out of the patriarchal structures of
> the home and into the French public sphere, and gave them the confidence
> and the ability to *resignify the wearing of the scarf*. (2006, 56)

So unlike Finkielkraut and others who characterize the stance of the
schoolgirls as premodern, anathema to the republican ideal, excluding them
as serious interlocutors in the debate, Benhabib creatively if not counterintuitively reads these students as essentially French and democratic, engaged in
"the very public act of resignifying the face of 'Marianne'." (2006, 61).[9]

This democratic iteration is a repetition with a difference, part and parcel
of producing what Benhabib (1992) calls "interactive universalism." The
Muslim girls are not victims, in need of France's *laïcité* to protect them and
ensure the recognition of their gender equality. Negotiating their place, their
cultural identities, in one of Europe's multicultural democracies is precisely
what these schoolgirls are doing. They (and Benhabib) reject the imputed
meaning of the scarf as an exclusive sign of male domination:

I defend the right of Muslim girls to wear the scarf precisely because I consider their continuing engagement with the public sphere of secular liberal
democracies, through which they are challenged to give an account of the
meaning of their actions to others, to be a healthy process of multicultural
and multifaith discourse, in the course of which meanings are negotiated,
articulated, and sifted through. . . . Such processes do not mean abandoning
one's core beliefs at all—if these entail observing women's modesty through
veiling their hair; rather, through the heightened pressure for justification
which subjects all religious beliefs, and not just Islamic ones, to the practice
of reason-giving in democratic publics, a more reflexive relation to one's
faith and identity claims can develop. (Benhabib 2004, 293)

Rather than aligning the schoolgirls with particularism, characterizing their
indocility as a stubborn attachment to their backward religion and way of life
(Finkielkraut's view), Benhabib sees the willful actions of the young Muslim
women as enriching both France's *laïcité*—refining it by making it respond
to today's challenges—and their own tradition, by opening Islam to the
forces of "decentering, reflexivity, and pluralization" (2004, 292). Benhabib's
universalism purports to accommodate difference, improving rather than
threatening the constituents of multicultural democracies; assimilation to
democratic liberalism does not entail the sacrifice or loss of the other's minority culture but a production of something new.

As with Balibar, Benhabib's "interactive universalism" thus foregrounds
context and pluralism. The normative underpinnings of Benhabib's universalism are not ahistorical/transcendental (as you find in Habermas) but
fashioned via interventions in the public sphere—the space of contestations
and negotiations. It is clear that the focus on embodiment, on the historically contingent, does not come at the expense of normativity and the universal. "Western philosophy," Benhabib stresses, "speaks in the name of the
universal" (Yancy and Benhabib 2015). And she has no desire to change that.
Her contribution to universalism lies in the ways she envisages the other—
the non-European other, to be more specific. She makes a crucial distinction
between the generalized other and the concrete other:

As humans, we are like one another, equally entitled to respect and dignity;
but we are also different from one another because of our concrete psychological histories, abilities, racial and gender characteristics, etc. Ethics and
politics are about negotiating this identity-in-difference across all divides.

ThE "CONCRETE" OThER *OThER"*
VS. *GENERALIZED OThER*

We live in a "post-racial" society only in the sense that we are all generalized others in the eyes of the law; but as we learn painfully, not in the eyes of
those who administer the law . . . . The history of discrimination, domination and power struggles among the concrete others trump the standpoint
of the generalized other. (Yancy and Benhabib 2015)

An "interactive universalism" acknowledges the need to account for both
dimensions of the other. It affirms a likeness with others while it recognizes
and respects differences in others (as individuals and communities) at the
same time. Benhabib's interactive universalism fosters an ethos of mutual
reciprocity and equality: "The guiding idea would be the principle of the
equal worth of every human being, the principle that the ideal of the human
would itself be open to these interactive encounters" (Benhabib 2018b). It is
thus in dialogue that interactive universalism emerges and is sustained.

If human rights aim to protect the most vulnerable, the would-be
victims of totalitarian regimes (whose generalized otherness—that is, their
humanity—is frequently suspended), Benhabib supplements traditional
human rights discourse with the concept of "the right to have rights," a formula she, like Balibar, freely borrows from Arendt. "The right to have rights"
is a foundational claim for moral politics; it affirms as axiomatic the equality
of every human being. "The recognition of the other as a right-bearing
person" (Benhabib 2018b) safeguards those others who find themselves outside the protection of the state. The first "right" in "the right to have rights" is
imbued with a normative force: it appeals "to humanity as such and enjoins
us to recognize membership in some human group" (Benhabib 2001, 16).
This right enacts an ethical injunction, a legal and moral cosmopolitan imperative about the intrinsic value of all human beings: "Cosmopolitanism
involves the recognition that human beings are moral persons equally entitled to legal protection in virtue of rights that accrue to them not as nationals,
or members of an ethnic group, but as human beings as such" (Benhabib
2011, 9).

COSMOPOLITANISM

Are Palestinian Rights Universal Rights?

Let us apply Benhabib's argument to Palestinians. What does a human rights
defense open up for the Palestinians? This question is from the start overde-
termined by Benhabib's overall position on the debate over Israel's status as a

settler colonial state, her refusal to denounce what Balibar rightly describes as Israel's belligerent "right of conquest" (2004). As noted earlier, Benhabib quickly dismisses the "incendiary" idea (incendiary for those who deem Israel to be untouchable—for its victim status, its strategic status, for its religious immunity, and so on), along with the analogy between Israel and apartheid South Africa. While there is nothing resembling an argument for dismissing the apt analogy, Benhabib informs Israel's leftist detractors about Zionism's complex history. Aside from normalizing Israel's founding violence by considering it typical of other (excessive) nationalist adventures, Benhabib insists on distinguishing between political Zionism and cultural Zionism, making it clear that there was no single Zionist position on how to deal with Palestine's indigenous population. Israel was never a straightforward colonial project. Zionism was split: cultural Zionists actively sought a form of coexistence with the Palestinians, whereas political Zionists were fully committed to pushing them out. Benhabib's historical reminder is welcome (Zionism is more than political Zionism), but it is also ripe for ideological manipulation. Dwelling on Zionist differences distorts the current realty of settler colonialism: a commitment to "the elimination of Native alternatives" characterized Israel's ethos toward the Palestinians shortly after its founding in 1948 (Wolfe 2013, 257).

The Israel that emerges from Benhabib's interactive universalism is an Israel that can be perfected (because of its participation in the democratic process: what the charge of settler colonialism forcefully contests)—the promise of *an Israel with a human face*. Israel's juridical framework, as in any liberal democracy, is equipped to recognize Palestinian basic human rights. To be sure, Benhabib does not give the Israeli government carte blanche. She repeatedly expresses her frustration and discontent with Israel's extreme Right and its influence on policies. Liberal Zionism, however, is spared. Its ideology is perfectly compatible with that of liberal democracy. Palestinian citizens of Israel are better off under Israeli juridical protection than anywhere else in the Arab world. But it is an inconvenient truth for liberal Zionism that these Palestinians are treated as second-class citizens. For example, Adalah (The Legal Center for Arab Minority Rights in Israel) has compiled "a list of over 65 Israeli laws that discriminate directly or indirectly against Palestinian citizens in Israel and/or Palestinian residents of the Occupied Palestinian Territory (OPT) on the basis of their national belonging. The discrimination in these laws is either explicit—'discrimination on its face'—or, more often, the laws are worded in a seemingly neutral manner, but have or will likely have a disparate impact on Palestinians in their implementation." Even if Palestinians citizens of Israel are afforded more rights, do we have to choose only between these stated options? Here, to the question, "Israeli (in)justice or Arab terror?" we might answer, *No thanks!*

Interactive universalism is present in all liberal democracies. Not unlike what France's republican model enables for female Muslim students in *l'affaire du foulard*, the same mechanisms of contestations are available to Palestinian citizens of Israel (far more than what the Palestinian legal system affords its subjects). With liberal Zionism, Israel gets a pass from the international community; its exceptional status is granted. *Pace* Balibar, a state *can* be Jewish and democratic! We might ask again: Is Israel a truly democratic state? Or is it merely passing as one? The liberal democratic supporter of Israel might point to Israeli courts as proof of the state's democratic bona fides. But isn't Israel merely projecting an image of juridical independence, disavowing, as it were, its complicity "in the colonial project itself," as Judith Butler points out? (Butler and Athanasiou 2013, 25). In *Justice for Some*, Noura Erakat (2019) powerfully demonstrates how Israel has manipulated international law so as to place Palestinians *outside* its protection and jurisdiction, furthering its colonial project and perpetual occupation of Palestinian land.

A universalist politics must see through the ideological performance of justice by the Israeli High Courts of Justice. As Žižek argues, "The condemnation of extra-statist anti-Palestinian violence obfuscates the true problem of *state* violence; the condemnation of 'illegal' settlements obfuscates the illegality of the 'legal' ones" (2013d, 9). While the courts, at times, do intervene to protect Palestinian rights from the violence of overzealous Israeli settlers, they, more often than not, turn a blind eye to the colonial situation, to the everyday, naturalized violence of the Occupation. What Benhabib's interactive universalism misses is precisely this settler colonial context— which blocks if not rules out the reformist gestures she endorses. Liberal Zionists are also implicated in the normalization of anti-Palestinian violence, that is, the default anti-Palestinian violence when nothing seems to be happening:

> Many peace-loving Israelis confess to their perplexity: they just want peace and a shared life with Palestinians; they are ready to make concessions, but why do Palestinians hate them so much, why the brutal suicide bombings that kill innocent wives and children? The thing to do here is of course to supplement this story with its counter-story, the story of what it means

to be a Palestinian in the occupied territories, subjected to hundreds of
regulations in the bureaucratic microphysics of power. (Žižek 2009c, 66)

Some liberal Zionists like Peter Beinart are waking up to the brute reality
that the two-state solution only feeds an ideological fantasy of hope that will
never produce peace and, by extension, is destructive to Palestinian lives. The
problem with the Occupation is not with its harshness (as if you could have
a kinder, gentler Occupation), but with Zionism's exclusionary commitment
to a Jewish state. To be a liberal supporter of Jewish statehood becomes a contradiction in terms. As Beinart puts it, "Liberal Zionists must make our decision, too. It's time to abandon the traditional two-state solution and embrace
the goal of equal rights for Jews and Palestinians. It's time to imagine a Jewish
home that is not a Jewish state" (2020). Israel's claim to exceptionalism—the
one Western nation that is allowed to violate the dictates of democracy, the
only state allowed to be Jewish and democratic—must be abandoned for the
universality of binationalism, for a just one-state solution, where rights are
open to all.

Can human rights discourse truly redress the situation in Occupied
Palestine? Through "the systematic 'micro-politics' of psychological
humiliations," as Žižek puts it, "the Palestinians are basically treated as evil
children who have to be brought back to an honest life through stern disci-
pline and punishment" (2002b, 145). Can human rights discourse counter
Israel's disciplinary and pedagogic practices of routinized humiliation
designed to reform Palestinians and make them compliant subjects of the
Occupation?

Unlike Balibar and Benhabib, Žižek's relationship to human rights discourse is far more strained. He, at times, describes the discourse as ideological through and through. For example, Žižek pushes back against
an unqualified praise of the republican model and its putative defense of
women's rights: "One cannot but note how the allegedly universalist attack
on the burqa on behalf of human rights and women's dignity ends up as a defense of the particular French way of life" (2010b, 1). Human rights are a ruse,
as underlined in chapter 1: they pretend to speak for humanity but in practice
they reinforce a Western and capitalist way of life ("abstract universalism").
From this critical, anti-ideological perspective, then, what the Left might
conclude about human rights is either that "their universality is false" (they
only pretend to be universal, privileging instead "a determinate set of particular cultural values") or that "'bourgeois' freedom and equality are *directly*

and only capitalist ideological masks for domination and exploitation" (Žižek 2012d, 105). In the first instance, universalism is a distortion of what is actually universal (applicable/available to all humans), and in the second, universalism is itself the lie and the vehicle of Western neocolonization.

Žižek acknowledges the veracity of these objections (his own examples lend credence to them), but still cautions against foreclosing the avenue of human rights. He stresses that human rights are dangerous and can turn on the same regime that exploits the rhetoric of human rights to subdue its citizenry (a point that is also made by Balibar). The deployment of human rights does often serve an ideological end (e.g., Israel speaks the language of inclusion; its progressive sexual policies and branding of sexual rights serve as a distraction from the government's mistreatment of Palestinians—a phenomenon known as "pinkwashing"), but it is only through them—through an antagonistic relation to them—that true emancipatory freedom can emerge: "If one prematurely abolishes 'formal' freedom, one loses also (the potential of) actual freedom—or, to put it in more practical terms, in its very abstraction, formal freedom not only obfuscates actual unfreedom, it simultaneously opens up the space for the critical analysis of actual unfreedom" (Žižek 2012d, 106). Abstract or formal freedom is not to be dismissed but radicalized—rendered concrete or actual.

Massimiliano Tomba sees this tension between abstract and concrete freedoms at work in the two versions of the French Revolution's Declaration of the Rights of Man and Citizen. He delineates two competing models: the "juridical universalism" of the original 1789 document and the "insurgent universality" of the 1793 version. The former follows a vertical or top-down logic and assumes "a subject of right who is either passive or a victim who requires protection," whereas the latter, horizontal in its orientation, declines to posit "any abstract bearer of rights," foregrounding instead "particular and concrete individuals—women, the poor, and slaves—and their political and social agency" (Tomba 2019, 32). A universal politics shares much with Tomba's vision of this forgotten "insurgent universality," but we locate the emancipatory seeds of the universal already in the 1789 Declaration— "The form is never a 'mere' form, but involves a dynamic of its own which leaves traces in the materiality of social life" (Žižek 2008c, 150). The original Declaration interpellated the "men" of the Third Estate as "citizens." But an ideological appeal is never foolproof. The logic dictating inclusion and exclusion can misfire. Why? Simply because we don't always act as we're compelled to act. The Haitian revolutionaries are a case in point. They "misread" the 1789 Declaration as addressed to them. Their *misreading*, as Žižek points out, "had explosive emancipatory consequences," politicizing the meaning of "human rights" (the 1793 Declaration is, in part, a response to the Haitian Revolution, which began in 1791): "Human rights were 'really meant' to be accepted only by white men of property, but their universal form was their truth. It was thus the first interpellation which was wrong, but the true interpellation could only actualize itself through the false one, as its secondary misreading" (Žižek 2016f, 64; see Martel 2017). This hermeneutic form of disobedience constitutes the ultimate act of fidelity to the event of the French Revolution, to the original idea of human rights, radicalizing it precisely by betraying its initial actualization (only open to white men of property, only accessible to the elite of the Third Estate), by making the rights available to all: women, the poor, and slaves—the parts of no-part. In this respect, Žižek considers Haiti a true "repetition" of the French Revolution, or even better: "It was perhaps even more of an Event than the French Revolution itself. It was the first time that the colonized rebelled not on behalf of returning to their precolonial 'roots' but on behalf of the very modern principles of freedom and equality" (2011, 108). Similarly, Paul Eisenstein and Todd McGowan praise the example of the Haitian revolutionaries, who elevated their plight as a universal concern, moving beyond "the particularity of culture" (2012, 80; see also McGowan 2020, 34–37).

What is valuable in human rights discourse, then, is not so much its content (as Finkielkraut would have it), which has historically reflected Eurocentric biases. Rather, it is first and foremost the "right to universality" (Žižek 2005a, 131). This right to be included, to be counted, is a right *open to all*. What makes the Palestinian question a universal cause (i.e., what makes the Palestinians candidates for the part of no-part—heirs to the Haitian Revolution) is not a Palestinian identity as such (a maligned subalternity that it is worth recovering, defending, understanding, ontologizing, and including in the existing social order): "This identification with the excluded [in this case, the Palestinians] is to be strictly opposed to the liberal sympathy for, and understanding of, their plight, and to the ensuing efforts to include them in the social structure" (Žižek 2010b, 124). To identify with the excluded Palestinians is to uphold their claim to universal values, values antithetical to the workings of the existing social structure. A universal politics jams consensus and the empty moves of inclusion; it is not an invitation to dialogue, an occasion for "dialogue of cultures." Rather, its investment lies in the unrealized potential of *égaliberté*—in the "solidarity of struggles" (Žižek 2015d).

Conclusion

Thus, the problem with the four versions of universalism covered in this chapter is that they fail to recognize or adequately face up to social antagonism, so crucial to a meaningful universalist politics. Finkielkraut is the most egregious here, fetishizing a nostalgic conservative republicanism (i.e., an abstract universalism) while conveniently sidelining France's (and Israel's) history of colonialism. Benhabib's interactive universalism is more critical but ultimately limited: human rights and debate are upheld only to improve the political status quo in Israel, while failing to contest the underlining project of colonialism and normalization of violence against Palestinians.

For their part, both Said and Balibar complicate questions of national identity, the former insisting on the humanist struggles proper to Jews and Palestinians, the latter foregrounding the challenge of new forms of democratic citizenship in Palestine/Israel. Yet both fail to adequately tackle the question of antagonism at the level of capitalist political economy. Said's humanist universalism tends to be restricted to an ethical-legal register, thereby defaulting to a reformist global capitalism, while Balibar settles on an ethico-political insurrectional universalism that elides the proletarian position of Palestinians in the global capitalist economy. This failure to tackle a thoroughgoing notion of antagonism not only obfuscates the socioeconomic contradictions of our global economic system, but equally leaves both Said and Balibar with an impoverished notion of subaltern agency: for, as Žižek maintains, it is on the basis precisely of antagonisms that shared struggle is made possible, most particularly in our late global capitalist times, when socioeconomic marginalization affects so many and on the basis of which political solidarity can take place.

A CENTRAL PROBLEM OF
THESE AUTHORS IS THAT
THEY PITCH THE CORE ISSUES
AROUND THE "MARGINALIZED" IT SHOULD
AND "EXCLUDED", WHEN "EXPLOITED
BE OPPRESSED". THESE ARE INDEED
ABOUT ALL NON ANTAGONISMS IN GLOBAL
THE CAPITALISM. BIASED LANGUAGE
SO TO BE INSTALLED IN THE BECAUSE
SEEMS DISCOURSE PROBLEMATIC
THEY ARE RIGHTS POLITICAL NOT
OF HUMAN ECONOMY.
THE CRITIQUE OF

3

Universal versus Decentralized Politics

Chapter 2 articulated the type of universality informing our call for universal politics by putting competing versions of the universal in critical dialogue. In this chapter, we hone our understanding of universal politics by considering a number of universality's foes. Angela Davis captures well, for example, common suspicions of the universal when asserting that "any critical engagement with racism requires us to understand the tyranny of the universal" (2016, 87). This resistance to the universal (which does not distinguish between universality and universalism) often takes the form of a retreat into difference—be it sexual, racial, or colonial—informed by a decentralized politics. With the demise of credible emancipatory narratives that would unify the plight of the marginalized and excluded, identity politics emerges on the interpretive scene, filling the void left by the absence of a global Left. Identity politics is, however, not the only critical mode that has emerged under such conceptual and material conditions. An anti-identitarian current has equally capitalized on this state of affairs, depicting universality as the enemy by (mis)identifying it as an expression of *being*, aligning the universal with positivity—a fetishized particularity: the sovereign, masculine, white, heterosexual subject of Western modernity.

In the pages that follow, we outline two strains or manifestations of decentralized politics. The first is informed by the linguistic/cultural turn, including postmodernism and radical democracy (as represented by Foucault, Lyotard, and Laclau and Mouffe). We believe these are key interlocutors for any discussion about the universal today, having laid the groundwork, each in their own way, for contemporary forms of skepticism, if not rejection, of universalism (as expressed by the likes of Jane Bennett or Walter Mignolo, as we shall see). The second strain operates under the ontological/affective turn, including New Materialism (Latour, Bennett), queer theory (Edelman, Ahmed), decoloniality (Mignolo), and Deleuzism (Hardt and Negri). In chapter 2, the Palestinian question served as a case study; here we will engage the question of workers' struggles in light of these two turns. What place do workers occupy in these turns or movements? Are they remnants of a prior,

Universal Politics. Ilan Kapoor and Zahi Zalloua, Oxford University Press. © Oxford University Press 2022.
DOI: 10.1093/oso/9780197607619.003.0003

now defunct mode of anticapitalist struggle, in need of replacement by more localized sites of resistance? If workers do not embody a " 'predestined' revolutionary subject" (Žižek 2008a, 289), what role can they play in universal politics?

The Linguistic/Cultural Turn: No Truth, No Working Class, No Revolution

As is well known, postmodernism is closely associated with the "linguistic turn"—the view that language is central to the construction of reality. In contrast to the Enlightenment position that language is constative, neutral, and stable, thus providing a "true" picture of the world, postmodernists contend that language is a constructed system of signifiers, each depending on other signifiers for meaning. The implication is that, far from unbiasedly representing reality, language is a sociohistorical construction that helps *constitute* reality and human identity. Because meaning is imprecise and insecure, moreover, it is no longer possible to hold on to the idea of a stable and rational subject. The postmodern belief in the partiality and instability of the subject puts into doubt questions of truth, objectivity, and universalism (including the universalism of the working class).

But what postmodernists ignore is the possibility of a negative universality/truth that stands not outside but at the limit of language and history, and indeed is constitutive *of* them.

Foucault and Lyotard: Universal Abandon

Throughout his oeuvre, but in *The Order of Things* (1970) and *Archaeology of Knowledge* (1972) in particular, Foucault makes the case that what constitutes truth changes through history: each episteme (which he later terms "discourse") sets out its own rules for ordering our view of the world, with the result that the construction of truth is historically contingent. For him, all social practices, institutions, and beliefs are historically defined and situated, each associated with discontinuous deployments of power. The will-to-truth is simultaneously the will-to-power, so that truth "is produced only by virtue of multiple forms of constraint, and it induces regular effects of power" (Foucault 1980, 131). Foucault associates universalism with domination—the forcible imposition of uniformity across social diversity. Thus, the privileging of rationality delegitimizes madness, the normalization of heterosexuality renders homosexuality abnormal, and the promulgation of criminal law outlaws deviancy.

Foucault's skepticism toward power causes him to abandon any type of universal politics in favor of small stories and everyday forms of resistance— what he famously coins as the "insurrection of subjugated knowledges." His aim is to "entertain the claims to attention of local, discontinuous, disqualified, illegitimate knowledges against the claims of a unitary body of theory which would filter, hierarchise and order them in the name of some true knowledge and some arbitrary idea of what constitutes a science and its objects" (1980, 81, 83). The concept of revolution recedes from his political horizon, his idea being not to take power but to change subjectivities. In his *History of Sexuality* (1978, 1985, 1986; see also Taylor 2017), in fact, he argues for the creation of the self as a work of art, valorizing autonomy, experimentation, and the deployment of "technologies of the self" to minimize the effects of power on the subject.

Lyotard has a similarly blistering critique of Western modernity. He draws on Wittgenstein to argue that language is an incoherent structure composed of ad hoc "language games," each with its mode of utterances (denotive, performative, prescriptive, etc.) and rules about what is and is not valid. As a result, for him, it is impossible to construct a meta-language or claim (scientific) objectivity; all that is possible are partial and incommensurable narratives. He thus famously expresses an "incredulity towards metanarratives" (1984, xxiv), taking aim at overarching and transhistorical Enlightenment views of history, progress, freedom, or working-class emancipation (advocated by the likes of Hegel and Marx). He sees universalizing theory as a stumbling block to understanding the global present, going so far as to characterize it as "terroristic" (1984, x, xviii) and echoing Foucault's concerns about it as exclusionary, arrogant, intolerant, and self-aggrandizing: "The grand narrative has lost its credibility, regardless of what mode of unification it uses, regardless of whether it is speculative narrative or a narrative of emancipation" (Lyotard 1984, 37).

Predictably, like Foucault, Lyotard favors knowledge in the form of plural stories, customs, myths. According to him, "Postmodern knowledge is not simply a tool of the authorities; it refines our sensitivity to differences and reinforces our ability to tolerate the incommensurable" (1984, xxv). Indeed, given his claim about the "heteromorphous nature of language games" (1984,

66), he deploys the notion of the "differend" (1988), whereby justice is about respecting the incommensurability of plural cultures, promoting dissensus and silence rather than consensus-based decision-making (à la Habermas), which for him tends toward uniformity, exclusion, and violation of social difference.

The problem with both Foucault and Lyotard is that they deny universal truth but ultimately assert the validity of their own. Habermas famously denotes this as a "performative contradiction" (1987, 185), pointing out (in a Hegelian vein) that the rejection of all metanarratives is itself a meta-theoretical position. To be sure, Foucault's critique of humanism is undermined by his own championing of personal autonomy and freedom as universal values. His characterization of coercion and subjugation as "dangerous" and his valorization of heterogeneity imply moral/normative judgments even as he eschews the latter (see Fraser 1981). The same is true of Lyotard: Benhabib (1984) accuses him of privileging his *own* language game over others and assuming the equal right to coexistence of plural language games (i.e., the presumption of universal moral worth). So like Foucault, Lyotard desires a pluralist society that consists of differends, all the while denying universalism.

Of particular concern here is Foucault's approach to history. As mentioned previously, whether in relation to the birth of prisons or the construction of homosexuality or reason/madness, for him, human bodies and social institutions are embedded in historically produced discourses. But the trap of such historicism is that it cannot account for its own position of enunciation. As Jameson indicates (1991, 323–24), to say that all knowledge is historically transitive requires an Archimedean point to establish the validity of that claim. So once again, while critical of metanarratives, historicism in fact requires a metanarrative.

Contrast this with the conception of history implied by negative universality. In this regard, Žižek makes it a point to distinguish between historicism and what he calls "historicity." The latter for him includes the all-important dimension of the Real, which, as we saw earlier, is to be seen "not as an underlying Essence but as a rock that trips up every attempt to integrate it into the symbolic order" (Žižek 2005b, 199). In this sense, the Real is an internally transcendent (i.e., unhistorical) traumatic kernel that returns to haunt each and every historical-discursive formation. The dimension of the Real is therefore what is missing in Foucauldian historicism, preventing the latter from including the element of universality needed to avert its performative contradiction. Žižek expresses this lacuna cally ("Historicity = Historicism + the Real"), underlining the anta dialectical relationship between the Real and historicism (1992, 81). For it is indeed the Real as the traumatic/excessive kernel at the center of sociohistorical reality that, as he puts it, "sets in motion the movements of history, propelling it to ever new historicizations/symbolizations" (Butler, Laclau, and Žižek 2000a, 232; see also Copjec 1994, 6–14; Vighi and Feldner 2007, 23–24; Žižek 1999, 256–57).

But also of concern, in this regard, are the political dimensions of Foucault's and Lyotard's postmodern gloss. In Foucault, the lack of any transcendental element, the reduction of subjectivity to relations of power, leaves little or no room for agency. The most he offers, as is well known, is resistance ("Where there is power, there is resistance"; 1978, 95). He upholds micropolitics and local struggles, to be sure, but he also doubles down on a voluntaristic politics of the self. Yet, without any universal dimension, he is unable provide a basis for collective action or solidarity. At worst, then, his discursive politics renders the subject docile, and at best it makes it resilient; but what it fails to provide is the possibility of a broad and transformatory political project.

Lyotard fares even worse on this score. While Foucault at least has a critique of power in all its forms, Lyotard falls into the trap of advocating an (unacknowledged universalist) idea of criticism that is localized, ad hoc, and untheoretical. Feminist critics worry that such a belief in the heterogeneous implies an absence of critique of the structural inequalities and injustice that cut across social and institutional practices. As Nancy Fraser and Linda Nicholson state, "There is no place in Lyotard's universe for critique of pervasive axes of stratification, for critique of broad-based relations of dominance and subordination along the lines of gender, race, and class" (1988, 88, 90). Worse still, Lyotard's defense of silence (rather than consensus) as a way of preserving incommensurability veers toward docility, if not acquiescence to domination, thereby reproducing the very totalizing power he stands against. As with Foucault, the problem here is the lack of a universalizing political organization such as the state to protect against encroachments on people's rights, to uphold the integrity of the local, indeed to keep "language games" in check.

Finally, there is the question of political economy, almost entirely absent in the work of both theorists.[1] Their jettisoning of Marx means that questions of socioeconomic inequality and the unequal division of labor recede into the background. What they forget is that, like them, Marx was himself very critical of "bourgeois" abstract universalism (see chapter 1), advocating instead for his own version of universalism (the proletariat as universal class), which although fraught, was nonetheless aimed at countering the universalizing proclivities of capital—its inexorable integration of cultures and social practices (1973, 408). It is precisely this inexorability that a negative universal politics is aimed at addressing and which postmodernism retreats from.

Now it is true that, toward the end of his life, Foucault did engage with neoliberalism. He saw it as a form of governmentality—composed of new market-based technologies that structure subjectivities. He suggested, in fact, that market openness to pluralism might actually help, rather than hinder, the proliferation of formerly subjugated knowledges, facilitating greater self-autonomy and enabling minority groups to occupy those spaces liberated by the state, thereby working to dismantle capitalism (2008, 130; Lemke 2016). Yet in retrospect, the opposite appears to have taken place: rather than constraining the reach of the market, neoliberalism has opened up new frontiers for advancing capitalism—new identities to commodify (LGBT+, environmental, health food, ethnic, etc.), new Third World markets for multinationals to colonize (facilitated by structural adjustment), new charity causes for celebrities to improve their brands, and so on. Ironically, Foucault's championing of personal autonomy/technologies of the self has proven quite compatible with theories of the "enterprising self"/"entrepreneurial self" put forth by such neoliberal gurus as Theodore Schultz and Gary Becker (see Zamora and Behrent 2016).

And then there is the issue of class: it may not be a privileged category of social organization and mobilization, but by discarding it altogether, Foucault and Lyotard are unable to arrive at a more systematic understanding and critique of global capitalism. Their neglect of workers' struggles in particular appears as a disavowal of the fundamental stumbling blocks of neoliberal capitalism—its dirty secrets (exploitation in the form of sweatshop/indentured/slave labor, mostly composed of women, children, and migrants) but also its points of potential disruption: the working class / lumpenproletariat may not be a privileged (or indeed the single) revolutionary agent, but its struggles do help bring out key socioeconomic crises / points of implosion (the Real) of the global market system that so dominates our lives. In this sense, sweatshop labor, for example, is not just one among many other potential agents of social change today (LGBT+, feminist, environmental, and other such groups) but, as part of the part of no-part (see chapter 1), a "concrete universal," a particular element that makes possible (and threatens) that most dominant of universal systems, global capitalism. By championing only narrow, single-issue movements (and most often cultural ones), it is as if Foucault and Lyotard have either given up on radical transformation or, as highlighted earlier, think that capitalism can be brought down by individual choice and micro-resistances. Žižek takes this argument further (Butler, Laclau, and Žižek 2000a, 97): drawing on Wendy Brown (1995), he claims that postmodernism's neglect of class struggle is a displacement of key social antagonisms onto a series of markers of social diversity (gender, queerness, disability, etc.) that, as we have just seen, align only too well with the capitalist commodification of identity. Such is the direct result of postmodernism's culturalization of politics, its jettisoning of political economy, its quasi-disavowal of issues of social injustice and exploitation, and whether by intent or neglect, its surrender to global capitalism. As Žižek puts it, *"Depoliticized political economy is the 'fundamental fantasy' of postmodern politics"* (1999, 355).

Radical Democracy: Unthreatening Universality

Laclau and Mouffe (L&M) share with Foucault and Lyotard the postmodern penchant for culture. For them, the world acquires meaning only through linguistic/discursive construction, as a result of which identities are not stable or innate but relational and contingent, each deriving from the play of differences. It is this embrace of the cultural that distinguishes L&M from classical (materialist) Marxist theorists. To be sure, they not only gladly adopt the moniker "post-Marxism" to describe their political-theoretical position, but also insist on doing so "without apologies" (1990), reflecting their aim to rethink socialism along postmodern lines.

In their groundbreaking book *Hegemony and Socialist Strategy*, L&M claim the "impossibility of 'society'" (1985, 122). According to them, the precariousness and instability of identity causes the social to be riven with antagonisms, rendering it fundamentally split and divided. Such instability underlies for them the *political* nature of society, foregrounding how identity is never given, but the result of political struggle. In turn, this anti-essentialist stance puts paid to the classical Marxist utopia of a harmonious society, and especially to the notion of the proletariat as a universal class. For L&M, the openness and political nature of identity means that the Left must abandon the idea of the working class as a privileged agent of change (87, 159). The contingent and changing social positioning of any group—whether workers or feminists—signifies that none can speak for everyone.

Implied here is not a rejection of universality but a certain suspicion (or circumscription) of it. L&M see it as contingent, that is, always in-the-making, never fixed or transhistorical. The universal is, in this sense, "empty" (75), ready to be filled by a contingent-particular content. Žižek usefully summarizes L&M's position this way: "Each Universal is the battleground on which the multitude of particular contents fight for hegemony . . . all positive content of the Universal is the contingent result of hegemonic struggle—in itself, the Universal is absolutely empty" (Žižek 1999, 101).[2]

Central to L&M's viewpoint is the notion of "articulation," which they define as "any practice establishing a relation among different elements such that their identity is modified as a result of the articulatory practice" (1985, 85, 105). The idea here is that discrete political movements may begin their struggle based on particular "subject positions" (87, 115), but through an act of political construction—through articulation—they can forge a common agenda. What matters to L&M is not sharing a horizon or building an alliance per se, but how the demands of each movement are articulated *equivalently* with those of others, resulting in the modification of "the very identity of [the] forces engaging in that alliance" (Laclau and Mouffe 1985, 182, 184). Thus for example, in their articulation with LGBT+ HIV/AIDS groups, healthcare groups will discover that to stand for universal access to health is also to stand for LGBT+ rights, while LGBT+ groups will realize that the broader fight for universal health coverage is equally a gay rights issue. Articulation is only meaningful, then, if political identities change equivalently on each side. Political movements thus build hegemony through articulation/equivalence, the goal being to construct a plural and radical democracy (Laclau and Mouffe 1985, 7, 170; Butler, Laclau, and Žižek 2000a, 302–3; Mouffe 2005b, 69). In this regard, L&M pin their hopes on the rise of "new social movements," which they see as enabling the multiplication of social spaces within liberal democracy.

Note here that hegemony creates universality by articulating particular positions in a chain of equivalence. This means that particularity can be transformed into universality only through hegemonic struggle. It also means that universality is always provisional and contingent—because hegemony itself is "permanently under threat and needs to be continuously redefined" (Laclau and Mouffe 1990, 124; Laclau 1990, 29). As a site of plural standpoints articulated in equivalence to each other, then, universality can never be decided in advance or out of context; for L&M it has to be deftly constructed and remains forever open and incomplete.

L&M's radical democratic perspective has much in common with Žižek's conception of universality: as discussed earlier (see chapter 1), negative universality is consistent with the notion of politics as responding to, and addressing, the fundamental incompleteness and instability of the social, as well as the paradoxical idea that the universal is contingent and can only be articulated from a partial/particular perspective. Yet there is also significant divergence between the two sides. To begin with, each has a very different understanding of antagonism (see Zerilli 1998; Brockelman 2003). L&M view antagonism as an *external* conflict between two subject positions (e.g., master/slave, man/woman). To wit, Laclau underlines that antagonism "does not originate from the 'inside' of identity itself but, in its most radical sense, *from outside*" (1990, 17). This means, as Žižek explains in his commentary in *Hegemony and Socialist Strategy*, that each subject position "is preventing the other from achieving its identity with itself, to become what it really is" (1990, 251).[3] In contrast, negative universality views antagonism as *internal*, reflecting the fundamental self-blockage of the subject: as Žižek avers, "It is not the external enemy who is preventing me from achieving identity with myself, but every identity is itself blocked, marked by an impossibility" (251–52).

Such a contrast lays bare two troublesome implications. First, the view that it is the Other/enemy prohibiting me from achieving my full identity appears as little more than a displacement of the problem of self-limitation. Žižek writes in this regard that "the negativity of the other which is preventing me from achieving my full identity with myself is just the externalization of my own auto-negativity, of my self-hindering" (252–53). In other words, such displacement is a way for one to avoid the trauma of auto-blockage (i.e., a refusal to face the Real of one's own identity). And second (and relatedly), dodging one's own limitations gives the "illusion that after the eventual annihilation of the antagonistic enemy, I will finally abolish antagonism and arrive at an identity with myself" (251). The fantasy here is in fact a double one, since it involves both deluding oneself that one can somehow free oneself of antagonism (i.e., refusing to admit that one never can) and pigeonholing or stereotyping the Other (e.g., viewing the Other as threat or exotic stranger to be kept at a distance or indeed eliminated). Ironically, then, L&M's position on antagonism veers toward essentialism (of the self and the Other); which is another way of saying that, despite all, it hides a universalist fantasy.

Paul Eisenstein and Todd McGowan take the argument further by claiming that, despite centering radical democracy on the notion of antagonism, L&M "sell antagonism short." This is because the latter fail to see the intimate link between universality and antagonism itself. As Eisenstein and McGowan pointedly underline, there is "no need to construct a universal ... because antagonism ... is already universal" (2012, 68). L&M spend so much time on issues of identity-related articulation and equivalence that they miss that which is in plain sight—what political struggles share is not identity but self-division. In fact, as underlined in chapter 1, it is precisely the focus on identity rather than self-division that has bedeviled social movements in our age of identity politics: so invested do people become in their identities (*jouissance*) that they get bogged down in battles over recognition and self-policing (i.e., "checking one's privilege"). A negative universal politics avoids this predicament by expressly focusing not on positive identities but on common auto-blockage.

The related issue is that, despite recognizing the problems of particularism (see Laclau 1996, 49), radical democracy's de facto fetishization of identity feeds (and has fed) too easily into liberal democracy's celebration of new subjectivities and fluid identities. Here the fate of L&M's position ends up mirroring Foucault's and Lyotard's in silently accepting, if not furthering, late capitalism's co-optation and commodification of multicultural/identity politics. Radical democracy may well aim at "deepening and expanding" the liberal democratic setup (Laclau and Mouffe 1985, 176), but it ends up remaining firmly within its horizon. In this regard, Žižek claims that it is not the capitalist economy that limits hegemonic struggle: "On the contrary, [capitalism] is its *positive condition*; it creates the very background against which 'generalized hegemony' can thrive ... [As a result, Laclau and Mouffe] *never* envisage the possibility of a completely *different* economico-political regime ... all the changes [they propose] are changes *within* this economico-political regime" (Butler, Laclau, and Žižek 2000a, 319, 223).

But Laclau counters by accusing Žižek of economism. He declares that Žižek fetishizes the economy in asserting a new version of the base-superstructure model and returning to "the nineteenth-century myth of an enclosed economic space" (Butler, Laclau, and Žižek 2000a, 293, 291). Here, Laclau is aligning Žižek with classical Marxism, which he and Mouffe sharply criticize for treating the market as the "Last Redoubt of Essentialism" (1985, 75). Yet the allegation does not stand up to scrutiny, since Žižek repeatedly talks about capitalism in terms of political economy, that is, as a system barred by class struggle. To wit, he writes that "the 'economy' .. be reduced to a sphere of the positive 'order of being,' precisely insofar as it is always political, insofar as political ('class') struggle is at its very heart" (2011, 198; see also Cowley 2014, 78). Class struggle for Žižek is therefore the Real of capitalism, underlining how the market is always already marked by socio-political antagonism (and thus never self-enclosed).

Yet Žižek remains adamant in claiming that the economy so conceived is not simply one among multiple spheres to be reckoned with: as stressed in chapter 1, the capitalist market is universal in scope, touching everything, articulating with ecology as much as disability and "race." For Žižek, capitalism is "more than ever . . . the concrete universal of today . . . overdetermin[ing] all alternative formations" (2012a, 184). It is for this reason that he pleads "for a 'return to the primacy of the economy' not to the detriment of the issues raised by postmodern forms of politicization, but precisely in order to create the conditions for the more effective realization of feminist, ecological, and so on, demands" (1999, 356).

Here Žižek's implicit if not explicit reproach to L&M is that by not wishing to "privilege" the economy under the pretext of anti-essentialism, they end up excluding the politicization of the economic sphere: "All the talk about new forms of politics bursting out all over, focused on particular issues (gay rights, ecology, ethnic minorities . . .), all this incessant activity of fluid, shifting identities . . . has something inauthentic about it, and ultimately resembles the obsessional neurotic who talks all the time . . . in order to ensure that something—what *really* matters—will *not* be disturbed, that it will remain immobilized" (1999, 354). Thus, because they preclude the prospect of radical change of the global socioeconomic system, "Laclau and Mouffe stand accused . . . of being ideologues" (Brockelman 2003, 196).

Finally, there is the thorny question of the working class: as we saw, because they claim that social movement politics cannot be reduced to economic positioning, they are critical of the classical Marxist view of the working class as a privileged political agent. They are of course right to point out that the working class is not homogeneous, and that workers' struggles are not necessarily anticapitalist (e.g., some, although certainly not all, unions and "labor aristocracies" can be politically placid if not conservative), nor are anticapitalist struggles necessarily workers' struggles (e.g., feminist, LGBT+, antiracism, and disability groups can also be anticapitalist) (Laclau and Mouffe 1985, 82, 86; Butler, Laclau, and Žižek 2000a, 203). Yet what they ignore is the unprecedented "re-emergence" of the working class under late capitalism. Žižek contends, in this regard, that "the result of the much-praised 'disappearance of the working class' is the emergence of millions of manual workers labouring in Third World sweatshops [most of whom are women, children, and migrants], out of the delicate Western sight" (Butler, Laclau, and Žižek 2000a, 322). Moreover, if anticapitalist struggles are not necessarily workers' struggles, neither are workers' struggles necessarily narrowly economic struggles: sweatshop (and forced/slave) labor exploitation most often has feminist, LGBT+, racial, and disability dimensions, so that labor action frequently involves more than just economic demands.

The broader point, though, is that, given that global capitalism is such a forceful and globalizing phenomenon, the importance of the working class, particularly although not exclusively the most exploited/marginalized among its ranks, cannot be overemphasized. As Žižek puts it, "My point of contention with Laclau . . . is that I do not accept that all elements which enter into hegemonic struggle are in principle equal: in the series of struggles (economic, political, feminist, ecological, ethnic, etc.) there is always one which, while it is part of the chain, secretly overdetermines its very horizon" (Butler, Laclau, and Žižek 2000a, 320). And that overdetermining element *is* the economic. So while the working class is not the predestined revolutionary agent, what cannot be ignored is the centrality workers embody under global capitalism, and the crucially attendant restructuring role that anticapitalist struggles can play. Workers' struggles are capitalism's uncanny, destabilizing it, preventing it from fully constituting itself. Thus, the *particular* truth of the socioeconomic position of sweatshop labor (or other forms of the abject working class) is universal in that it is a distilled version of what is rotten about the system. This is why the proletariat for Žižek is not the mythical Marxist idea of the Subject of History, but rather, as we have noted before, the Rancièrian notion of the part of no-part that draws out the universal injustice of the system: "To take Marx's classic example, 'proletariat' stands for universal humanity not because it is the lowest, most exploited class, but because its very existence is a 'living contradiction'—that is, it gives body to the fundamental imbalance and inconsistency of the capitalist social Whole" (Žižek 1999, 173, 225). In this precise sense, when workers are fighting for their own *égaliberté* (equality-freedom), they are fighting for everyone's.

To conclude, what is striking is that, even though L&M proclaim a Marxist orientation, politically they end up remarkably close to Foucault's and Lyotard's decidedly non-Marxist position. This is likely because what they all share is a postmodern bias toward the cultural. Such a bias, as we have seen, causes Foucault and Lyotard to abandon universality altogether, in favor of localized particularism, which multicultural global capitalism has been only too happy to accommodate. And while L&M embrace rather than discard universality, it turns out to be a placid form of it, placing its bets mostly on cultural struggles that once again are unthreatening to, and easily co-opted by, global capitalism. L&M may well affirm antagonism, yet it appears as a timid version, yielding to particularized struggles over identity rather than more challenging and disruptive struggles over labor exploitation, resource extraction, or dispossession (i.e., material struggles). While political economy struggles might not be the only struggles worth waging, they truthtell about the real stakes in the capitalist global economy. Thus, the only way to break out of globalization's colonization of (culturalized) particularities is to reassert (a negative) universality, that is, to expose its antagonisms, to affirm the primacy of the economic sphere and its accompanying political/class struggle.

The Ontological/Affective Turn: A "Passion for the Real"

The ontological/affective turn presents itself as a correction to the overreach of the linguistic/cultural turn, to its overemphasis on the subject and its vicissitudes. What brings these diverse voices together is a certain "passion for the real," to borrow Badiou's expression, a desire for the spontaneous and unmediated, a desire to frame what is at stake in terms of ontology and exposure. This turn shifts attention back to the external world, to "the great outdoors [*le grand dehors*]," as Quentin Meillassoux puts it (2008, 7). In *After Finitude*, Meillassoux blames Kant and his "Ptolemaic counterrevolution" (2008, 119) for the unfortunate state of philosophy, with post-Kantian movements of thought only prolonging this philosophical catastrophe. From Marxism and phenomenology to psychoanalysis and deconstruction, continental philosophy has suffered the limitations of "correlationism": the crippling view that contends that "we only ever have access to the correlation between thinking and being, and never to either term considered apart from the other" (Meillassoux 2008, 5). Since we do not have a rational access to things-in-themselves, all we have after Kant, all we are allowed to discuss philosophically, are the transcendental conditions for human knowledge.[4] Any claim of knowledge is immediately followed by a qualification: "for us," that is, *for us finite beings*. On Meillassoux's reading, the linguistic turn is only the latest phase of correlationism. Against this decidedly wrong turn, Meillassoux and others move to usher in a new philosophical ethos, marked by its receptivity to exteriority, to what lies outside the prison house of language and subjectivity.

Among the divergent philosophers and critics of the ontological/affective turn is a concerted effort to approach the question of identity (be it that of the subject or what lies beyond the subject) in ontological terms, beyond culturalization, or in other words to see "being/becoming" as at odds with the symbolic order, in excess of its cultural containment and gentrification. Žižek is by no means hostile to this (re)turn to ontology. Indeed, a universal politics cannot be solely preoccupied with the epistemic conditions of possibility; it cannot give up on "big metaphysical questions."[5] Reality *as such*—a matter all too quickly dismissed by the "easy relativism" of a popularized version of postmodernism—is the *matter* of a universal politics. The return to the "great outdoors" is first and foremost for Žižek a return to politics: the materialist practice of a "ruthless critique of all that exists" (Marx 1975, 142) and/as the affirmation of the ontological incompleteness of reality itself. Politics begins with a *no!*—a contestation of the status quo. As we argued in previous chapters, politics happens when one declares the established order contingent—affirming that it could be otherwise—insisting on the *gap* between the existing, administered social order and the ontological lack that bolsters it.

New Materialism: The Fantasy of Postcritique

Žižek's unwavering commitment to ideology critique in the pursuit of a universal politics puts him at odds with the flat ontology of New Materialism (NM) championed by Bruno Latour and Jane Bennett. For Latour and his acolytes, ideology critique is outdated; not only did it *run out of steam*, but it is also effectively doing more harm than good, arming the enemies of science with fallacious arguments about "objective world" and distorting the realities of impending ecological disasters. For Bennett and her wing of NM, the very idea of universal politics harks back to a violent and anthropocentric model that does little to acknowledge and respond to the challenges of the Anthropocene. Latour and Bennett frame their interventions as fundamentally egalitarian, democratizing the value of all beings, " 'horizontalizing' the ontological plane" (Bennett 2015, 230). Consequently, the key Heideggerian distinction between being-in-the-world and being-in-the-midst-of-the-world vanishes. With flat ontology, *there are only beings*; or, as Levi Bryant puts it, in a way that decentralizes the human subject and its relevance further, "There is only one type of being: objects" (2011a, 20). NM degrades the human subject's historically elevated status in the Great Chain of Being (*scala naturae*), curbing its narcissistic and solipsistic aspirations in order to bear witness to the long-neglected "capacity of things" themselves. NM is a non-human politics, or, better yet, a politics of objects/things—of those who do not belong or count *from the standpoint of the human subject*.

Latour's impact in this ontological/affective turn cannot be overstated. His hit-job on leftists for their alleged hubris and their general neglect of or disparaging attitude toward the common man—who is reduced to a "hapless victim of domination" (2004b, 243)—was instrumental in marginalizing the labor of critique, creating optimal conditions for a new generation of critics to embrace the postpolitical in its righteous and phantasmatic form of postcritique. If fantasy teaches one to desire, the fantasy of postcritique teaches today's critics to desire a politics beyond antagonisms, a politics that can unproblematically operate alongside global capitalism. Part of Latour's rhetorical appeal is that he presents himself as a guilty party, one who was complicit with critique: "The mistake we made, the mistake I made, was to believe that there was no efficient way to criticize matters of fact except by moving away from them and directing one's attention towards the conditions that made them possible" (2004b, 231). Mea culpa aside, Latour paints the practice of denaturalization—the "*critical barbarity*" (2004b, 240) of the Left, its enjoyment of debunking people's hard-felt beliefs—as shortsighted at best, and detrimental to the social fabric at worst. In his self-congratulatory apology of the common man, Latour contests critique's myopic attachment to demystification and antifetishism. The consequences of critique are simply devastating: too much subtracting and not enough adding to people's Lebenswelt. What is a universal politics other than a positing of its exponents in the position of an all-powerful God? This deity, "the Zeus of Critique," as Latour describes him, "rules absolutely, to be sure, but over a desert" (2004b, 239, 248).

Latour's corrective to critique's obsession with ideology is actor-network theory. Rather than foregrounding critique—by putting the human agent at the center of the critical interpretation of what *is*—actor-network decentralizes the subject of critique by multiplying the sites of agency and extending the privileges of autonomy and hermeneutics to nonhumans:

> *Any thing* that does modify a state of affairs by making a difference is an actor—or, if it has no figuration yet, an actant. Thus, the questions to ask about any agent are simply the following: Does it make a difference in the course of some other agent's action or not? (Latour 2005, 71)

> Hermeneutics is not a privilege of humans but, so to speak, a property of the world itself. (Latour 2005, 245)

Similarly for Bennett, it is paramount to place humans and things on equal footing, and not rob the latter of their anarchic powers to contest. From this vantage point, a truly universal politics would at once reconsider its elevation of workers' struggles and call for a radical rethinking of Rancière's notion of part of no-part by making it available to nonhumans as well. Asking Rancière about this very possibility, Bennett recalls her disappointment in the answer given:

> When asked in public whether he thought that an animal or a plant or a drug or a (nonlinguistic) sound could disrupt the police order, Rancière said no: he did not want to extend the concept of the political that far; nonhumans do not qualify as participants in a demos; the disruption effect must be accompanied by the desire to engage in reasoned discourse. (2010, 106)

A nonhuman part of no-part is a priori ruled out by Rancière. Lacking Logos, nonhumans are not ascribed a contesting will; they are precluded from occupying a "'proletarian' position," from "stand[ing] for the position of universality" (Žižek 2012d, 434). Nonhumans are "deprived of a discourse" but denied the ontological means of doing something about it. From the perspective of NM, the workers' capacity to struggle against capitalist exploitation, to voice their grievances (to "act," in its Lacanian sense), is a human privilege—the privilege of resistance, that is, of becoming candidates for the part of no-part. But new materialists assure us that there are moments when objects do rise up and speak (back) to the *anthropos*. We just have to be more attentive to the ways they unsettle the normal order of things. As Bryant puts it, "These moments where nonhuman agents such as cane toads, natural gas leaks produced through fracking, and hurricanes can rise up and disrupt the orderly auto-reproduction of systems look suspiciously like the agencies of *political subjects*" (2011b, 27). It is thus not beyond the reach of nonhumans to alter the human-centered "field of experience" (Rancière 1999, 35), to upset the unjust "distribution of places and roles," and to exert pressure on the "order of the visible and the sayable" (Rancière 1999, 28–29). If nonhumans in Rancière's political schema are kept in their place of subordination, as second-class beings, they are welcomed and recognized as full-fledged democratic agents in Bennett's and Latour's non-anthropocentric model of democracy, where *"the voices of nonhumans"* (Latour 2004a, 69) count in this "parliament of things" (Latour 1993, 144–45).

After the obsession with critique comes an appreciation for the non-human; a better and more holistic approach to the external world—a world marked by a non-anthropocentric orientation. A Žižekian rejoinder, how-ever, questions this framing of the problem. Žižek does not see a focus on nonhuman factors as mutually exclusive with ideology critique. Far from it: an eye for the ways actants relate to one another at a polluted trash site (drawing on Bennett's own example) promises to yield a critical perspective, since it effectively brings to light "how not only humans but also the rotting trash, worms, insects, abandoned machines, chemical poisons, and so on each play their (never purely passive) role. There is an authentic theoret-ical and ethico-political insight in such an approach" (Žižek 2016f, 60). The virtues of a wider account lie in its disruption of an anthropocentric vision of the external world. But whereas Bennett promotes the cultivation of non-human perspectives as something intrinsically valuable, Žižek locates its de-sirability in its capacity to mobilize adequate resistance to capitalism's ruling ideology (Bennett 2010, 4–6).

Moreover, the question of the nonhuman in NM often appears to be nothing more than virtue signaling: look at the ways we conscientious (post) humans care about nonhumans. "I will emphasize, even overemphasize, the agentic contributions of nonhuman forces . . . in an attempt to counter the narcissistic reflex of human language and thought," writes Bennett (2010, xvi). A decentralized politics declines to erect its politics around a narcis-sistic subject, opting for a perpetual decentering of the human/subjectivity per se:

> Another way to cultivate this new discernment might be to elide the ques-tion of the human. Postpone for a while the topics of subjectivity or the nature of human interiority, or the question of what really distinguishes the human from the animal, plant, and thing. Sooner or later, these topics will lead down the anthropocentric garden path, will insinuate a hierarchy of

subjects over objects, and obstruct freethinking about what agency really entails. (Bennett 2010, 2)

NM's objections to anthropocentrism and critique are essentially moralist (a mode of analysis that is increasingly flourishing in a postpolitical climate): "Ethical motivation needs ... to draw upon *co-feeling or sympathy with suffering*, and also upon a certain love of the world, or enchantment with it" (Bennett 2004, 361, emphasis added). Our hubris—our inextinguishable will to critique (as opposed to love or enchant)—is effectively to blame for the suffering of nonhumans: it is keeping us from a life of enchantment, from truly living with nonhumans, from making and embracing assemblages, which, following Deleuze and Guattari, Bennett describes as "ad hoc groupings of diverse elements, of vibrant materials of all sorts. Assemblages are living, throbbing confederations that are able to function despite the persistence of energies that confound them from within" (2010, 23–24). They are contingent associations of human and nonhuman entities. Humans are decentered in assemblages. As Jasbir Puar points out, assemblages "de-privilege the human body as a discrete organic thing" (2012, 57). The essentialization of the object/thing/body is anathema to the workings of an assemblage. Embodying a model of coexistence between humans and nonhumans, assemblages bring to the forefront objects that are multiple and unstable, always available to alteration and mutation. Indeed, an assemblage stresses complexity and process, deriving its "agentic capacity" from "the vitality of the materialities that constitute it" (Bennett 2010, 34).

To be sure, Žižek is not unsympathetic to assemblage thinking per se. Rather, it is NM's repeated under-theorization of the subject, folded in a fantasy of postcritique (read as a posthuman re-enchantment of the given), that gives him, and us, pause. NM's assemblages are the product of premodern magic:

If, then, New Materialism can still be considered a variant of materialism, it is in the sense in which Tolkien's Middle-earth is materialist: as an enchanted world, full of magical forces, good and evil spirits, etc., but strangely without gods—there are no transcendent divine entities in Tolkien's universe, all magic is immanent to matter, as a spiritual power that dwells in our terrestrial world. (Žižek 2014a, 12)

Against Bennett's regressive neoanimism—to the extent that it "takes the step back into (what can only appear to us moderns as) premodern naivety, covering up the gap that defines modernity and re-asserting the purposeful vitality of nature" (Žižek 2014a, 12)—Žižek maintains that assemblages hold a "subversive potential" as long as we keep in mind the status of the subject. The operation of seeing the world from "inhuman eyes"—disclosing, as it were, *the world of objects*—can only be enacted or performed by "an (empty) subject," a subject who has dislodged himself from his human coordinates— from his symbolically constituted reality—and whose "violent abstraction" from his particular situation enables him to see himself as an object among other objects in the world (Žižek 2018, 57).

In a way, we might say that a universal politics supplements an ethics of NM with a psychoanalytical framework. And this supplement begins with the structure of fetishistic *disavowal* (*I know very well, but all the same*). Žižek interprets this refusal to fully attend to the suffering of nonhumans not merely as evidence of humanist hubris and callous speciesism but as emblematic of ethics as such. At some profound level, every ethics performs a fetishistic disavowal, choosing to "draw a line and ignore some sort of suffering." Žižek keenly asks:

> What about animals slaughtered for our consumption? Who among us would be able to continue eating pork chops after visiting a factory farm in which pigs are half-blind and cannot even properly walk, but are just fattened to be killed? And what about, say, torture and suffering of millions we know about, but choose to ignore? Imagine the effect of having to watch a snuff movie portraying what goes on thousands of times a day around the world: brutal acts of torture, the picking out of eyes, the crushing of testicles—the list cannot bear recounting. Would the watcher be able to continue going on as usual? Yes, but only if he or she were able somehow to forget—in an act which suspended symbolic efficiency—what had been witnessed. This forgetting entails a gesture of what is called fetishistic disavowal: "I know it, but I don't want to know that I know, so I don't know." I know it, but I refuse to fully assume the consequences of this knowledge, so that I can continue acting as if I don't know it. (2008c, 53)

Bennett and new materialists would lament liberalism's strong anthropocentric tradition, which prevents its indoctrinated subjects from extending the vibrancy of humanity to animate and inanimate objects, and thus to register and connect with the suffering of nonhumans. Failure to appreciate the "vitality of matter" can only perpetuate "our earth-destroying fantasies of conquest and consumption" (Bennett 2010, ix). But a Žižekian approach tells a different story. The problem is not an attachment to human exceptionalism per se. As liberal subjects, we maintain a split attitude. We know that we experiment on animals, mistreat and slaughter them. But we want to forget about their suffering. We want to remain ethical but don't want to assume the consequences: the need to radically transform the order of things, society's unequal distribution of values—the determination of who counts and who doesn't. The structure of fetishistic disavowal enables the liberal subject to "know" but without making that knowledge paralyzing, disruptive, or detrimental to the well-being of society.

A universal politics must confront the fetishistic disavowal that neutralizes this knowledge and makes possible the smooth functioning of quotidian existence, that feeds the belief that life under liberal democracy is a life without genuine misery: no factory farms, sweatshops, sex trafficking, slums, and so on. NM misfires when it blames the "earth-destroying fantasies of conquest and consumption" almost exclusively on our Cartesian humanist legacy. Today's humanists are liberal and enthusiastically tolerant of nonhumans. They not only acknowledge evolution but also fight for its teaching in school and even support animal rights. But as psychoanalysis helps to disclose, liberal subjects are anti-speciesists in theory but speciesists in practice when it comes to *their* humanity.

So Žižek asks again: "Does not *every* ethics have to rely on such a gesture of fetishistic disavowal? Yes, every ethics—with *the exception of the ethics of psychoanalysis* which is a kind of anti-ethics: it focuses precisely on what the standard ethical enthusiasm excludes, on the traumatic Thing that our Judeo-Christian tradition calls the 'Neighbor'" (2008a, 15–16). Assemblage thinking is at its most subversive not when it enchants or mystifies the world but when it effectively produces an "'inhuman' view" of things, when it compels us to confront the subject *as neighbor*, as a faceless object. As we have seen, a universal politics avows the "traumatic Thing," foregrounding this unnerving image of the neighbor in its critical engagement with global capitalism and its pursuit of solidarity. Postcritique masquerades as more egalitarian and less anthropocentric. It does so by mischaracterizing the penchant for universality as inescapably anthropocentric. A universal politics is clearly not in the service of anthropocentrism, especially when it is inflected with a psychoanalytical bent. It is NM that does little to weaken the prevalent attitude of fetishistic disavowal, which enables anthropocentrism to strive while allowing "woke" liberal subjects to pretend to have overcome its ideological hold. Psychoanalysis, as Žižek frames it, insists that any form of solidarity must pass through (an encounter with) the neighbor—and, contrary to Bennett, what or who stands for the neighbor (as a figure for the part of no-part) does not a priori exclude nonhumans.

In *Less Than Nothing*, Žižek takes up the question of the animal in relation to the subject's own animality:

> The cat's gaze stands for the gaze of the Other—an inhuman gaze, but for this reason all the more the Other's gaze in all its abyssal impenetrability. Seeing oneself being seen by an animal is an abyssal encounter with the Other's gaze, since—precisely because we should not simply project onto the animal our inner experience—something is returning the gaze which is radically Other. The entire history of philosophy is based upon a disavowal of such an encounter. (2012d, 411)

If philosophy always seeks to positivize the subject—" 'Man,' 'human person,' is a mask that conceals the pure subjectivity of the Neighbor" (Žižek 2008a, 16)—psychoanalysis is in the business of emptying the subject, reminding us of the faceless other, the animal, the animalized human.

To make his point, Žižek offers the example of a lab cat: "I remember seeing a photo of a cat after it had been subjected to some lab experiment in a centrifuge, its bones half broken, its skin half hairless, its eyes looking helplessly into the camera—this is the gaze of the Other disavowed not only by philosophers, but by humans 'as such' " (2012d, 411). Žižek's cat bears a striking resemblance to the *Muselmann* of Primo Levi's account, that living-dead, faceless figure of Auschwitz, whom he identifies with the biblical figure of the neighbor. Again, Žižek considers the neighbor, the injunction to "love thy neighbor," the "most precious and revolutionary aspect of the Jewish legacy," highlighting, as chapter 1 outlined, the ways the neighbor "remains an inert, impenetrable, enigmatic presence that hystericizes" (2006b, 140–41). While Greek philosophy never accounted for this hysterical presence ("Nothing is farther from the message of Socrates than *you shall love your neighbor as yourself, a formula that is remarkably absent* from all that he says," Žižek writes, quoting Lacan [Žižek et al. 2006, 4]), Jewish law bears witness to the Real of the neighbor, the neighbor as the "bearer of a monstrous Otherness, this properly *inhuman* neighbor" (2006b, 162).

The *Muselmann* is the paradigmatic example of the neighbor. The Auschwitz camp produced the *Muselmann*, a "neighbor with whom no empathetic relationship is possible" (Žižek 2006b, 162). With the *Muselmann*, "We encounter the Other's call at its purest and most radical," and "one's responsibility toward the Other at its most traumatic" (Žižek 2006b, 162). Žižek's lab cat is a feline version of the *Muselmann*. The lab cat is a cat laid bare, stripped of its symbolic veneer as a *domestic* pet. We are in the presence of a "real" cat, a neighbor that is neither *like* other domestic cats nor a radical alterity mysteriously exempt from symbolic mediation (a cat with a Levinasian face, if you will). Žižek's lab cat simultaneously hystericizes and implicates me:

> What if that which characterizes humans is this very openness to the abyss of the radical Other, this perplexity of "What does the Other really want from me?" In other words, what if we turn the perspective around here? What if the perplexity a human sees in the animal's gaze is the perplexity aroused by the monstrosity of the human being itself? What if it is my own abyss I see reflected in the abyss of the Other's gaze. (2012d, 414)

"*Che vuoi?*" What does the cat (as neighbor) want from me? The Žižekian response sends us (back) to the subject. The terrifying abyss that I see in the cat's gaze, that prompts my hystericization, is paradoxically *also* my own. An (anti-)ethics of solidarity is not satisfied with simply attending to the alterity of the Other (be it worker or cat); it equally stresses the need to come to terms with the abyssal neighbor *within*, with what the structure of fetishistic disavowal is constantly trying to cover up or over. A struggle against anthropocentrism (a struggle against the human domination on nonhumans) must, then, begin not with a phantasmatic suspension of subject, but with the subject as neighbor, which might very well lead to a solidarity with nonhumans, say, of workers with lab cats.

Edelman and Ahmed: Queering the Universal

Queer theory's attitude toward the universal is also one of suspicion. The universal has stood for heteronormativity, whiteness, male particularity, and the values of Western civilization. Queering the universal for queer theorists as divergent as Sara Ahmed and Lee Edelman has meant contesting the rhetoric of the universal that has systematically marginalized gender-nonconforming bodies. The act of queering perverts (from the Latin *pervertere*, meaning to subvert, to turn upside down) society's normalizing and disciplining practices, that is, the identities that it promotes and universalizes. Most queer theorists do not subscribe to the script of postcritique. Queer critique scrutinizes the making of sexual or gender normativity, questioning society's operative logic of exclusion. Edelman proceeds by a frontal attack on identity as such, defining queerness as what is antithetical to all forms of identitarianism—"queerness can never define an identity; it can only ever disturb one" (2004, 17)—whereas Ahmed pursues alternative forms of identity, cultivating and sustaining a sense of "discomfort" that stems from "*inhabiting norms differently*," beyond "assimilation or resistance" (2014a, 155), beyond strict conformity or absolute subversion.

For Edelman, it is figure of the Child—denoting not actual or historical children but functioning symbolically "as the emblem of futurity's unquestioned value" (2004, 4)—which crystallizes the ideological trappings of identity, underpinning a future horizon determined by the promise of an innocent wholeness regained. The ethico-political injunction to make a future "for the children" locks us into an insidious reproduction of the status quo. Queer negativity is Edelman's uncompromising response to liberal society's heteronormativity and the prospects of "reproductive futurism." Queering the universal thus breaks with a politics thoroughly invested in the Child, which incarnates the "citizen as an ideal, entitled to claim full rights to its future share in the nation's good, though always at the cost of limiting the rights 'real' citizens are allowed" (Edelman 2004, 11). It involves the pure negation of the phantasmatic child, declining its redemptive value: the Child, as an embodiment of universal hope and innocence, will not save us—nor, for that matter, does Edelman's queer subject want to be saved, that is, included in Western civilization's fold. No, the queer—as the anti-Child, the homosexual subject who cannot reproduce—stands for the destruction of that civilization. Contrary to the typical well-meaning liberal responses to homophobes in power (e.g., Donald Wildmon, founder and head of the American Family Association, who rejects and demonize queer sexualities, depicting them as a threat to America's way of life, to the "very foundation of Western Civilization"), Edelman does not make any rhetorical or imaginary appeals to homophobes (i.e., queers are like them, that they are equally committed to society's values—they want to be able to marry, to adopt, to serve in the military, and so on—the stuff of homonormativity and homonationalism). Queer oppositionality acknowledges the right-winger's charge and boldly affirms it: "Rather than rejecting, with liberal discourse, this ascription of negativity to the queer, we might . . . do better to consider accepting and even embracing it" (Edelman 2004, 4). Queerness is, indeed, pursuing the destruction of Western civilization (spurring the view that Edelman is unapologetically promoting what has been called the "anti-social thesis"). Queerness refuses its integration in the Symbolic, always insisting on its heterogeneity. Thus antithetical to the survival of the status quo, queer negativity "*should* and *must* redefine such notions as 'civil order' through a rupturing of our foundational faith in the reproduction of futurity" (Edelman 2004, 16–17).

The engine of this rupturing of the symbolic order is the psychoanalytic notion of the death drive. It "names what the queer, in the order of the social, is called forth to figure: the negativity opposed to every form of social viability" (Edelman 2004, 9). What the death drive signals is the limitations of the pleasure principle, that there is an excess, a self-sabotaging structure at work in the Symbolic, a structure principally at odds with the well-being or fortification of the ego. Edelman pairs the death drive with Lacanian notion of jouissance, "a movement beyond the pleasure principle, beyond the distinctions of pleasure and pain, a violent passage beyond the bounds of identity, meaning, and law" (2004, 25). Edelman explores jouissance in two distinct scenarios, each with its particular version of the death drive. In the first instance, jouissance manifests itself as a result of a fetishistic attachment "to a particular object or end," resulting in a "congealing identity around the fantasy of satisfaction or fulfillment by means of that object" (Edelman 2004, 25). Here jouissance translates as a "fantasmatic escape from the alienation intrinsic to meaning" (Edelman 2004, 25); it "lodges itself in a given object on which identity comes to depend, it produces identity as mortification, reenacting the very constraint of meaning it was intended to help us escape" (Edelman 2004, 25). The death drive lies in the dissolution of the ego, an overcoming of the vicissitudes of meaning, in the hope a retrieving a blissful state of being. But this affective investment in the phantasmatic object has the effect of reifying the subject ("identity as mortification"), enacting a form of jouissance that ties it to a permanent mode of stasis. This death drive registers the subject's "craving for self-annihilation" (Žižek 2006c, 62).

If this form of jouissance is identified with the promise of plenitude, jouissance in the second instance derives from disrupting this very desire for completeness, halting its logic and procedures, "tear[ing] the fabric of Symbolic reality as we know it, unraveling the solidity of *every* object, including the object as which the subject necessarily takes itself" (Edelman 2004, 25). This form of jouissance is beyond or bereft of meaning. It foregrounds "the death drive that always insists as the void in and of the subject, beyond its far self-realization, beyond the pleasure principle" (Edelman 2004, 25). Edelman aligns the Child with the first scenario of jouissance, and the queer with the second. To queer the universal here is to choose the queer over the Child.

It is this emphasis on queerness that has led Madhavi Menon to counterintuitively align queerness with the universal as opposed to the particular: "What is universally queer is the ontological impossibility of self-identity. Everything is queer because nothing—peoples, events, desires—can achieve ontological wholeness" (2015, 19). For Menon, the negation introduced by Edelman is analogous to Badiou's universal. The queer is anti-identitarian, declining identity's seductions and manipulations. Unlike queer theorists who turn to difference as the antidote to heteronormativity/homonormativity, Menon urges, following Badiou, an *indifference to difference*. To queer the universal is to reject identity itself: "Identity is the demand made by power—tell us who you are so we can tell you what you can do. And by complying with that demand, by parsing endlessly the particulars that make our identity different from one another's, we are slotting into a power structure, not dismantling it" (2015, 2).[6]

And yet, is there an emancipatory politics to be found in this version of the universal? Is Edelman's queer protean subject truly compatible with Badiou's Pauline or cosmopolitan universalism? Menon's "queer universalism" irons out too quickly the friction between the two models. Žižek shares with Badiou a skepticism toward what presents itself as subversive and emancipatory. As Badiou says, "Tout ce qui bouge n'est pas rouge" (literally, "All that moves is not necessarily red," punning on *bouge/rouge*, meaning whatever agitates is not necessarily leftist). For example, the Yellow Vests *appear* as a leftist populist movement—anticapitalist, antiglobalization. But its potential to advance workers' struggles is aborted when the movement is successfully interpellated by Marine Le Pen's right-wing nationalist politics. With (Menon's) Edelman, we have another case of a fake emancipatory model. The elevated queer subject, this protean self along with "its unleashing of. . . radical negativity," remains fully compatible with global capitalism. Edelman's elevation of the "death drive" amounts to little more than a strategy of capitalist flexibilization, matching capitalism's "own nihilistic self-destructive aspect" (Žižek 2017c, 141).[7] Capitalism does not really have a problem with a subject who insists on the void/crack at heart of its being. Edelman's "ethics of now" (Žižek 2012d, 124)—his anti-politics of prosperity—never touches the Real. While Edelman's queerness does promote "the negativity of the death drive," which, in principle, nihilistically aims at a "withdrawing from reality into the Real of the 'Night of the World'" (Žižek 2012d, 141), his queer subject, in practice, still operates from *within* the ideological coordinates of capitalism, subversively dwelling, as it were, in the postpolitical, where capitalism can and does accommodate Edelman's "radical" apolitical demands, his drive for an undifferentiated unity of everything.

If, with the death drive and his "radical ethics of *jouissance*" (Žižek 2012d, 141), Edelman rejects the Child for its promise of future wholeness—which creates an opportunity for challenging capitalism and its reproductive logic—he stops short of exerting actual pressure on the system—of touching the Real. The queer subject is not (a priori) a revolutionary subject.[8] Queer universalism—which amounts to the fetishization of the protean self—misconstrues who the enemy really is: normativity rather than capitalism. The generalizability of queer jouissance (the becoming queer of the world) and the expansion of capitalism (the becoming black of the world) are not mutually exclusive phenomena. *All that is bereft of meaning is not necessarily left-leaning.* The Child and the Queer, though in different ways, do the bidding of capitalism: more of the same.

Now for Ahmed, queering the universal makes no pretensions to universalism. Ahmed does not follow Edelman's uncompromising brand of queer theory. She refuses to fetishize movement, a jouissance-inducing mode of becoming, since "the idealisation of movement, or transformation of movement into a fetish, depends upon the exclusion of others who are already positioned as *not free in the same way*" (2014a, 152). Queering the universal means declining the lure of transcendence. Queerness takes place against the backdrop of normativity; its negativity is never absolute. This is not a limitation but a fact of queerness, something constitutive of queer feelings:

> It is the non-transcendence of queer that allows queer to do its work. A queer hope is not, then, sentimental. It is affective precisely in the face of the persistence of forms of life that endure in the negative attachment of "the not." Queer maintains its hope for "non-repetition" only insofar as it announces the persistence of the norms and values that make queer feelings queer in the first place. (Ahmed 2014a, 165)

Universalisms of all kinds ignore the messiness of queer feelings. Ahmed disparages what she calls the "formalist universalism of philosophers such as Alain Badiou and Slavoj Žižek" (2014c, 160). For her, to queer the universal means to turn to what universalism leaves behind or ignores. It means giving voice to neglected particulars, valuing their irritant force, what she calls their "willfulness."

Ahmed's resistance to the universal is exemplified in her dispute with Žižek over multiculturalism's hegemonic status in society. She rejects Žižek's observation that multiculturalism's dominance is an empirical fact. She accuses Žižek of crude literalism, of failing to distinguish between multiculturalism as a reality and multiculturalism as a fantasy: "Multiculturalism is a fantasy which conceals forms of racism, violence and inequality as if the organisation/nation can now say: how can you experience racism when we are committed to diversity?" (2008). Diversity functions as an "ego ideal" (Ahmed 2008);[9] it is not there to support the vulnerable and the racialized but rather is put on display for the big Other to see: look at our workshops and mandatory seminars; see how we are endlessly contributing to the multiculturalism of the nation, the organization, the university, and so on. As "champions" of diversity, liberals imagine themselves as open-minded and enlightened multiculturalists, but in practice they are myopic monoculturalists:

> The best description of today's hegemony is "liberal monoculturalism" in which common values are read as under threat by the support for the other's difference, as a form of support that supports the fantasy of the nation as being respectful at the same time as it allows the withdrawal of this so-called respect. The speech act that declares liberal multiculturalism as hegemonic is the hegemonic position. (Ahmed 2008)

Žižek's response is twofold: first, yes, it is true that dominant multiculturalism functions as a fantasy; second, the problem with this multiculturalism is not that it hides the reality of monoculturalism but that it wants a toothless form of coexistence with difference—a being-with that does little to challenge the racism of multiculturalism. Ahmed misdiagnoses the problem; what is needed to cut through the fantasy multiculturalism is not a robust, queer, or willful difference but the universality of the part of no-part. A universal politics is not seduced by the moral discourse of cultural tolerance. It insists on figuring out who the true enemy is, and against today's political correctness, it urges *intolerance* toward who/what is actually responsible for society's ills. To do so necessitates a turn to society's antagonisms, along with the injunction to politicize them:

One should thoroughly reject the standard multiculturalist idea that, against ethnic intolerance, one should learn to respect and live with the Otherness of the Other, to develop a tolerance for different lifestyles, and so on—the way to fight ethnic *hatred* effectively is not through its immediate counterpart, ethnic *tolerance*; on the contrary, what we need is *even more hatred*, but proper *political* hatred: hatred directed at the common political enemy. (Žižek 2000a, 11)

So both Žižek and Ahmed reject the phantasmatic multiculturalist solution to racism, seeing it as part of the problem insofar as it obfuscates society's "civil racism." They condemn multiculturalists for making racism an exclusive problem of fringe groups and ideologies outside liberal sensibilities. The paradigmatic racist is not the white supremacist or neo-Nazi, but everyday liberals who consider themselves "woke" and socially refined, oblivious to their inscription and participation in "civil racism," the naturalized racism of quotidian life.

But this is where Žižek and Ahmed's convergence ends. What follows is a different set of prescriptions. Ahmed urges a defense of difference, holding out for a queer multiculturalism that does justice to the plight of the excluded, whereas Žižek exposes multiculturalism's misadventure with the universal in the hope of reviving or actualizing an antiracist form of universality (the more effective counter to fake universalism):

Multiculturalism is a racism which empties its own position of all positive content (the multiculturalist is not a direct racist, he doesn't oppose to the Other the *particular* values of his own culture), but nonetheless retains this position as the privileged *empty point of universality* from which one is able to appreciate (and depreciate) properly other particular cultures—the multiculturalist respect for the Other's specificity is the very form of asserting one's own superiority. (Žižek 1999, 216)

Multiculturalism traffics in *false* universality, or what we've been calling (abstract) universalism. It only purports to respect cultural difference; indeed, the enthusiastic multiculturalist is the first to defend the right for the other's particular way of life. The former does so from a position of power—only those with privilege, with the self-appointed privilege of speaking for humanity and hence not needing to claim their particularity—tolerate difference.

We must contrast multiculturalism's empty point of universality with that of the part of no-part. Ahmed ignores the relevance of this distinction, since for her, all universalisms are alike in their investment in a "theoretical brick wall"—a wall that reinforces the divide between those who count as universals (privileged white males) and the rest, those delegated to the purview of mere "identity politics." The consequences of Ahmed's neglect are significant. Žižek is accused of parochialism (as if he and Finkielkraut were saying the same thing), ironically when he is making this very point about multiculturalism. Žižek is all too cognizant of universalism's ideological framework, how it hides its racism by assuming that the multiculturalist's own culture is the norm, a norm from which others are denied from enjoying and claiming: "Multiculturalism is a disavowed, inverted, self-referential form of racism, a 'racism with a distance'—it 'respects' the Other's identity, conceiving the Other as a self-enclosed 'authentic' community towards which he, the multiculturalist, maintains a distance rendered possible by his privileged universal position" (1997a, 46).

De-universalizing multiculturalism, Žižek discloses how the respect for the non-European is never a respect for an equal. Multiculturalism's celebration of all cultures is a lie. Upon close scrutiny, we discover that only Western subjects are capable of mutuality, the privileges of disagreement; with cultural others, the Western subject must proceed with patronizing caution as if he or she were dealing with children, not full-fledged Kantian subjects: "When multiculturalists tell you to respect the others, I always have this uncanny association that this is dangerously close to how we treat our children: the idea that we should respect them, even when we know that what they believe is not true" (Reul and Deichmann 2001).

If Ahmed is correct in exposing how liberal multiculturalism produces what she dubs "non-performatives" ("speech acts that do not do what they say, and that *do not bring into effect what they name*" [Ahmed 2008; see Žižek 2011, 43]), she draws the wrong conclusion, according to Žižek, in saying that when multiculturalism claims to promote cultural difference (what it says), it is really after cultural homogeneity (what it does). For Žižek, multiculturalism is neither for cultural difference nor for cultural homogenization: what it wants is "cultural apartheid."

Queering multiculturalism, for Ahmed, takes the form of demystifying Europe's claim to the universal, provincializing the Western way of life, the unmarked standard of the rest of humanity. Ahmed advocates a true multiculturalism, one that starts by questioning "the coherence of the 'we' of the nation," learning to see "cultural difference" not as something to "abolish" or overcome but as constitutive of this national "we." Ahmed's multiculturalism is thus "always contested, whether at the level of government policy, or whether in critical scholarship and resistant political activity" (2000, 101). This multiculturalism avoids the traps of what passes for multiculturalism today, which is really a "liberal monoculturalism." But this is not enough for Žižek. "'True' multiculturalism" is itself a fantasy which reintroduces a questionable "neutral universal legal frame enabling each particular culture to assert its identity" (Žižek 2011, 53). Žižek doubts that this frame is capable of yielding any emancipatory potential. Rather, to repeat the passage quoted in chapter 1, "the thing to do is to change the entire field, introducing a totally different Universal, that of an antagonistic struggle which, rather than taking place between particular communities, splits each community from within, so that the 'trans-cultural' link between communities is one of a shared struggle" (Žižek 2011, 53).

Ahmed's purported "theoretical wall" comes not from universality per se but from an ideology of universalism that either elevates one form of life over another (by keeping Western subjects tacitly protected from non-European alterity: "Others should not come too close to us, we should protect our 'way of life'" [Žižek 2011, 46]) or unwittingly assumes a universalism that relativizes and flattens difference. In the first instance (multiculturalism's universalism), the protection of the Western "way of life" is framed as an ethical choice, a way of recognizing and sustaining the specificity of the Other's being-in-the-world: don't let go of your authentic (natural, innocent, whole, eternal, etc.) "way of life"; don't become like us compromised and alienated by our modernity. This disingenuous warning against Western homogenization recalls the type of arguments unsuccessfully used by South Africa's Afrikaners whose "official regime's ideology was multiculturalist," outrageously maintaining that "apartheid was needed so that all the diverse African tribes would not get drowned in white civilization" (Žižek 2011, 46).

In the second instance (Ahmed's queer or true multiculturalism), universalism returns as a leveling force, offering to ontologize each particular culture's claim to identity. Ahmed repeatedly accuses Žižek of producing a "caricature of identity politics," since he considers (along with many others in the Pauline tradition of universal cosmopolitanism) any minority group's desires to "find their voice," or assert a "way of life," ineffective, if not reactionary, due to its attachment to the defunct model of identity politics. Ahmed retorts: "Perhaps some have 'ways of life' because others have lives: some have to find voices because others are given voices; some have to assert their particulars because others have their particulars given general expression" (2014c, 160). But isn't this Ahmed's own caricature of universal politics? Žižek's point is not to chastise others for seeking a voice or a way of life and ignoring the emancipatory path of universality. Ahmed is blaming Žižek for conceptual narcissism. Simply put, Žižek never acknowledges the givenness of his own voice and life, seemingly unaware of his male and white privileges—which allow him the luxury of musing about universality. Such objections, however, miss their mark. To be sure, Žižek is often excessively dismissive of identity politics, but his critique does not stem from an unscrutinized attachment to a European way of life (a universal life that needs, according to Ahmed, provincializing).

Žižek's part of no-part stands for these very minority subjects. Queering the universal here means thinking the universal *with* the part of no-part. Queer subjects are not to be aligned exclusively with the partisans of difference. To short-circuit the smooth functioning of the system, queer subjects must assume the proletarian position and engage in the shared struggle against global capitalism and its reproduction of the status quo. Their struggle must become a universal struggle—irreducible to an ethical struggle against domination, which, as we have seen, plays into the hands of a postpolitical system. Leaders in global capitalism have repeatedly expressed their moral support of LGBT+. Take for example Apple CEO Tim Cook, who can, on one hand, openly condemn North Carolina's 2016 anti-LGBT+ law in "solidarity" with the transgender community while, on the other, disavowing Apple's abysmal labor practices outside the United States: "Tim Cook can easily forget about hundreds of thousands of Foxconn workers in China assembling Apple products in slave conditions—he makes his big gesture of solidarity with the underprivileged by demanding the abolition of gender segregation" (Žižek 2017a, 204).

If queer theorists do not elide economic exploitation altogether (Edelman), they narrowly focus on the labor of trans/queer people of color or migrants (Ahmed). But queering the universal, if it is going to be politically viable and transformative, must fully harness universality's negativity and be reread as a rallying cry to struggle against the implacable logic that divides the world between the included and the excluded, between those who count, whose lives matter, and the ever-expanding wretched of the earth (including whites among the labor force and the permanently unemployed)—at home and abroad.

Decolonial Pluriversality:
The Reactionary Authenticity of Geography

Like queer theory, decoloniality tends to approach the question of identity in ontological terms, rejecting Western modernity wholesale, while valorizing decolonial ways of knowing and living, especially as manifested in the global South. We focus here on the work of one of the leading decolonial theorists, Walter Mignolo, who accordingly repudiates Euro-North American "identity politics," seeing it as imposed on colonial subjects and preferring instead "identity in politics," which he takes as "open to whoever wants to join" (2011, 137; 2010, 346). For him, the geopolitical location of knowledge/identity matters (2007, 469). This is because European modernity has been violently foisted on the rest of the world while parading as universal. In this sense, universalism for him is "always imperial and war driven" (2018, xii).[10] His aim, instead, is to retrieve a "pluriverse" of decolonized (particularly Latin American) subaltern epistemologies.

Mignolo borrows from Aníbal Quijano (2000, 2007) the notion of "coloniality of power" (or "colonial matrix of power"), which refers to the systematic application of material, epistemic, and aesthetic resources required to create and maintain empire. To be sure, coloniality is seen as continuing in the former colonies despite the formal end of colonialism, and describes how colonial power manifests in the pervasiveness of Eurocentric knowledge systems, as much as in continuing patterns of racial oppression and socioeconomic exploitation. For Mignolo, as for Quijano, such coloniality cannot be disentangled from (Western) modernity: modernity and coloniality are co-constitutive, with the former acting as model for the latter, and the latter providing both the material wealth and cultural resources that have enabled Western superiority. As Mignolo puts it, " 'modernity' is a complex narrative whose point of origination was Europe; a narrative that builds Western civilization by celebrating its achievements while hiding at the same time its darker side, 'coloniality.' Coloniality, in other words, is constitutive of modernity—there is no modernity without coloniality" (2011, 2–3).

For Mignolo, the "rhetoric" of modernity/coloniality not only imposes a universal rationality on its subjects, but discursively creates and manages what he calls "colonial difference" (2012, xxv). The colonial subject is incorporated into Europe's orbit, most often relegated to the periphery, while subaltern knowledges are either erased or classified as "backward" in accordance with European norms. This has made it difficult for the colonial subject to imagine alternative ways of knowing and being.

Accordingly, Mignolo advocates for "epistemic disobedience and delinking from the colonial matrix in order to open up decolonial options" (2011, 9, 54).[11] The idea here is to decolonize the colonial subject's mind and imaginary, to "fracture the hegemony of knowledge and understanding that have been ruled, since the fifteenth century . . . [by] the theological and ego-logical politics of knowledge and understanding" (Mignolo 2010, 313). For Mignolo, only such an epistemological shift will be able to change both the content and the *terms* of the modernity/coloniality matrix. Drawing on Gloria Anzaldúa (1987), he argues in favor of "border thinking," as a result of which the cosmologies neglected and denied by coloniality become resources for constructing "alternatives *to* modernity" (2010, 320; 2011, xxviii). Border thinking for him entails "absorbing and displacing hegemonic forms of knowledge into the perspective of the subaltern"; it means that "the reason of the master is absorbed by the slave," enabling the subaltern to incorporate "another reason to his or her own" (2012, 12, 157).

Mignolo sees such epistemological decolonization and delinking as producing decolonial "pluriversality."[12] Relying on the Zapatista motto of creating " 'another world' in which many worlds will co-exist," he argues for "pluriversality as a universal project" aimed "not at changing the world (ontology) but at changing the beliefs and understanding of the world (gnoseology), which can lead to changing (all) praxis of living in the world" (2010, 323; 2011, 21, 23; 2018, x). Implicit here again is the critique of modernity's claim to universalism and the assertion of a world of multiple coexisting ontologies and temporalities. The aim is to bring about not a single global future but plural ones, in which decoloniality would be one option standing alongside several others, including what Mignolo (2011, 27ff.) calls "rewesternization"—attempts by Western powers to save their declining political-economic power in the face of an increasingly multipolar world—and "dewesternization"—the rise of "emerging powers" such as the BRICS (Brazil, Russia, India, China, and South Africa), who refuse to toe the Western line. For Mignolo, the decolonial pluriverse will emerge (and is already emerging) through the efforts of "global civil society," engaging in such activities as "deracializing and depatriarchizing projects, food sovereignty, reciprocal economics and the definancialization of money, . . . [and] decolonization of aesthetics as a way to liberate esthesis, etc." (2018, xii–xiii).

There is much to appreciate in Mignolo's decolonial perspective, including its critique of modernity's abstract universalism (which we readily endorse), its multidimensional analysis of coloniality, and its prescriptions for demystifying and decolonizing the colonial matrix. The problem, however, is that his analysis inclines toward the romanticization of decolonial spaces. He has nary anything critical or negative to say about them,[13] as if they are somehow "originally good," free from antagonistic struggle, immune to failure, disagreement, or internal violence.

This is evident, for example, in the work of the modernity/coloniality/ decoloniality (MCD) research program, a collective research project associated with Latin American scholars that Mignolo is part of (along with the likes of Arturo Escobar),[14] which emphasizes "non-Eurocentric" forms of knowledge and lived experience.[15] Mignolo and his colleagues often draw on many of the same examples to illustrate decolonial ways of knowing and being: communal living and organizing among the Zapatistas in Mexico; Ecuador's granting of rights to "nature" (*Pachamama*); Bolivia's constitutional commitments under Morales to *buen vivir* and *sumaq kawsay* (Spanish and Quechua terms, respectively, signifying human-nature well-being or "living well"); Afro-Latina women's movements fighting for indigenous rights, and so on (see for example, Escobar 2008, 27ff., 43, 254ff.; 2018, 71–77; Mignolo 2011, 11, 328, chap. 6; Asher 2013, 838). Yet when Mignolo praises, for example, the Zapatistas for their participatory politics and collective consensus-making, he too easily forgets that consensus-based politics runs the risk of suppressing dissent (especially by the subaltern) and imposing a single decision on the community (thereby excluding minorities) (see Rancière 1999; Kapoor 2008, 107–8; 2020, chap. 7). And when he lauds indigenous ways of knowing and living, he elides, for instance, Ecuadorean state co-optation of indigenous leaders, the Morales regime's compromises with capitalist extraction despite commitments to indigenous self-determination (see chapter 4), ideological divisions between and among indigenous groups across North, South, and Central America, or the anti-Muslim politics of sections of Adivasi (aboriginal) communities in India in collaboration with right-wing Hindu supremacists (Merino 2016, 275–76; Cadena and Starn 2007, 3–4, 10, 19; Baviskar 2007). What is absent in Mignolo's representations of the subaltern are the warnings by the likes of Freire and Fanon about the possibility of internalized subaltern oppression, racism, and co-optation (which is ironic, given that Fanon is one of Mignolo's key decolonial exemplars; see Mignolo and González García 2006, 47). Here

Mignolo seems not to even take seriously the implications of the colonial matrix of power that is so central to his argument: he conveniently evades the fact that coloniality can brutalize the colonial subject (as it would anyone), resulting in internalized oppression. Even were delinking/decolonization possible, it seems difficult to defend the position that the subaltern (or anyone) is somehow able to remain immune to ideological interpellation.

The problem is compounded by Mignolo's construction of stark and simplified binaries, such as when he pits universalism (which for him, as we saw, is "always imperial and war driven") against pluriversality, in which communities are "convivial, dialogical, or plurilogical . . . decolonial and communal personalities are driven by the search for love, conviviality, and harmony" (2018, xii, xiv; see also 2011, 313). He even goes so far as to contend that border thinking "points toward a new way of thinking in which dichotomies can be replaced by complementarity of apparently contradictory terms" (2012, 338): such radical complementarity, as Michaelson and Shershow demonstrate (2007, 53), would imply an eventual withdrawal from the need for any critique or deliberation "into a space in which nothing need ever be decided."[16]

What is missing in Mignolo's decolonial viewpoint, in other words, is the dimension of the Real—the fundamental deadlock that prevents the subject from realizing its identity with itself. True, he does speak about the "colonial wound" inflicted by modernity/coloniality on the colonial subject (2012, xiv; 2011, xxi, 48, 114), but like L&M, the source of the wound is always located in the (Western) Other. The illusion is that once that blockage is removed, the decolonial subject can recover a lost wholeness, finally achieve its identity with itself, and become what it "truly" is. Hence Mignolo's resort to a romanticized pluriversality devoid of blemishes: a space where there is apparently neither hierarchy nor structural opposition, indeed not even the need to criticize, debate, or deliberate. This appears as the textbook definition of ideology—the erasure of the political, the covering over of social antagonism (Žižek 1989). The irony is that, as Žižek puts it (2014c, 325), "His [Mignolo's] goal—harmony, plenitude of life—is a true Abstract Universal if there ever was one."

This is why our earlier quibble was not with the Zapatistas-as-subaltern, but with Mignolo, who, in his search for pluriversality, ends up producing a romanticized subaltern space. As Kiran Asher, echoing Spivak, suggests, Mignolo and his MCD research peers are "turning to subaltern knowledge to fulfill [their] desire to create a just world for humans and non-humans"

(Asher 2013, 838–39; see also Kapoor 2004). There appears to be no self-reflexivity on the role and position of the intellectual in representing the subaltern; it is as if the subaltern is transparent to itself, with the intellectual as an equally transparent relay capturing and communicating the pure subaltern voice. This absence of impediments/imperfections (the Real) is precisely what allows Mignolo to cherry-pick his favorite heroes for his own political purposes (echoing the proclivities of New Materialism). And it is indeed such a process of decontextualization that makes Mignolo's move an abstract universal one, as Žižek is right to underline.

Yet if pluriversality for Mignolo is about retrieving an ideological past devoid of blemishes, then (negative) universality for Žižek is a mode of arriving expressly at society's fundamental antagonisms. To be sure, such antagonisms are not simply external but fundamentally *internal* to the subject, as we saw earlier, revealing of the subject's irreducible conflict with itself, and demanding that the subject squarely face and work through them rather than avoid or erase them. The "colonial wound," then, is not a reason to nostalgically produce past glory or wallow in victimhood and resentment, but to reinvent a new universality, one that is more universal than that of the Master. Negative universality would here mean being forever marked by and learning from colonial history, from Europe's violent and murderous past. Thus, the onus on oppressed groups such as Ecuador's indigenous groups or India's Dalits ("untouchables") would be to become proficient with and use European discourses of emancipation and freedom to fight for equality (as indeed they sometimes have):

> The true victory over colonization is not the return to any "authentic" pre-colonial existence, even less any "synthesis" between modern civilization and pre-modern origins—but, paradoxically, the fully accomplished loss of these pre-modern origins. In other words, colonialism is not overcome when [for example] the intrusion of the English language as a medium is abolished, but when the colonizers are, as it were, beaten at their own game—when the new Indian identity is effortlessly formulated in English, i.e., when English language is "denaturalized," when it loses its privileged link to "native" Anglo-Saxon English-speakers. (Žižek 2014c, 327–28)

In this sense, negotiating the Real internally (self-reflexively) rather externally (locating it only in the European Other) implies not a delinking from, but a more radical incorporation and destabilization of, the colonial matrix of power. It means fully immersing oneself in the matrix so as to exploit its liberatory potential and outsmart Europeans on their own terrain. Žižek frequently turns to Malcolm X to illustrate this point: the latter saw racism and slavery as traumatic, depriving Black people of their roots, yet he nonetheless esteemed it as opening up a creative space—the "X" in Malcolm X—by inventing a new universal (Islamic) identity (Žižek 2013b, at 65:30; 2014c, 326–27; 2018b, 60–61). Here though, one must quickly recall that, even were such a universalizing tactic to prove successful, it is one that would continue to leave the colonial subject at odds with itself. For there is no escaping the Real: it abides stubbornly, serving as a constant impediment but also as an opportunity to create a new universal (in this case, a more radical modernity). The Real, we might say, enables as it disables.

But we must take issue with Mignolo's representation of not just the subaltern, but also the "West." Since, for him, modernity/coloniality means the "imposition of one perspective and one type of consciousness [e.g., rationality, binary thinking, European racial superiority, etc.] over others" (2010, 346), European thought is inescapably tainted and problematic. This is why he insists that Western thought cannot be opened up or expanded by decoloniality; it must be superseded (2002, 80). But the problem is that such a view borders on caricature, painting Western intellectual production as monolithic and prompting Linda Alcoff to note that "Mignolo is often operating with what appears as an overly simplified account of Western philosophical positions" (2007, 91; see also Michaelsen and Shershow 2007, 41). He conflates *hegemonic* European (colonial) thought with European thought writ large.[17] He fails to acknowledge the many European intellectual counterdiscourses to colonial rationality or binary thinking (anti-imperialism, nondualism, communitarianism, etc.) with which, for all intents and purposes, much of decolonial thought is allied. Worse still, Mignolo fails to account for his own debt to so-called Eurocentrism. The trouble here is not just that his anti-Eurocentrism appears as a knee-jerk reaction to Eurocentrism, but also that the decolonial "critique of Eurocentrism is, in its intellectual background and the tools it mobilizes, a 'Eurocentric' endeavor par excellence" (Žižek 2002c, 580). The Western legacy may well be (and is indeed) imperialist domination and plunder, but it is also, as Žižek underlines, "that of the self-critical examination of the violence and exploitation the West itself brought to the Third World . . . the West supplied the very standards by which it (and its critics) measures its own criminal past" (2009a, 115). To posit authentic "non-European" decolonial intellectual space(s), discrete and untainted, as

GATEKEEPING OF
DECOLONIAL SCHOLARS

Mignolo is wont to do, is therefore to deny both the ongoing violence of co-lonialism and the subversive intellectual background that enables Mignolo's Eurocentric critique in the first place.

Mignolo's position vis-à-vis postcolonial thought provides a helpful il-lustration here. He makes it a point to distinguish decoloniality from post-colonial studies, arguing that each has a different intellectual trajectory, with among other things, the former inspired by non-European thinkers and activists (Fanon, Gandhi, Mariátegui, Menchú, Anzaldúa) and the latter by European ones (Foucault, Lacan, Derrida, etc.): "The de-colonial shift, in other words, is a project of de-linking while post-colonial criticism and theory is a project of scholarly transformation within the academy" (Mignolo 2010, 306). Yet, as Kiran Asher indicates, it is far from unprob-lematic that Mignolo sees it fit to draw from Fanon and Gandhi (who, it should be underlined, were themselves inspired by such "Western" thinkers as Ruskin, Thoreau, Sartre, Freud, and Lacan), yet does "*not* engage with postcolonial theories on the grounds that they come from metropolitan institutions of higher learning. This seems odd given that most decolonial thinkers are also based at universities in the West [Mignolo himself works at Duke University in the United States and writes in English] . . . why ignore Spivak and claim Gandhi? Far from going beyond binaries, classifying whose work contributes to decolonial thinking and whose is to be rejected on the basis that it is tainted by modernity gives the impression that MCD scholars are patrolling theoretical and political borders" (Asher 2013, 839). Implied here then is an unmistakable politics of authenticity, with demarcations of an "inside" and "outside" and a concomitant tendency to engage in gatekeeping.

We'd like to suggest that such a politics of authenticity is tied to an incon-sistent notion of power/hegemony.[18] Indeed, Mignolo appears to take two mutually exclusive positions. On the one hand, he is scathing in his critique of "500 years of Western hegemony" (2011, xiii), which he sees (rightly, in our view) as having dominated the colonial subject in the multifarious ways suggested by the expression "colonial matrix of power." But on the other hand, he undertakes the political project of founding an identity outside the prison house of coloniality. This conception of radical decolonial difference is clearly indicated by such formulations as "the de-colonial shift belongs lit-erally to a different space," and border thinking enables a delinking from "the Totality of Western epistemology," resulting in "unheard and unexpected" forms of knowledge "outside" European "cognitive patterns" (Mignolo 2010, 339, 347; 2012, 81, 154). But it remains indeterminate how such a radical distinction between modernity and decoloniality can be maintained, how pluriversal subaltern spaces are immune to the reach of global capitalism or uncontaminated by European thought after five hundred years of coloniality. Apparently, delinking/border thinking is what enables this radical alterity, yet border thinking appears not as a mechanism to work *through* hegemony, but rather a way of somehow overcoming colonial/capitalist violence and restoring an original colonial difference. Delinking is not a (difficult) negotiation with hegemony but an almost superhuman cleansing of it from a position of subordination.

The only consistent position on (the Gramscian notion of) hegemony[19] is to treat coloniality precisely as *dominant*, implying that subordinate groups must operate within the lines of power laid down by the hegemon (otherwise they wouldn't be subordinate).[20] In other words, whether Mignolo likes it or not, in the wake of European imperial domination, the European symbolic order is the de facto global symbolic order (Kapoor 2018), so that the decolonial subject has no choice but to work with it. This is why an anti-Eurocentric viewpoint cannot escape a Eurocentric background. It is also why the non-European's search for roots can never recover a pure or authentic local tradition: the search is always a retroactive one, made possible only in *the* terms of the dominant European (and capitalistic) Symbolic, so that a search for roots is always a tainted one. Undoubtedly, there are innumerably important "non-European," decolonial philosophical texts, past and present, but these are inescapably written, read, and practiced in the light of the postcolonial present. No wonder that for Žižek, a (decolonial) emancipatory project lies in retrieving from both the European Symbolic and (retroactive) "tradition" their respective antagonistic dimension, from which to invent a new universal identity.

So indeed, Mignolo does appear to want it both ways: a radical critique of colonial power, but a decolonial space uncontaminated by (colonial) power. It is precisely this inconsistency—or rather, his refusal to acknowledge this contradiction—that enables him to produce romanticized spaces and resort to a politics of authenticity so often associated with notions of radical alterity. What he misses is that pluriversal spaces cannot be protected from contamination because they are always already contaminated, both internally, as a result of the impossibility of the social, and from the "outside," as a result of colonial/capitalist hegemony.

Finally, we must broach the exclusion of the state and political economy in Mignolo's Weltanschauung. As to the former, Mignolo stands fiercely against it, seeing it as the political expression of the European logic of coloniality. According to him, pluriverses would "exist independently of the state and corporations" by delinking "from state forms of governance, from the economy of accumulation, and from ego-centered personalities that both enacted and reproduced Westernization" (2018, xii, xiv). As a result, "The future would be composed of 'communal nodes' around the planet cooperating rather than competing with each other"; and pluriversality would not be a "cultural relativism, but the entanglement of several cosmologies connected today in power differential" (2011, 283; 2018, x).

But once again, Mignolo's rhetoric appears as politically naive (not unlike Foucault's and Lyotard's): in the absence of a state,[21] who or what would ensure the security and well-being of these (presumably relatively small) "communal nodes"? What guarantee is there that these nodes *would* cooperate, rather than squabble among and between themselves, especially if they are connected "in power differential"? And how would the nodes withstand the continuing onslaught of global capitalism, or threats from the Western and indeed "dewesternized" powers that Mignolo envisages as part of the global multipolar future (discussed earlier)?

What strikes us is that Mignolo's conception of pluriversality secretly *requires* a (national, regional, transnational) state to safeguard the coexistence of "many worlds." It is able to conjure up a depoliticized pluriversal vision only based on the assumption that such things as peace enforcement, cooperation, provision of universal education and healthcare, regulation of multinationals, campaigns against global viral infections, and so forth, will somehow be taken care of. Mignolo thus conveniently elides the (Hegelian) point we stressed in chapter 1—that pluriversal nodality/particularism actually needs a universality to be understood and recognized as particular, distinct, different. Autonomous spaces such as Chiapas in Mexico or self-determining indigenous communities in Canada, Peru, Ecuador, and Australia necessitate a universalizing political authority like the state to respect their alterity and guarantee their coexistence.[22]

As to the question of political economy, it is conspicuous by its relative absence. As with the case of hegemony, Mignolo is happy to mention it as part of his critique of the colonial matrix, but remains practically silent about it when it comes to his vision of an alternate pluriversality. He does not see fit to engage with Marxist political economy because, according to him, the latter is a "Eurocentered critique," restricting itself to confronting capitalism, whereas decoloniality "confronts all of Western civilization, which includes liberal capitalism and Marxism" (2011, xi, xviii; see also Asher 2013, 840). Not only does such a view conveniently neglect the plethora of "non-Eurocentric" Third World Marxisms (in India, Nepal, Cuba, China, South Africa, Peru, Ecuador, etc., many of which are not just intellectual but political projects, including, for instance, democratic communism in Kerala and Bengal), but it also does not live up to its claim. Having thrown the political economy baby out with the bathwater, Mignolo resorts to "delinking from capitalism" epistemologically: we are meant to believe that examining the "partiality and limitations" of Eurocentric discourse and expanding the "geo- and body-politics of knowledge and understanding" (2010, 339) will somehow dismantle not just the ideology of, say, free trade, but also the reach of such powerful organizations as multinationals and the Word Trade Organization. The overwhelming evidence to date is that such a strategy, even at the hands of social movements, has not meaningfully succeeded. Quite the opposite: it is corporate capitalism that has succeeded in colonizing and co-opting social movement claims (e.g., the commodification of minority identities, the corporatization of "Pride," the marketing of ethnic "chic," the institutionalization of participation—by the likes of the World Bank, and even the logoization of Gandhi and Subcomandante Marcos).

It is equally significant that Mignolo makes no mention of workers' movements. He looks approvingly on cultural and identity-based groups (indigeneity, gender and queer movements, racialized minorities, etc.), but shies away from the more materialist struggles involving workers and unions, most likely once again for ideological reasons. Yet Latin America, for example, has a strong history of labor organizing, in several cases successfully challenging transnational capital and helping secure socioeconomic rights (improved labor conditions, the right to unionize, gender equality, minimum wage rises in maquiladoras, etc.) (Lazar 2017; Bronfenbrenner 2007). To the extent that such organizing targets capitalism, sometimes globally through cross-national campaigns, it is attempting to dismantle at least one arm of coloniality. There is no reason, therefore, not to conceive of labor struggles as decolonial. While workers may not be a privileged revolutionary subject and are not immune to internalized strife (e.g., the development of a labor aristocracy, as discussed earlier), they bring to the fore the political struggle at the heart of capitalist political economy, in this sense serving as a Real to the contemporary colonial matrix of power (and hence acting as universal mediation). But Mignolo will have none of it, putting all his eggs in the decolonization-through-epistemological-delinking basket.

Thus, deprived of any state and any significant materialist analysis, mediation, or strategy, Mignolo's upholding of pluriversality amounts to little more than multicultural diversity. Despite outward protestations against coloniality, decoloniality ends up aiding and abetting that most dominant form of colonial power—global capitalism. Particularism and localism, as we have seen, suit imperial economic interests well—you do your own thing, celebrate your language, identity, and festivals, as long as you don't interfere with the free mobility of capital. As with multiculturalism, pluriversal politics appears as a quite suitable politico-cultural arrangement for global capitalism. Decolonial difference remains unthreatening to the smooth functioning of the system and can be quite readily accommodated (assigned a "proper" place) and commodified. So by opting for particularism with no meaningful dimension of universality, Mignolo ends up (like Foucault, Lyotard, Edelman, and Ahmed) enabling the unfettered globalization of capital.

Consequently, while Mignolo's conception of decoloniality mounts an effective critique of the colonial matrix of power, its resort to pluriversality tends toward depoliticization and political naivete: by ignoring social antagonism (the Real), it inclines toward the production of romanticized and authentic spaces; by thinking radical difference outside of (colonial) power and political mediation, it suffers from the illusion of being able to delink from, and operate independent of, the reach of Western hegemony and global capital; by shutting the door to "Western" counter-discourses, the state, political economy, and the working class, it considerably weakens its ability to fight against postpolitical global capitalism or forge political allyship within and across the North-South divide; and by backing a pluriversality devoid of universality, it ends up helping sustain global capitalism. What Mignolo misses is precisely the dimension of universality, which, as we have argued, avoids the pitfalls of abstract universalism by being rooted in the (decolonial) particular, while at the same time transcending the latter to open up to a shared universality (the Real) across particularities.

Hardt and Negri: Multitude and Biopolitics, or the Postpolitics of Becoming

Unlike decolonial theorists, Hardt and Negri (H&N) share Žižek's suspicious attitude when it comes to the politics of difference. They underscore how global capitalism willingly adopts a rhetoric celebrating (racial, cultural) difference: "This new enemy not only is resistant to the old weapons but actually thrives on them, and thus joins its would-be antagonists in applying them to the fullest. Long live difference! Down with essentialist binaries!" (2000, 138). And rather than unplugging from "Empire" (postmodern globalization as a global form of domination), H&N seek to take it to its next emancipatory phase, unleashing capitalism's full productivity—"radicalis[ing] Marx, who held that if we just cut the head off capitalism we'd get socialism" (Žižek 2012c). *Pace* decoloniality, the logic of global capital is inescapable. The inside/outside and local/global dichotomies obfuscate the reality that all of us, in some way or another, "feed into and support the development of the capitalist imperial machine" (Hardt and Negri 2000, 45). It is thus an ideological fantasy to claim that we can resurrect an authentic, precolonial reality or alternative modernity, "to claim that we can (re)establish local identities that are in some sense *outside* and protected against the global flows of capital and Empire" (Hardt and Negri 2000, 45). Capital's decentered flow structures Empire's new imperial sovereignty:

> We insist on asserting that the construction of Empire is a step forward in order to do away with any nostalgia for the power structures that preceded it and refuse any political strategy that involves returning to that old arrangement, such as trying to resurrect the nation-state to protect against global capital. (Hardt and Negri 2000, 43)

Any leftist critique of the global order—universalist or not—that relies on the assumption that nation-states are the primary actors of power is ill-advised.

H&N introduce the "multitude" as Empire's "living alternative" (2004, 61). The multitude is an anti-vanguard phenomenon; its powers emanate "from below" (2017, 78). It is constituted by "radical differences, singularities, that can never be synthesized in an identity" and forms the new agent of change and resistance, the "new proletariat" of globalization (Hardt and Negri 2000, 335). The meaning of singularity is clearly indebted to Deleuze's thinking and should not be confused or conflated with the notion of *cultural* difference. For Deleuze, a singularity is defined by its "internal difference"; in other words, it is univocal and (linguistically or culturally) unmediated, dwelling, as it were, in "a world *without* others" (1990, 301–21; qtd. Hallward 1997, 531). Deleuze's rhizomatic thinking and postidentitarian metaphysics— often characterized by his acolytes as *a politics of becoming*—lay the ground for H&N's positive biopolitics and their ideal of "absolute democracy" (2000, 410).

As "a collective biopolitical body" (Hardt and Negri 2000, 30), H&N's multitude promises radical change; its resistance will take place either as "a *proliferation of creative activities* or as a diversity of relationships and associative forms" (Negri 2008, 102). Against an understanding of biopolitics that "strips it of every possibility of autonomous, creative action" (Hardt and Negri 2009, 58), that is always haunted by the Nazi catastrophe of bare life, H&N foreground biopolitics' affirmative dimension or force, stressing its difference from the normative/destructive regime of biopower. Far from eradicating inventiveness and subjectivity, biopolitics—incarnated in the multitude, its putative collective body—opens up the possibility of managing life differently, gesturing to an alternative politics of life, one that is less controlling, regulating, and exploitive. Unlike Agamben's nightmarish version—where we are all virtual *homines sacri*, reducible at any moment to bare life— H&N's biopolitics of the multitude is resolutely a *biopolitics with a human face*.

Distinct from the traditional proletariat, the labor of the multitude is not confined to the factory; rather, their labor is said to be immaterial or affective, reflecting the shift from industrial to postindustrial or "cognitive" capitalism (Negri 2008, 64). It is the type of labor that "immediately involves social interaction and cooperation," a type of labor, for example, common in service industries: "Since the production of services results in no material and durable good, we define the labor involved in this production as immaterial labor—that is, labor that produces an immaterial good, such as a service, a cultural product, knowledge, or communication" (Hardt and Negri 2000, 294, 290). What immaterial labor produces are not objects "but new social or interpersonal relations; immaterial production is bio-political, the production of social life" (Žižek 2012c). Revising the meaning of labor (and its revolutionary potential), H&N define the proletariat of Empire as including "all those whose labor is directly or indirectly exploited by and subjected to capitalist norms of production and reproduction" (2000, 52).

What purportedly brings the multitude together, constituting them as a collective entity, is their rhizomatic movement along with the will to contest:

> One element we can put our finger on at the most basic and elementary level is *the will to be against*. In general, the will to be against does not seem to require much explanation. Disobedience to authority is one of the most natural and healthy acts. To us it seems completely obvious that those

FALSE!

REBELLION!

SPONTANEOUS

who are exploited will resist and—given the necessary conditions—rebel. (Hardt and Negri 2000, 210)

Unruliness, "being-against," characterizes the "proper of the multitude" (Laclau 2004, 27). Its rebellion takes a new form appropriate to its new enemy:

If there is no longer a place that can be recognized as outside, we must be against in every place. . . . Whereas in the disciplinary era *sabotage* was the fundamental notion of resistance, in the era of imperial control it may be *desertion*. Whereas being-against in modernity often meant a direct and/ or dialectical opposition of forces, in postmodernity being-against might well be most effective in an oblique or diagonal stance. Battles against the Empire might be won through subtraction and defection. This desertion does not have a place; it is the evacuation of the places of power. (Hardt and Negri 2000, 211–12)

But H&N's migrating, nomadic multitude—this Deleuzian-inspired rhizomatic indocility—strikes us as romantic and misguided in its view of human agency, and this, in turn, throws into question the overall value of Deleuzian theory for a universal politics.[23] This is precisely Žižek's point. Deleuze's politics of becoming does not fare any better than Edelman's fetishized protean subject. As with Edelman's, Deleuze's much-vaunted "infinite potential field of virtualities," its form of "critical resistance," is compromisingly suitable to the cultural logic of late capitalism to the extent that it mimics rather than disrupts the deterritorialized flows of capitalism, making him "the ideologist of late capitalism" (Žižek 2012a, 185).[24]

H&N's project to go beyond capital is plagued by its Deleuzian, romanticized vision of the multitude as the rhizomatic agent of change. The fault lines separating Žižek's universal politics and H&N's decentralized micropolitics could not be clearer. While H&N want to enact a biopolitics (via the liberatory praxis of the multitude) that is through-and-through life-affirming—cultivating the new forms of life that have emerged under the conditions of immaterial (as opposed to material) labor—Žižek is after a politics that exposes the gap between the administered social order and the ontological lack that avers the negativity constitutive of politics as such. That is to say, there is politics only when there is a contestation of the order's positivity, an affirmation of "the inconsistency and/or non-existence of the big Other—of the fact that there is no Other of the Other, no ultimate

RHIZOMATIC MULTITUDE: NEW NODES CAN EMERGE ANYWHERE

TRYING TO DISRUPT THE WHOLE SYSTEM AT ONCE

EXTREMELY ABSTRACTED

guarantee of the field of meaning" (Žižek 2005b, 200). For Žižek, the system never coincides with the Real. Politics wages war against all fantasies (of national unity, of personal and social wholeness) that would seek to suture the Symbolic's inherent discord. If insisting on the system's irredeemable discord constitutes the task of politics, then touching the Real, rearranging the symbolic order, we might say, is the task of a universal politics. After the gap is exposed, the coordinates of the system must undergo a radical disturbance and reinvention.

But for H&N, the Real is never a concern; or at the very least, it falls outside the purview of biopolitics. This is why Žižek describes biopolitics as postpolitical (2005a). Though H&N talk about communism (the move beyond capital), theirs is a communism as a *"capitalist* fantasy," as Žižek puts it (2017c, 260). H&N are overtly enthusiastic about the emancipatory character of capitalism's new organization of production and its multi-centered cooperation, hopeful of the multitude's seizure of what Marx's called the "general intellect," that is, "collective knowledge in all its forms, from science to practical knowhow." Žižek sums up their adoption and adaptation of Marx's term from the *Grundrisse* (Marx 1973, 706):

> Marx, as they see it, was historically constrained: he thought in terms of centralised, automated and hierarchically organised industrial labour, with the result that he understood "general intellect" as something rather like a central planning agency; it is only today, with the rise of "immaterial labour," that a revolutionary reversal has become "objectively possible." This immaterial labour extends between two poles: from intellectual labour (the production of ideas, texts, computer programs etc.) to affective labour (carried out by doctors, babysitters and flight attendants). (2012c)

But, as with Deleuze, H&N's decentralized micropolitics[25]—which purports to be subversive of Empire by framing the new form of labor "as the unique chance to overcome capitalism"—is paradoxically "celebrated by the ideologists of the information revolution as the rise of a new, 'frictionless' capitalism" (Žižek 2012c). If Deleuze is "the ideologist of late capitalism," H&N are unequivocally *the ideologists of immaterial capitalism.* The rhizomatic multitude cannot deliver on its emancipatory promise. Worse, H&N's quasi-populist solution defangs politics as such; their "ethics of affirmation . . . eliminates negativity from the political" (Dean 2006, 120). Politics in turn is naturalized, an "immanent . . . part of the nature of things"

(Dean 2006, 120). H&N's version of biopolitics sends us back to Jameson's opposition between domination and exploitation: the struggle against domination is the stuff of biopolitics (constantly countering an immunological paradigm and its dreadful production of bare life), whereas the struggle against exploitation compels us to confront class antagonisms and seriously consider the "eternal idea of communism" (Badiou 2010).

To probe the contours of this dialectical tension between domination and exploitation, we turn to Todd Phillips's 2019 film *Joker* and to its entanglement of political economy and libidinal economy, its nuanced depiction of the multitude as Empire's new gravediggers. While conservatives feared the film would incite violence,[26] liberals were quick to demonize its depiction of the working class, (mis)reading it as legitimizing white male rage, giving cover to racist Trump supporters and/or incels.[27] What *Joker* actually stages, however, is, in the words of Achille Mbembe, the "*becoming black of the world*" (Mbembe 2017, 6). The distinction between the worker and the slave is disappearing under the devastating logic of neoliberal capitalism, where life of the increasingly excluded is the object of endless domination. But *Joker* is not about biopolitics. Its intervention, its concerns, cut much deeper. The film offers no life-affirming micropolitics. *Joker* refuses to endorse a phantasmatic narrative of overcoming—a conceptual journey in which the multitudes move from being-against "the One of sovereign Power," the elite of Gotham City—such as billionaire mayoral candidate Thomas Wayne (Brett Cullen), father of Bruce Wayne (the future Batman)—to triumphantly "directly ruling themselves" (Žižek 2006c, 263). No, *Joker* tells another story.

Joker recounts the origin story of Batman's archenemy, Arthur Fleck (Joaquin Phoenix). Arthur is a struggling party clown and an aspiring comedian who lives with his mother Penny (Frances Conroy) and who suffers from mental illness. He is literally out-of-joint, out of sync with the world: he has a medical disorder that causes him to laugh at the wrong moments. Arthur diligently seeks out help in the services of a social worker. But a garbage strike has paralyzed Gotham City, throwing it into a disarray that is especially harsh and disruptive for its less fortunate. The city is particularly cruel and inhospitable to those who do not seem to fit in. Arthur laments in his notebook, "The worst part about having a mental illness is people expect you to behave as if you don't." Most significantly, the austerity measures the government implements in response to the crisis have devastating results for Arthur; they terminate his access to medication and therapy. The film traces his derailment, or in other words, his becoming Joker—the fall into madness and nihilistic despair that leads him to lash out violently at Gotham's elite and those who have wronged him. Though Arthur/Joker states that he isn't "political," his actions spark an anticapitalist, populist surge (one headline reads: "Kill the Rich—A New Movement?"), causing mass destruction and rioting throughout the city. This Joker is not the quintessential enemy of the people, but is rather *of* the people, of the workers, of the excluded of Gotham City.

And yet what is appreciable about *Joker* is that it politicizes rather than moralizes the plight of the excluded. It declines any didactic rendering of *what's next*: the proletarian or multitude must or will do X. That is not the point of the film. Rather, as Žižek observes, *Joker* spends its aesthetic and intellectual energy elsewhere; it performs a climate of hopelessness, and we pass through this fog of despair before "something new" has any chance of happening (Žižek 2019f). Without such a "zero level of clearing the table," without emptying the mind of ready-made liberal solutions, nothing new can occur (Žižek 2019f). Indeed, without "go[ing] through the self-destructive zero-level" (Žižek 2019a) embodied by Joker's position, no universal politics can ever take shape. *Joker* is our conceptual midwife, so to speak. The film compels us not only to scrutinize our libidinal economy, what we desire from this world, but also to consider what kind of desire is a desire for "something new." One thing is clear: this "something new" cannot be conflated with liberal or democratic-leftist desires.

Joker throws us back to the beginning of neoliberalism's rise: the early 1980s, the era of Reagan and Thatcher. Gotham—this incarnation of late capitalism and hub of democracy, which is said to embody "our 'best ever' political order" (Žižek 2019f)—is also the site of rampant misery and cruelty. Neoliberalism imposes its own (mis)management of life, customizing biopolitics to serve its needs and agenda. Capitalism is all there is (a precondition for postpolitics). Crimes and unemployment, by this logic, are more or less the result of poor decisions. In Thomas Wayne's words, someone who rises up against such a system is merely "someone who's envious of those more fortunate than themselves, yet too scared to show their own face. And until those kind of people change for the better," he continues, "those of us who've made a good life for ourselves will always look at those who haven't as nothing but clowns." It is within the capacities of individuals to "make a good life" for themselves under capitalism. The role of the government is to maintain law and order, and fiscal responsibility—that is, austerity; the marketplace, or so it goes, will take care of the rest. In this light, asking for "something new" entails a significant break with the status quo. In the wake of Reaganesque austerity measures (implemented by the economic elite to protect the upper classes from "political and economic annihilation" [Harvey 2005, 15]), is the desire to reinvest in the welfare state—to return to what David Harvey calls "embedded liberalism" (2005, 11), a compact, or rather compromise, between labor and capital offering a social safety net and a commitment to full employment—an instance of a desire for "something new"? *Joker* suggests that it is not; it is yet another liberal cultural fantasy.

Michael Moore's insightful review of *Joker* discloses the strength of the democratic-leftist reading as well as its shortcomings. Moore rightly points out that "the fear and outcry over *Joker* is a ruse" (Moore 2019). The liberal outrage about *Joker* functions as an ideological distraction: it tells us, "Don't look at the real violence tearing up our fellow human beings" (Moore 2019). The panic over the film centered on potential acts of what Žižek terms "subjective violence," that is, a form of violence in which the victimizer and the victim can be clearly delineated (e.g., an incel shooter killing movie-viewers at a showing of *Joker*—a scenario the FBI and Homeland Security warned about); this hysteria thereby obfuscated the realities of "objective violence" (Žižek 2008c, 2) such as the normalization of trauma-inducing "active shooter drills," the lack of healthcare for thirty million Americans, or overcrowded schools in poor cities and neighborhoods. Objective violence denotes the background violence that goes on when nothing seems to be happening. It is this dominant form of violence—the naturalized violence of everyday life—that Moore is powerfully decrying.[28] For this reason as well, Moore objects to identifying Joker with Trump (two figures who do not conform to liberal sensibilities—though for radically different reasons) and aims instead to shift our attention back to structural problems. To focus on Trump is to attend to America's symptoms, whereas what the Left needs is an account of the causes that led America to vote for Trump, the underlying structures that produced an "America which feels no need to help the outcast, the destitute," a country "where the filthy rich just get richer and filthier" (Moore 2019). To avoid a repeat of Trump (either by re-electing him or by voting similar candidates into power in the future), liberal democrats must fear not the Joker but rather what is facing them if nothing changes: "What if one day the dispossessed decide to fight back? And I don't mean with a clipboard registering people to vote. People are worried this movie may be too violent. . . . *Joker* makes it clear we don't really want to get to the bottom of this, or to try to understand why innocent people turn into Jokers after they

)nger keep it together" (Moore 2019). *Joker* is a timely warning. Isn't
al outrage simply a case of "shooting the messenger"?

Where Moore's review falters is in his speculation regarding what *should*
follow from an encounter with *Joker*: "You will thank this movie for connecting you to a new desire—not to run to the nearest exit to save your own
ass but rather to stand and fight and focus your attention on the nonviolent
power you hold in your hands every single day" (Moore 2019). Moore's conclusion betrays a liberal faith in the system: the democratic nation-state can
reform itself. It can pay sufficient attention to the needy—ignored or rather
punished by Republicans and Wall Street Democrats alike who have systematically weakened America's welfare state. Connecting the audience "to
a new desire," then, means reversing or tempering America's capitalist logic
whereby the "filthy rich just get richer and filthier." Desiring a new welfare
state, however, is not the same as desiring "something new," if "new" is to re-
tain its emancipatory potential. The former emerges from *within* the system,
whereas the latter insists on the system's bankruptcy and the need for its
overhaul.

Conclusion

For democratic leftists like Moore, *Joker* serves as a moral epiphany, moti-
vating, or rather frightening, Americans into doing the right thing and
looking at available solutions for redressing the situation of the most unfortunate: to resignify what it means to be a caring American. For Žižek—and
for those of us committed to a universal politics—what *Joker* solicits from its
audience is "the courage of hopelessness":[29] it is the only thing that will allow
us to overcome the "system deadlock" (Žižek 2019f). Seeking an alternative
to the status quo *within* the coordinates of the existing system—as not just
H&N, but all said and done, all our previous interlocutors in this chapter have
done—is a fool's errand, evidence of a debilitating pragmatism, "a sign of theoretical cowardice" (Žižek 2017a, xi). Keeping in mind the May 1968 slogan,
Soyons réalistes, demandons l'impossible, we wonder: Are Moore and H&N—
and indeed, Foucault, Lyotard, Laclau/Mouffe, Edelman/Ahmed, Latour/
Bennett, and Mignolo—asking for the impossible? As Žižek makes clear, it is
those leftists who believe that things can be reformed from *within* (more tolerance, more diversity, and so on), that the system can improve itself, who are
fleeing from reality: "It is the advocates of changes and resignifications within

the liberal-democratic horizon who are the true utopians in their belief that their effort will amount to anything more than the cosmetic surgery that will give us capitalism with a human face" (Žižek 2000b, 326). "The true courage" is not avoiding despair by staying positive (things will moderately get better) but to pass through the dreadfulness of despair, the trials of nihilism. It is "to admit that the light at the end of the tunnel is probably the headlight of another train approaching" (Žižek 2017a, xi–xii). Nihilistic despair enables as it disables and disabuses. Without it, there would be no touching the Real. We would be stuck in the Symbolic, with no desire to intervene in the social order of things.

Importantly, Joker is not to be identified with, nor a model to imitate, and he is certainly not to be fetishized as the collective voice of an emerging multitude:

> It is wrong to think that what we see towards the end of the film—Joker celebrated by others—is the beginning of some new emancipatory movement. No, it is an ultimate deadlock of the existing system; a society bent on its self-destruction. The elegance of the film is that it leaves the next step of building a positive alternative to it to us. It is a dark nihilist image meant to awaken us. (Žižek 2019f)

If Joker "remains a stranger up to the end" (Žižek 2019a), it is because he undergoes subjective destitution: his self-destructive transformation from Arthur to Joker. Arthur's self-annihilation—his becoming Joker—is ethical in the Lacanian sense; the mutation of being resulted from his radical subtraction from every aspect of the symbolic order, declining to follow the dictates of "morality," that which "regulates how we relate to others with regard to our shared common Good" (Žižek 2019a). Joker does not subscribe to the common good. His presence is a shock to the system.

But as Žižek points out, there is also no politics to the Joker. He is not inaugurating a "new emancipatory movement" (Žižek 2019f); he is not after a politics of becoming. So what is he doing? Or better yet, how is the film positioning Joker? Do we see Joker engaged in his own form of self-fashioning, one that is not amenable to the biopower of the state? Is Joker announcing the rhizomatic multitude, constituted by a multiethnic cohort of followers, that will enact his desire and bring down Gotham City / Empire, ushering in an age of positive biopolitics? Žižek cautions with good reasons against this leftist reading (a H&N-inspired one, as is Moore's or indeed Foucault's,

Bennett's, or Ahmed's), since Joker is positioned in the film as a "being of drive" rather than as a "being of desire":

> The "new desire" Moore mentions is not Joker's desire: to see this, one has to introduce here the psychoanalytic distinction between drive and desire. Drive is compulsively-repetitive; in it, we are caught in the loop of turning again and again around the same point, while desire enacts a cut, opening up a new dimension. Joker remains a being of drive: at the film's end, he is powerless, and his violent outbursts are just impotent explosions of rage, actings-out of his basic powerlessness. (Žižek 2019a)

A "new desire" is not what Joker voices, or is capable of voicing, in the film. To speak as the "new tribal leader" (Žižek 2019a) of the multitude or a radical democracy would entail an articulation of such a "new desire" in a programmatic fashion. But this is not Joker. "In order for the desire described by Moore to arise, one step further is needed," adds Žižek (2019a). What separates Joker from the likes of Moore, Bennett, or Mignolo is their respective position vis-à-vis the symbolic order. Whereas Moore/Bennett/Mignolo possess a certain hold in the Symbolic, enjoying the privileges of inclusion while speaking *for* the silenced (society's forgotten working class, nonhumans, the Third World subaltern) and *against* the oppressors (the Donald Trumps and Thomas Waynes of the world), Joker resides among the living dead of Gotham City. Becoming Joker is, however, a refusal to simply occupy the position of the victim, resigned to his circumstances (Arthur under the control of maternal superego Penny): "The act that constitutes the main figure as 'Joker' is an autonomous act by means of which he surpasses the objective circumstances of his situation. He identifies with his fate, but this identification is a free act: in it, he posits himself as a unique figure of subjectivity" (Žižek 2019a).

But what kind of subjectivity is Joker's? His is not a sovereign subjectivity. It is a paradoxical subjectivity. As mentioned earlier, it is a subjectivity with which I cannot / must not identify. He is the "real" neighbor—"He remains a stranger up to the end." Even as Arthur, he declines the racist interpellation of his coworker Randall after his assault at the hands of a few Black and brown teenagers: "I heard about the beatdown you took. Fucking savages." Arthur calmly responds, "It was just a bunch of kids. I should have left it alone." He is not Randall's imaginary racist neighbor, and as Joker, he becomes the real neighbor for Randall, who never imagines "Arthur" as someone capable of brutally killing him.

The shift from Arthur to Joker elevates the Real above the Imaginary and the Symbolic. The ungentrified neighbor—from the perspective of Gotham City's capitalist elite—is the clown. As a figure of the big Other, Thomas Wayne legitimizes disparities, naturalizing the divisions in the world. To recall, he callously attributes the motives for revolt to envy, cowardice, and laziness, separating those who count from the "clowns": "Someone who's envious of those more fortunate than themselves, yet too scared to show their own face. And until those kind of people change for the better, those of us who've made a good life for ourselves will always look at those who haven't *as nothing but clowns.*"

The becoming Black of the world is a *becoming clown of the world* (see Manoharan 2019). If democracy had once shielded the white workers from the (worst of the) ills of capitalism, which they experienced phantasmatically and concretely as white privilege, the marriage of democracy and capitalism is quickly deteriorating under neoliberalism's global regime of austerity and its encroachment on the commons (Žižek 2013a, 30). Domination and exploitation are deeply intertwined. The struggle of one must implicate the other. Joker is the clown that says no to the big Other, no to his (and others') domination and exploitation by the rich. But Joker's emphatic no follows the impotent path of (self)destruction, introducing no actual change to the system. This is the deadlock of Joker/*Joker.* If Moore moves too quickly from Joker's violence to democratic-leftist nonviolence, a universal politics pauses and dwells in that question of "zero point." It is imperative that a universal politics passes through this self-destructive zero-level. Without this exposure to self-annihilation, the hold of the Symbolic remains too strong: "Only in this way can one break out of the coordinates of the existing system and envisage something really new" (Žižek 2019a).

If Joker does not / cannot desire "something new" (as he is locked in his being of drive), Moore's "new desire" or L&M's radical democracy is not quite a desire for "something new" (a leftist democrat remains a feature of the system). Hardt/Negri and Mignolo, by contrast, gesture toward a break with the system (Empire/pluriversality). But if Hardt/Negri and Mignolo put their faith in the powers of the multitude/pluriverse to push through this deadlock, substituting the decentralized multitude/pluriverse (as the new revolutionary subject) for the classic working class, a universal politics returns to the question of the excluded as embodied in the figure of the "pure prole-tarian" (Žižek 2002d, 291): *this worker which is not one.*

Arthur represents "the potentiality of a worker who cannot work" (Žižek 2002d, 291). His employment is not contingent or temporary but becomes a permanent feature of his being—he is part of "the structurally unemploy-able" (Žižek 2002d, 291). No true remedies *within* the system are available. His sustenance in this world is at best precarious and fragile. Arthur as come-dian is a slave to the will of others; he is there for their enjoyment of others. His job (when he is lucky to have one) is not to produce anything but en-tertainment (though, of course, entertainment in capitalism is a commodity much sought after).

A universal politics takes the Arthurs of the world seriously. They are the "slum-dwellers"—the " 'living dead' of global capitalism" (Žižek 2006c, 269)—and as such candidates for the part of no-part. Žižek stresses that these "slum-dwellers" are not merely a "redundant surplus," an "unfortunate acci-dent" of the System, "but a necessary product" of its "innermost logic" (2008a, 424). Žižek designates the slum-dwellers as "the counter-class to the other newly emerging class, the so-called symbolic class (managers, journalists, and public relations people, academics, artists, etc.)" (2008a, 424).

So let's say the slum-dwellers meet the immaterial laborers of the mul-titude: what emerges from this encounter? Suspicion, hostility, a doubling down on a "new axis of class struggle" (Žižek 2008a, 424)? Most likely, but miracles do happen—"not a miraculous thing in the sense of God or reli-gion, but a miraculous event in the sense that something can emerge out of nowhere. We cannot predict anything" (Žižek 2013a, 99). People are not de-termined by their class position. One's class is not destiny. The unpredictable *does happen.* Defections from one's class are miraculous. To be sure, the sym-bolic class is ripe for its emancipatory betrayal insofar as it "is also uprooted and perceives itself as directly universal" (Žižek 2008a, 424). Unlike the middle class—which enjoys the structures of capitalism and willingly accepts its ideological purpose to stabilize the system—the symbolic class is not as affectively tied to its organic community. A universalist politics nurtures the antagonism or inherent split at the heart the "symbolic class." Its progres-sive members can break from their putative class and join forces with the excluded. This is the wager of a universal politics: the possibility of a non-identitarian coalition "between slum-dwellers and the 'progressive' part of the symbolic class" (Žižek 2008a, 425).

Does *Joker* display examples of such defection? The short answer is no. The film ends with a thematization, and even a reification, of the struggle between the poor and the rich, the excluded and the included. We never move from Joker's impotent ressentiment to an emancipatory ressentiment: a ressentiment, we might imagine, constituted by its stubborn refusal to play nice, to play "the game of those in power" (Žižek 2019a) and fueled by a political project, a desire for another Gotham.[30] It declines the pathos of vengefulness by passing through the despair of nihilism. But *Joker* does hint at different possibilities, alternative genealogies of Joker and Batman.

In a key scene, Arthur approaches Wayne Manor in an attempt to speak to Thomas Wayne, having just heard his mother confess that Wayne, her former employer, is his father. We see Arthur having a playful exchange with young Bruce through the bars of the entrance gates to the property when Alfred, the Waynes' butler, interrupts their game, as if to separate the two classes, denying any rapprochement (biological or not).[31] What if young Bruce had understood the corruption of his father? What if he had seen through his philanthropy and the endless lies propagated by the system itself? What if the adult Bruce Wayne went one step further and disidentified with his subject position, with the regressive quality of his symbolic class? Maybe then Batman wouldn't have become a superhero of the privileged rich, a defender of the establishment and status quo. Miracles do happen.

A universal politics must attend to the miraculous—looking for "signs of the new forms of social awareness that will emerge from the slum collectives"—while also actively engaging in a political doing, forestalling the co-optation and neutralization of this new consciousness by forging political solidarity across the identity/class divide, ensuring that "they will be the germs of the future" (Žižek 2008a, 425).

INCREDIBLY DISAPOINTING CHAPTER ABOUT
HOW "MIRACLES DO HAPPEN"!
THE CRITIQUES OF OTHERS IS GOOD,
BUT ZIZECK'S ALTERNATIVE IS
PITIFUL A WASTE OF TIME!
THEY MAKE SO MUCH OF JOKER
BECAUSE THEY FALSELY ASSUME THAT
HE REPRESENTS THE REVOLUTIONARY
MARGINAL "PART OF NO PART" — THIS
VIEW COMPLETELY ELIDES THE REAL
POLITICAL ECONOMY THAT MATTERS TO
KM.

4

What a (Negative) Universal Politics Might Look Like Today

In our previous chapters, we have articulated the contours of a universal politics: how it avoids the pitfalls of prior universalist interventions without retreating to communitarian boundaries or succumbing to the passions for authentic difference (be it sexual, ethnic, or nonhuman), a nostalgic or re-enchanted return to the premodern, pre-capitalist, non-Western, and so on. Such a politics does not compromise on its desire for universality in favor of the liberally sanctioned public good. In making our case, we drew on the Palestinian question and workers' struggles as touchstones for thinking and imagining the system's parts of no-part. A defining feature of this universal politics is its dual struggle against both exploitation and domination, its re-fusal, as it were, to disentangle the two, to separate neatly the political from the ethical, the *is* from the *ought*. The biopolitical may be postpolitical, but the universal politics envisioned here—underpinned by a psychoanalytic mode of critique—is never simply post-ethical, as its affective investment in, and critical engagement with, the ethico-political injunction of "Love thy neighbor" makes abundantly clear.

The neighbor constitutes an endless source and locus of negativity. The questions *Who/what is my neighbor? What does the neighbor want from me?* and *What are the state's duties toward its citizens and global neighbors?* preoc-cupy if not "hystericize" (Žižek 2006b, 140) a universal politics. This chapter pursues further the stakes of a universal politics in a variety of case studies that serve as key global sites of resistance and antagonism, spanning the West and the East, or the global North and South. We look here at the ways the diverse phenomena of climate change, refugee crises, Black Lives Matter, #MeToo, political Islam, Bolivia under Morales, the European Union, and Covid-19 open up emancipatory spaces when they manage to short-circuit the democratic liberal script, exhorting us to see to what extent the script works against (most of) us. To that end, the revolutionary potential of these *events* lies in their capacity to shake our postpolitical myopia by inciting us

Universal Politics. Ilan Kapoor and Zahi Zalloua, Oxford University Press. © Oxford University Press 2022.
DOI: 10.1093/oso/9780197607619.003.0004

to read politically and dialectically—to read with an eye for capital and political economy, race and gender, and the libidinal economy that subtends their global circulation.

Climate Change: It's the Political Economy, Stupid!

Ecology—and climate change—has become one of the main terrains of ideology today. Žižek characterizes it as the "new opium of the masses" (2008b, 55), pointing to how it takes up real problems (global warming, pollution, etc.) but mystifies them. The very term "climate change" is an ideological displacement, a way of obfuscating the causes and targets of our global predicament: the word "change" gentrifies what is a palpable crisis, and the focus on "climate" deflects from the socioeconomic underpinnings of the crisis (more on this later). The discourse of ecology/climate change thus engages in mechanisms of duplicity and self-deception, which for Žižek take two main forms.

The first is the notion that nature is harmonious—an intrinsically balanced ecosystem, derailed by human hubris and technology gone wrong (Žižek 2011, 80). The idea here is that because nature cannot be mastered, we must treat it with more respect and refrain from disturbing its natural stability. For Žižek, this is a social fantasy constructed to escape the trauma of nature's inherent imbalance and contingency: societies need, and are premised on, (the construction of nature as) a stable background in order to ensure human freedom and justify the exploitation of "natural resources" to fuel capitalist accumulation. It has taken the present environmental crisis to wake us up to the fact that such a background cannot be taken for granted anymore and that human life is inextricably linked with nature (i.e., nature is a thoroughly social construct). Worse still, the underlying political message of the fantasy of nature-as-balance is "a deeply conservative one—any change can only be a change for the worse" (Žižek 2008b, 55); it acts as a brake on radically rethinking our liberal capitalist order.

A truly radical ecology for Žižek is therefore a "nature without ecology." Extending Lacan's famous motto—"The big Other doesn't exist"—to ecology, he argues that "nature doesn't exist" (2008b, 56). Not only is nature inherently chaotic and violent—catastrophes and disequilibrium are integral to natural history—but since the Industrial Revolution in particular (i.e., since the onset of the Anthropocene), nature has been so adapted and controlled by humans that it has been thoroughly denaturalized, so much so that human intervention is now part and parcel of nature's fragility and imbalance. What this implies, importantly, is the groundlessness and contingency of human existence: "Humanity has nowhere to retreat: not only is there 'no big Other' (self-contained symbolic order as the ultimate guarantee of Meaning); there is also no Nature qua balanced order of self-reproduction, but only one whose homeostasis is disturbed and derailed by human interventions. Not only is the big Other 'barred,' Nature is also barred" (Žižek 2008b, 56).

The idea, then, is to become not less but *more* artificial, to increase our alienation from "nature," not lessen it, to face such catastrophes as climate change head-on by more effectively intervening in nature. Indeed, on the question of climate change, there is no comfort zone: act we must to squarely address the crisis, but we are left entirely to our own devices, with no guarantees, no certain knowledge of the consequences of our actions: "We are not impotent, but on the contrary, omnipotent, [yet] without being able to determine the scope of our powers" (Žižek 2008b, 64).

A second ideological mechanism is fetishistic disavowal (see chapter 3): "We know the (ecological) catastrophe is possible, probable even, yet we do not believe it will really happen" (Žižek 2011, 328). So libidinally captivated (jouissance) are we by the comforts and stability of our global capitalist order that we are unwilling to make any radical changes to our lives. Even in light of such catastrophes as Chernobyl and Fukushima, total destruction seems unimaginable. The profound changes required to face and tackle the ecological crises appear too traumatic: they would entail a reduction (or loss) of all those things we hold dear (consumerism, accumulation, entrepreneurialism, etc.). So instead, we engage in halfhearted half measures.

These often take the form of individual responsibilization: the capitalist liberal order makes addressing such problems as climate change a question not of serious structural change but of personal burden—superegoic pressures to recycle, consume less, buy organic, and so on. The ideological ruse here is to make us feel good that we are at least doing something to help nature, even if—or rather, *because*—it does not add up to much (i.e., it does not seriously threaten the system). And when structural change does happen, it is usually in the shape of band-aid or reformist measures, most often ones that maintain and reproduce the system. Here, rather than questioning the capitalist market, market mechanisms themselves become the solution: emissions trading (which commercializes our atmosphere), the marketization of fish stocks or water, green subsidies and taxes, the privatization of sewerage or garbage collection, the production of green or organic products—all are neoliberal environmental retrofitting devices that create new opportunities for accumulation and market penetration. Frequently such green capitalism ("The market can save us") goes hand-in-hand with technofetishism ("Technology can save us"); hence the resort to such (market-oriented) solutions as biodiversity and carbon offsets, geoengineering to capture and store atmospheric carbon, and so on. Yet while technology may indeed help in addressing climate change, we should not forget that it has itself been a major contributing factor to the problem: mainstream science's close association with industry (the commercialization of carbon-based energy/technologies) is what has helped produce the climate crisis in the first place. But the overall intent of such techno-managerial green capitalism nonetheless is to exhaust the imaginary of what is possible today: transformation *is* happening . . . but only within the parameters of neoliberal capitalism; climate change *is* being addressed structurally . . . but only in a way that conforms to the liberal-capitalist horizon. The stamp of fetishistic disavowal ("I know very well, but . . .") remains unmistakable here.

To be sure, what is remarkable is a wary acknowledgment of the climate crisis but the resort to deflection and gentrification to avoid any real change. Thus, the West sometimes engages in a blame game with the Third World as a diversion tactic, for example accusing the likes of Brazil for wantonly destroying the "lungs of the earth" (the Amazon rainforests), all the while disavowing the West's own role in the massive deforestation of its ex-colonies and Europe itself. Or China normalizes its smog crisis by issuing new rules and procedures to cope with urban pollution as a new fact of life: "An event first experienced as impossible but not real (the prospect of a forthcoming catastrophe which, however probable we know it is, we do not believe will effectively occur and thus dismiss as impossible) becomes real but no longer impossible (once the catastrophe occurs, it is 'renormalized,' perceived as part of the normal run of things, as always already having been possible). The gap which makes these paradoxes possible is the one between knowledge and belief: we know the (ecological) catastrophe is possible, probable even, yet we do not believe it will really happen" (Žižek 2017b).

The darker side of such deflection/normalization, though, is an "ecology of fear": the use of catastrophe to both reproduce global capitalism *and* advance postpolitical authority. In the face of the climate crisis, the above-mentioned techno-managerialism, involving the neoliberal retrofitting of the environment, is increasingly being imposed by states (Hungary, India,

Turkey, Italy) without debate or contestation. Capitalist market mechanisms to mitigate climate change are taken for granted (i.e., imposed by "consensus") without consideration of alternative articulations of economy or more inclusive democratic governance (Swyngedouw 2011). The result, as underlined in chapter 1, is the replacement of politics by postpolitical expert administration, often rationalized by the need to urgently address the climate crisis. In the *Shock Doctrine* (2009), Naomi Klein points to how catastrophes (earthquakes, tsunamis, wars, economic downturns) can be, and have been, exploited to eliminate old socioeconomic and political constraints and impose new (corporate) agendas. The atmosphere of fear, chaos, and panic caused by such hazards as climate change thus becomes not a limit but a boost for late neoliberal capitalism and its attendant postpolitical tendencies; this is why Klein (2009) refers to the phenomenon as "disaster capitalism."[1]

What thus emerges is that climate change discourse (and broader mainstream ecology) seeks to cover over the antagonisms of global capitalism. The frantic activity, the halfhearted measures, the deployment of a politics of fear—all aim at ensuring the system is left unthreatened, and indeed at securing its reproduction in the face of crisis. The crucial conclusion to draw is that climate change is not really the problem, but the *symptom*; hence to address climate change, one has to address the contradictions of global capitalism. As Žižek puts it,

> In the relation between the universal antagonism (the threatened parameters of the conditions for life) and the particular antagonism (the deadlock of capitalism), the key struggle is the particular one: one can solve the universal problem (of the survival of the human species) only by first resolving the particular deadlock of the capitalist mode of production. In other words, the common sense reasoning which tells us that, independently of our class position or our political orientation, we will all have to tackle the ecological crisis if we are to survive, is deeply misleading: the key to the ecological crisis does not reside in ecology as such. (2011, 333–34; see also Klein 2014; 2019, 70–103)

So as the slogan goes, what a universal politics requires is "system change, not climate change."

But climate change discourse elides not just the economic but also the social roots of the crisis. Global warming may well affect everyone, but it impacts people and places differently across the planet. This is hardly surprising, since sociospatial inequality is inherent to capitalism (see chapter 1), ensuring that poor and marginalized communities are the hardest hit by climate change. Faced with pollution, drought, hurricanes, land degradation, deforestation, or coastal erosion, the rich can afford to retreat to exclusive, protected neighborhoods; subalterns cannot, often paying with their lives and livelihoods. The problem is exacerbated by state-induced neglect and dispossession of communities/neighborhoods (women and children, migrants, the disabled, the homeless, indigenous and racialized people) deprived of the resources and infrastructure to withstand natural or economic crises. The recent upsurge of climate refugees—escaping hunger, dispossession, smog, droughts, earthquakes, tsunamis—testifies to this phenomenon.[2] The overall result is what many in the climate justice movement now refer to as "climate apartheid" (see Perkins 2020); it means that the current global climate change regime is founded on the exclusion and disposability of the part of no-part.

In this sense, without addressing the climate apartheid, without centering the antagonism between the excluded and included, environmental / climate change discourse deprives itself of any subversive edge and becomes just another problem of techno-managerial "sustainable development." The latter, as we have seen, focuses on the included, whose interests represent only private concerns, aimed at protecting and promoting the privileges of the wealthy, most often derived on the backs of the excluded. In contrast, a radical and universalist ecology, if it is to have any meaning, focuses on the excluded, who, as "rejects" with no proper place or stake in the system, represent the interests of all. It is to the latter's call for *égaliberté* that the universal politics we are advocating is meant to respond. But how?

The advantage of the climate crisis is that (negative) universality is already built into it: it brings home the idea of humans as a "species" facing a common threat. While this threat impacts people and places differently, it nonetheless impacts everyone; no one can fully escape it, and everyone encounters it as a traumatic loss (of life, livelihood, etc.). It makes us "aware that, with all the universality of our theoretical and practical activity, we are at a certain basic level just another species on planet Earth. Our survival depends on certain natural parameters which we automatically take for granted" (Žižek 2011, 332). Climate change thus provides the opportunity for collective mobilization around a universally experienced antagonism.

True, the climate crisis is the symptom, not the cause, of a larger systemic deadlock, and the risk is that by targeting this particular crisis we might reproduce the previously outlined ideological mystifications. There are of course real dangers here, but focusing on the particular can sometimes help open up more far-reaching avenues for change; negative universality after all can only be approached and concretized through the particular, as chapter 1 delineated. Žižek claims in this regard that "we must insist on the dialectical link between the particular and the universal, as a result of which the very focus on an apparently particular problem can trigger a global transformation" (2011, 398). Just as the Tunisian revolution had a domino effect across the Middle East, resulting in what came to be known as the "Arab Spring,"[3] so it is not impossible that seriously addressing climate change could set in motion broader processes of radical change to the global capitalist order.

Faced with a common crisis requiring shared solutions, what climate change brings forth is the very idea of the "commons"—its reinvigoration to better think through how we can move away from private ownership toward new collective forms: the commons of nature, of course, but also of intellectual property (knowledge, software). While private property is certainly dominant today, we should not forget that the natural commons are still prevalent: it is estimated that the lives of about two billion people across the planet revolve around access to the commons of fisheries, forests, water, wild game, and land (Weston and Bollier 2013, 1). Crucially, these two billion are composed of the part of no-part, those whose well-being is often the most threatened by climate change (and state-facilitated dispossession), as underlined earlier. Prioritizing the commons in a universal politics of climate change, then, is at the same time centering the most marginalized. Expanding the commons is not only a way of protecting our natural habitat, thereby helping address such problems as drought, desertification, or declining fish stocks, but by putting the excluded first, it is also a way of repoliticizing the stale discourse of mainstream environmentalism, of ensuring subaltern contestation and more bottom-up decision-making, of bringing the sphere of politics back into the postpolitical climate of climate change.

Moreover, at a time when the very idea of collective decision-making has been discredited (in favor of neoliberal individualism and entrepreneurialism), climate change offers the (pressing) opportunity to sign on to a universalist ethico-politics: the idea that we all live on a single planet ("Spaceship Earth") facing a serious threat demands universal solidarity, cooperation, and coordination. Practically speaking, this implies the need for collective decision-making at a global scale, vitiating our current nation-state setup, which is most often the main obstacle in this regard: "Ecological threats make it clear that the era of sovereign nation states is approaching its end—a strong global agency is needed with the power to coordinate the necessary measures" (Žižek 2019b). If the most powerful neoliberal global economic organization today—the World Trade Organization—can be given the power to override national sovereignty in favor of "free trade," then it appears not unrealistic to envision the establishment of a World Environmental Organization, with the power to protect and regulate the global commons, support trans-local civil society climate change networks, override (or shield) national sovereignty where necessary, and punish corporate, national, or local violators. Thus, Žižek asks: "Are these not all measures destined to protect our natural and cultural commons? If they do not point towards communism, if they do not imply a communist horizon, then the term 'communism' has no meaning at all" (Žižek 2017b).[4]

Such an institutionalization of universal politics, it must be noted, is a way not only of meaningfully addressing climate change at a global scale, but also concretizing *égaliberté* so that when the next environmental shock hits, it is liable to impact people and places around the world more equally: regulating the commons will better ensure that the part of no-part does not pay the highest price (in order that the wealthy pay the lowest). We cannot fully guard against crisis—it is part and parcel of human-nature relationships, as argued earlier—we can only try to make sure that when it strikes, it does so in more equal ways. In this context then, engaging in universal politics is a method of aligning the unpredictability of life/nature with egalitarian justice, that is, laboring for the public good.

There is of course no getting around the fact that any such universal politics would entail substantial loss. It would mean that, rather than resorting to reformism or welfare-state measures that mostly leave capitalism intact, we would all have to give up many things, particularly those of us located in the West and/or wealthy urban centers. This is what the advocates of "degrowth" have been calling attention to (see Daly 1992; Victor 2008; Martínez-Alier 2012; D'Alisa, Demaria, and Kallis 2015): any movement toward a non-fossil fuel, recycling economy would entail "steady state" economics and "managing without growth"—not just rethinking and dismantling the neoliberal economy (a massive undertaking), but coming to terms with the accompanying loss of such things as the expectation of (huge) profits, dependence on personal automobiles, high and cheap energy consumption, reliance on packaging/plastic (and landfills), production of excessive garbage and waste, and so on. Such is the price to pay for being in the ranks of the included—the loss of privilege and security. It is also the price of identifying with the excluded: simply declaring, "We are all the wretched of the earth" is easy; actually experiencing the loss of privilege is much more painful: "Acts of solidarity depend on the abandonment of the security that comes from existing inside. We are united only insofar as we don't belong" (Eisenstein and McGowan 2012, 108). A universal politics is thence unpleasant, traumatic, perilous—both personally and politically.

But many opportunities may also be (and are being) opened up by a universal politics of climate change. In keeping with the notion of facing nature's imbalance, the idea would be, not to resort to a Luddite "return to nature," but to readily harness nature's turbulence: this is what alternative green technologies and renewable energy (hydro, wind, solar, biomass, geothermal, tidal) aim to do after all, although the important consideration here will be ensuring not corporate monopoly of such technologies, which enclose the commons, but public control to protect, expand, and regulate the commons for all.

Of late, one of the most innovative ideas gathering support worldwide is the proposition for a "Green New Deal" (Klein 2019, 29–30; Aronoff et al. 2019). Inspired by Roosevelt's New Deal, which responded to the socioeconomic devastation of the Great Depression in the form of large public works projects, the proposal is to tackle the climate crisis by investing in massive socioenvironmental infrastructure projects (green energy, reforestation, low-cost housing, public transit, protection of workers' jobs in the move from high-carbon to green industries, etc.) that would create well-remunerated employment and invest systematically in the excluded. The objective is to transition toward a zero-carbon world, while also addressing issues of inequality, poverty, and exclusion. The proposal has gathered steam in the United States especially (championed by the likes of Congresswoman Alexandria Ocasio-Cortez), but many have also warned against seeing it as an isolated, nation-based project, arguing in favor of a coordinated global vision so as not to ignore the significant risk of global climate apartheid (see the earlier discussion) (Varoufakis and Adler 2019). A modified "International Green New Deal" is thus proposed as a kind of planet-wide equivalent of the Marshall Plan—but centering on an "environmentalism of the poor" to ensure that progressive climate change measures do not themselves reproduce climate colonialism, for example by ignoring or sanctioning forced/child labor in the extraction of minerals (lithium, tellurium, neodymium, etc.) needed for the production of electric cars, solar panels, or wind turbines.

Yet the main challenge for a universal politics of climate change may not be so much ideas—there are many creative experiments happening at the local level around the globe, from community forestry to wind farms and farmers' cooperatives—as effective leadership and mobilization. Here, Greta Thunberg, the de facto teen leader of the global climate movement, can be seen as a model for the type of *leadership* required for a universal politics today: she takes not a stereotypically soft, "feminine" approach to politics (which would conform well to the capitalist liberal status quo), but a more dogmatic and uncompromising one. Her message is that, faced with the climate crisis, it is time to act—to stop with the compromises, halfhearted responses, and rhetorical games (as represented by the toothless Paris Climate Agreement, for example)[5] and take the crisis deadly seriously. To this end, she sees breaking the law as an act of ethical duty, thus, for instance, helping organize student strikes across Europe and North America (during 2018–19). Her approach can be viewed as a way of cutting off the fetishistic disavowal ("I know very well, but . . .") that so grips and immobilizes us today. In fact, she frequently declares, "We children are doing this to wake the adults up" (2019), prompting Žižek to remark: "They (adults) know very well what is going on but . . . they add the usual 'but nonetheless . . .' which prevents us from acting upon our knowledge. Children [like Greta] just know it. The only really 'complex' thing is the emperor's new clothes, and children simply see that the emperor is naked, and demand from us that we act upon it" (2019e). In this regard, Thunberg's publicly declared autism, which she often refers to as her "superpower," is an important part of the story: "Far from being a disturbing factor, it is what gives her strength . . . [it is] exactly what is needed if we are to confront global warming: repetitively insisting on scientific results and ignoring all the rhetorical tricks that obfuscate the scientific message" (Žižek 2019e; see also Klein 2019, 9–10).[6]

Principled yet uncompromising leadership such as Thunberg's is thus important in revealing several key features of a universal politics. It insists that the climate catastrophe is not in the distant future (a typical procrastination technique to avoid dealing with the problem) but already here—affirming that catastrophe is our lot in life so that we are forced to make collective decisions as if the future is now (Žižek 2008b, 68). It shows that the solution to the climate change crisis is not merely more democracy, but also the need to sometimes impose unpopular solutions as a result of which many stand to lose: this is befitting of a negative universal politics, since the latter would address itself to everyone, while still dividing people (i.e., fighting climate change deniers or those who stubbornly seek to defend their private interests) (Žižek 2019c). Finally, an uncompromising universal politics is also a hysterical politics, one required to rupture, rather than compromise with, the ancient régime; one, that is, that demands the impossible: "not demanding the impossible from the system but demanding the 'impossible' changes of the system itself. Although such changes appear 'impossible' (unthinkable within the coordinates of the system), they are clearly required by our ecological and social predicament, offering the only realist solution" (Žižek 2018b).

Love Thy Refugee

As with climate change, current refugee crises call for immediate leftist involvement—matters are urgent, lives are a stake. The cultural Left is asked to intervene on behalf of the vulnerable. If Western governments, under pressure at home from an unruly populist Right, are faltering on their moral duty, failing to act as global leaders, a common refrain from leftist activists and academics is the need to fight for open borders: to welcome in the refugees as our "neighbors"—*to love them as ourselves*—and not let the artificiality of geographical divides determine their worth or humanity. Geography, after all, is not destiny. If universal equality means anything at all, where you are born should not condemn you to a lifetime of hardship. From a multiculturalist standpoint, what is standing between Us (the included) and Them (the excluded) is a myopic investment in our way of life: only our lives matter, only our lives deserve state protection. The refugee discloses the fear of postcolonial scholars and critical multiculturalists that Europe's rhetoric of cultural openness is fake, that it has always masked an insidious monoculturalism. Liberal multiculturalists may have been duped by, if not complicit with, the system's rhetoric of diversity and tolerance, but critical multiculturalists—made up predominantly not of white elites but antiracist and anti-colonial people of color—were suspicious from the start of the promoted narrative of inclusion and racial progress. Advocating open borders is a way to disabuse Europe of its exceptionalism, its claims of sovereignty and superiority. The barbarians, the wretched of the world, are now at the gates. Is Europe going to the turn its back on the refugees? Don't these former colonial European nations bear some responsibility for the current state of affairs?

It is hard to deny the appeal of open borders. We might even consider the idea of open borders as another way of expressing the radical Left's cherished ideal of cosmopolitanism (so dear to Žižek and Badiou, among others). It would be reasonable, then, to expect that a universal politics would endorse the ethico-political position of open borders. As tempting as that idea may be, its seductive simplicity—no more borders, no more nation-states—obfuscates deeper concerns. Žižek rightfully cautions against the multicultural solution. Why? Contrary to his objectors, it is not due to Žižek's Islamophobia or cold indifference to the plight of Muslims and non-Europeans. Quite the opposite, what Žižek is after is not the protection of Europe but its radical transformation. What he is after is an effective engagement with Europe's symbolic order (its laws and language)—an intervention that would "touch, and change the Real" (Dean 2006, 181), disrupting its societies' seamless representation of reality. Anything short of that can only compound the problem of the refugees. Accordingly, the proposed solution of open borders is likely to worsen the living condition of refugees, since it simultaneously solicits the ire of a large population of (mainly working-class) Europeans, who themselves feel betrayed by the promises of their neoliberal political leaders (on the right *and* the left), and, perhaps more importantly, distracts leftist activists and critics from actually addressing the causes of the crisis: Why do we have refugees in the first place? What is the status of refugees in the age of the postpolitical?

As an intervention, the plea for open borders does little to orient us toward the antagonism of the social order. Here we must resist the liberal framing of the problem. It is not a question of being for or against border enforcement. It certainly is not about liberals or "radicals" feeling good about themselves for scoring a moral point. The intervention of multiculturalists depoliticizes the situation, amounting to "self-flagellation" (Žižek 2020g, 40) and virtue signaling: the call for open borders is tantamount to telling Europeans (the West, or global North at large) to check their First World privilege (human rights do not only pertain to their lives; thinking is not an exclusive capacity of whites [see Dabashi 2015], etc.). Consequently, multiculturalists "play the Beautiful Soul which feels superior to the corrupted world while secretly participating in it" (Žižek 2016d, 7). Their goal is never "to break out of the global capitalist deadlock" (Khader 2015).

If the logic of liberal multiculturalism "humanizes" capitalism, supplying it with the moral aura of tolerance and diversity (we should do a better job with refugees; we were once refugees; we're better than this; this is not who we are, etc.)—and thus distracting us from capitalism's ongoing devastating impact, is critical multiculturalism's logic any better at figuring (out) society's true antagonisms? Yes and no. Critical multiculturalists are also suspicious of the surplus enjoyment of "woke" liberals: an empathic or compassionate attitude toward refugees "can just be another way those with privilege can feel good about themselves," as Sara Ahmed points out (2014c). But this scrutinizing of liberal ineffectuality or complicity has its limits.

In the struggle against domination, the refugee crisis is often framed as a crisis in relationality. How should Western nations treat refugees? How should the European Union process their mounting requests for asylum? We know that the ongoing war in Syria remains "the biggest driver of migration" (BBC 2016a) and that the continuing turmoil in Afghanistan and Iraq is only aggravating the crisis. "Hospitality or hostility?" is the leftist moral question shaping our response to this human catastrophe, to this catastrophe of humanity. The populist Right is rightfully criticized for its heartless reactions, its criminalization and animalization of the refugees. But the moral high ground of the liberal Left does not really change the long-term predicament of refugees: more humanitarian assistance, more resources devoted to accommodating the fact of makeshift camps. Yes, but what comes next? Important as the question "hospitality or hostility?" is (and its importance should not be diminished—lives are at risk, people's dignity and sanity are at stake), it tacitly treats the refugee crisis as an isolated or isolable situation. Under a postpolitical horizon, the question directs us away from the causes of the crisis, obfuscating the degree to which refugees *are* a constitutive feature of global capitalism. A universal politics must keep in mind the distinction between symptoms and causes when it comes to the refugee crisis. The call for open borders is a case in point. The multicultural slogan still believes in the perfectibility of capitalism, in a capitalism with a multicultural face, one that would flourish alongside "green capitalism" (neoliberalism's ideological version of climate justice). A world without borders posits the existing system without its refugee crisis. It is a capitalism without its nasty symptoms (Žižek 2020g, 63). The multicultural champions of open borders never really ask: "How to strike back at global capital?" (Žižek 2020g, 61).

This is true for critical multiculturalism as well. The true enemy on this view, as we saw in chapter 3, remains liberal monoculturalism, not capitalism. The cause of the mistreatment of refugees is a pervasive Eurocentrism (from white supremacy to white victimhood). Culture trumps economics. Calling out the hypocrisy of the Western nations seems to exhaust the multicultural labor of critique. *Respect the Others, Open your borders*, and *Don't judge the refugees* are ways to bombard the system with moral injunctions. But do they work? The idea of open borders, at best, is a wishful but ineffective shortcut in the emancipatory struggle (a belief in cosmopolitanism *with* capitalism); at worst, it is a liberal democratic fantasy, a demand made in bad faith, where the open-borders advocates never intend the policy to take hold, never want it to come to fruition or to actually change the coordinates of the system— which would necessarily involve self-violence, destroying the coordinates that actually ground them within the system.

As with climate change, a universal politics repeats and restates a basic insight: *It's the system, stupid!* In order to avoid another refugee crisis down the line, "We have to change the system itself" (Žižek 2020g, 63). Treating symptoms is a short-term concern that Western nations must be committed to doing, but the Left, while supporting the struggle against domination, working to ameliorate the living conditions of the refugees, cannot neglect the political economy, "the logic of antagonism" (Žižek 2012d, 34) that animates the system; it cannot lose sight of its long-term goals: the demise of the system. What is needed is

> the properly dialectical tension between long-term strategy and short-term tactical alliances: although, in the long-term, the very success of the radical-emancipatory struggle depends on mobilizing the lower classes that are today often in thrall to fundamentalist populism, one should have no problems with concluding short-term alliances with egalitarian liberals as part of anti-sexist and anti-racist struggles. (Žižek 2016d, 62–63; see also Žižek 2007, 201–2; Žižek 2004a, 189)

The rhetoric of open borders—which "follows the logic of recognition of difference, of defusing antagonisms into coexisting differences" (Žižek 2012b, 34)—plays into the hands anti-immigrants and race-baiters who gleefully redirect populist anger at global capitalism (a legitimate target) to refugees (scapegoats).[7] The liberal defense of refugees does more harm than good when it engages the anti-immigrants on their own terms, pleading with them that the refugees are not a "real threat to Europe" (Žižek 2017, 169). Liberals and multiculturalists fail to reorient the question about what this paranoid obsession means for European identity, what it discloses "about the weakness of Europe" (Žižek 2017, 169) and the West at large. Why do European

racists need the figure of the refugee? What self-identity are they pathologi-
cally invested in? It is a pristine image of the European subject, whose mythic
land is now contaminated by non-Europeans, foreigners, racialized as
Muslims. Populist and nativist anxieties are offered an explanation. There is
nothing intrinsically problematic about the current state of European identity. A world without refugees would restore the greatest of Western nations
(Trump mastered this trope by blaming in no small part Mexican immigration for the economic ills and decline of America). This ideological explanation overwhelms any liberal cognitive intervention (refugees are not like
that . . .); more empathic imaginings (refugees are really like you and me . . .)
will not do the trick either. A universal politics shifts the register, stubbornly
returning to the source of the problems: Where does the responsibility for socioeconomic disorder actually lie? Is it refugees who threaten Western lives,
or the system itself? Positing an "Islamization of Europe" (Žižek 2017, 169),
as the putative struggle for the future of the West, acknowledges that Western
nations are indeed in trouble but misdiagnoses the *cause* of the trouble. The
populist anticapitalist sentiment—the raw affect of the real antagonism—
gets "mystified or displaced" (Žižek 2012b, 23), shifted onto the external and
contingent enemy that is the refugee. *Non-Europeans are stealing, or threatening to steal, our enjoyment.*[8]

Between the refugee, the populist fundamentalist, and the liberal, it is
the last figure who is the most reluctant to welcome revolutionary change,
to construe the system as the problem. While the alliance between refugees
and the traditional working class is fraught with tensions, it is also pregnant
with emancipatory possibilities. Refugees belong to what some on the left
have characterized as "nomadic proletarians." This identification of refugees
as "the core of a new revolutionary subject in Europe" (Žižek 2017d, 437) is
marked by a liberatory euphoria reminiscent of Hardt and Negri's multitude.
Frustrating the Left's impulse to romanticize the refugees, which amounts
to a kind of "out-sourcing" of the revolution, Žižek proceeds to formulate
a more complex and inclusive vision of the today's new exploited class. The
challenge is obvious: how to make this class a *universal* class rather a coalition of discrete, *positive* identities. In chapters 2 and 3, we discussed Žižek's
opening up of the category of the proletariat, leaving behind "a 'predestined'
revolutionary subject" (Žižek 2008c, 289), as in the days of Marx, in favor
of "different proletarian positions." The question of the refugees, we would
argue, provokes a further expansion.

To be sure, refugees are a challenge to a universal politics; they occupy a position in transition, in between the included (those who count) and the excluded (those who don't count) of global capitalism:

> "Nomadic proletarians" are not simply outside the cupola but somewhere in between: their premodern substantial life-form is already in ruins, devastated by the impact of global capitalism, but they are not integrated into the cupola of the global order, so they roam in an in-between netherworld. (Žižek 2020g, 30)

Can the refugees be subsumed to the revolutionary class *à venir*? Leftist optimism (refugees as multitude) is matched by suspicion from Marx himself. From a traditional Marxist perspective, refugees occupy a position analogous to that of the lumpenproletarians—those who are "outside the production process," lacking a "place in a social totality," and thus bereft of "any emancipatory potential" (Žižek 2020g, 30). Should we adhere to Marx's warning about the lumpenproletarians? Or are the refugees candidates for the parts of no-part, an intrinsic part of a universal politics?

Žižek's intervention in this debate shifts the debate itself, turning the focus back on the proletarians and their phantasmatic *privileged non-privilege*. The refugees are looking to join the proletariat; they want to become "nothing"— divested of all substantial content, the subjectivity of the proletarians is "reduced to the 'nothing' of their working force"—because they are strictly speaking "less-than-noting" (Žižek 2020g, 31). Proletarian anxiety, anti-immigrant populist rage—what happens after proletarians encounter refugees—is linked to a loss of their *positive* "nothing":

> The problematic elements are, more and more, (local) proletarians themselves who, when confronted with the nomadic "less-than-nothings," all of a sudden realize "nothing" (the zero-level, the "place of no-place" in the existing social order) is nonetheless a determinate nothing, a position within the existing social order with all the privileges (education, healthcare, etc.) that this implies. No wonder, then, that when "local" proletarians encounter the nomadic "less-than-nothings," their reaction is the rediscovery of their own cultural identity. (Žižek 2020g, 39)

The fantasy of privilege is at stake in the proletarian resistance to the refugees: "The 'local' proletarians discover," Žižek adds, "that their 'nothing' is nonetheless sustained by a series of particular privileges, and this discovery, of course, makes them much less prone to engage in radical emancipatory acts—they discover that they have much more to lose than their chains" (2020g, 39). Whiteness—the proletarian privilege in the world of racial capitalism—stands in the way of transformative change.

Populist movements on the right and the left articulate their anger at *global* capitalism. Take for example the 2018 Yellow Vest movement in France which was sparked by high costs of living and increases in fuel prices. The Yellow Vests (*gilets jaunes*), named after the fluorescent safety vests kept in vehicles for wear in emergencies, leans left but its members are constantly enticed or recruited by Marine Le Pen's far-right party. Their anger attests to economic pain; they seek remedies: lower taxes, higher pensions, increased salaries, and even unplugging from global capitalism by means of a French exit from the European Union. But the Yellow Vests disclose the limitations of a populist Left, which rails exclusively against *global* capital without offering "a feasible alternative to the system" (Žižek 2020g, 142). What they want is national sovereignty; what they want is also the system without its symptoms. Open borders or isolationism? It doesn't matter—both options preserve the existing system. For the multiculturalists, a capitalism with a multicultural face means a capitalism that can smoothly integrate the refugees. For the Yellow Vests, it is a capitalism that looks out primarily for French citizens (a "France first" attitude, a contagious nationalist sentiment that is dangerously spreading throughout the world).

The demand for economic justice is, then, a necessary condition for revolutionary change but not a sufficient one, especially if the universality of that demand is curtailed by a nationalist script, that is, if its call for justice is *not* open to all. For this reason, the Yellow Vests' political agenda can only receive a "conditional 'yes'" (Žižek 2020g, 142). A universal politics can never be partially emancipatory: it insists that "the whole paradigm will have to change" (Žižek 2020g, 142). For a universal politics, emancipatory change is global or it is not. At present, it is hard to see how the Yellow Vests can be considered candidates for the parts of no-part. They do not stand for something more than themselves. They fall far short of the "singular universal." In making their demands, the Yellow Vests still occupy "a determined place" in France's social totality; they are not "'out of place' in it." Consequently, they do not stand for "the universal dimension" (Žižek 2012d, 831).[9]

And what about the refugees? Is their plight elevated to the level of a universal cause? A universal politics must proceed with caution here. The refugees are not a mere trope for thinking revolutionary change. They are not to be romanticized or instrumentalized. *What do the refugees want?* is a question that cannot be answered in advance. What the Left can and should do is to engage refugees. It must reject the "unconditional" support of refugees preached by many cultural leftists, which is really a patronizing attitude (we must tolerate the refugees as they are; who are we to judge them?) rather than a sign of respect (at least not a respect of equals). The point is obviously not to callously add to the suffering of refugees but to create the conditions to politicize their plight rather than ontologize their pain or settle for their state of passivity, locking the nomadic proletarians, as it were, in their victimhood, where only liberal benevolence can save them. Again, never solidarity without criticism.

The refugee crisis confronts Europeans with ethico-political decision: "The Christian motto 'love your neighbor as yourself' acquires here its full weight: true social love is the love for the unaccountable less-than-nothings" (Žižek 2020g, 35). Love thy refugee does not follow the path of liberal multiculturalism, the impulse to humanize the stranger, making him or her available for empathy. A universal politics begins by affirming that there is no "friendly neighbor" (Žižek 2006b, 144) behind the mask of cultural difference; there is no shared positive identity. It assumes that "most of the refugees are *not* 'people like us'" (Žižek 2016d, 82). But this is no attempt at ontologizing the Other, fixing the refugees in their cultural difference, subjecting them to an Us versus Them logic, to yet another clash of civilizations scenario. No, the purpose here is to substitute negativity for positivity. If we share something with the refugees, and we do, it is a universality constituted by an irreducible alterity, a void or inhuman core. The universality that underpins our universal politics is a "universality of 'strangers,' of individuals reduced to the abyss of impenetrability in relation not only to others but also to themselves" (Žižek 2016d, 79).

A universal politics foregrounds this understanding of the stranger (the Other as neighbor and the subject as neighbor to itself). This self-division is mirrored in one's community or civilization: "The true clash is the clash within each civilization" (Žižek 2002b, 44). The refugees stand for the parts of no-part when they disidentify with the image that reifies them in their monolithic identity—as a *particular* way of life (arousing either compassion/tolerance or contempt/violence)—when they disrupt, and thus politicize, the naturalized order of things by asking "to be heard on equal footing" (Žižek 1998, 989). The refugees are not a romanticized exception to Europe, "those who resist (universal) subsumption," fetishized as a new "site of resistance" (Žižek 2020g, 44). Rather, they disclose a Europe whose subsumption is without exception, a Europe that is non-all (Žižek 2020g, 44). In this respect, it is the refugees, as the parts of no-part, who stand as the latest heirs to the emancipatory European tradition (the French Revolution and the dissolution of eastern European socialism are powerful reminders that Europe cannot be totalized), making, in turn, the anti-immigrant Europeans ironically the greatest peril Europe faces: "A Europe where Marine Le Pen [in France] or Geert Wilders [in the Netherlands] are in power is no longer Europe. So what is this Europe worth fighting for?" (Žižek 2018a, 98). Against a nostalgic and self-enclosed vision of Europe—an idea of Europe governed by the logic of the exception—the refugee crisis creates the possibility for a left-infused Europe "to redefine itself" (Žižek 2016d, 10) (more on this later).

Black Lives Matter and Solidarity Struggles

On July 13, 2013, the #BlackLivesMatter hashtag began trending on Twitter. Sparked by the acquittal of Trayvon Martin's murderer (George Zimmerman), Black Lives Matter's cofounders—Alicia Garza, Patrisse Cullors, and Opal Tometi—miraculously interrupted liberal America's postracial script, "destabilizing the 'natural' functional order of relations in the social body" (Žižek 1998, 989). What made it miraculous was the responsiveness that life-altering hashtag #BlackLivesMatter generated: the movement moved the underground of postracial discourse. The illusion that racism is an anachronism was shattered. Black Lives Matter (BLM) disclosed to the world a racist America engaged in a daily assault on Black folks. After BLM, politicians could no longer play the postracial card, recycle aspirational claims of color-blindness, and disregard systemic Black suffering without consequential pushback.

With the police murder of George Floyd in Minneapolis on May 25, 2020, and the global protests that it sparked, BLM's crucial contribution to debates about racial injustice and formulating an antiracist project worthy of its name has become painfully clear once again. David Theo Goldberg rightly perceived the emancipatory force of BLM from its inception: " 'Black Lives Matter' is gathering steam as the compelling human and social rights movement of our time" (2015). What makes BLM different from other progressive movements? At the top of the list is its refusal to pursue the predicable paths of identity politics; it does not foreground race to fetishize racial identity, but to draw attention to race as "the site of inequality" (McGowan 2020, 183). With its focus on inequality, BLM signals its principled unwillingness to play the game of liberal politics: (negligible) social recognition for (unconditional) party support. We should recall how its members refused to endorse Hillary Clinton in her 2016 presidential bid. Would you endorse someone who willfully capitalized on America's long-history of antiblackness by championing the notorious 1994 crime bill and characterizing "gangs of kids"—meaning Black youth—as "superpredators"?

BLM refused to follow the predictable path of identity politics, declining their interpellation by the Democratic National Committee. Its activists did not let their message be claimed by the Democratic Party. Their request was not for inclusion, since "to demand inclusion in the structure of society as it is means forfeiting the possibility of structural change" (Haider 2018, 22; see McGowan 2020, 183–84). To the chagrin of the Democratic leadership—which is in the business of recognizing, or rather paying lip service to, diversity—BLM's message exceeded the confines of American politics, taking on a global dimension when its members unexpectedly aligned themselves with the Palestinian cause.[10] Racialized state violence is a global problem. Israel and the United States not only practice it, but join forces and learn from each other about the best ways to neutralize racial "threats." The American-Israeli Cooperative Enterprise (n.d.) celebrates this alliance: "With the United States on constant terror alert since the events of September 11, 2001, American police and law enforcement officials are taking advantage of Israel's expertise in various facets of counter-terrorism and first response to better protect the American people." Many US police departments are indeed "taking advantage" of Israel's art of domination, repeatedly offered the opportunity to attend counterterrorism training in Israel or at home from Israeli experts (Collins 2012; Garwood 2016; Weiss 2020; Khalel 2020). And to be clear: what is being imported from Israel is not antiblackness (the US police has it in spades) but the most brutal strategies of containing and disciplining racialized, dangerous (dangerous *because* racialized) bodies.

Against police brutality and state-sanctioned violence, BLM fostered an atmosphere of critical collaboration, inviting activists to couch their struggle against racial domination in global terms. Black-Palestinian solidarity was (re)born:

We know Israel's violence toward Palestinians would be impossible without the US defending Israel on the world stage and funding its violence with over $3 billion annually. We call on the US government to end economic and diplomatic aid to Israel . . . We urge people of conscience to recognize the struggle for Palestinian liberation as a key matter of our time . . . We reject notions of "security" that make any of our groups unsafe and insist no one is free until all of us are.

("2015 Black Solidarity Statement with Palestine")

This type of cross-racial solidarity, so vital for a universal politics, did not go, however, unchallenged by critical Black scholars and activists. A key voice of dissent emanated from critics associated with the movement of Afropessimism. Suspicious of a revival of Black-Palestinian solidarity, Afropessimists argue for the singularity of antiblackness and its seeming incompatibility with any universal project of emancipation—Marxist or otherwise. What is at stake here are the challenges that an Afropessimist "separatist ideology" (Haider 2018, 37) poses for a universal politics and, as a countervailing point, the critical viability of BLM's cross-racial and transnational political mode of resistance. A fault line opens between BLM and Afropessimism: the Black subject can be politicized; its being is in excess of its given symbolic identity and open to reviving an "Afro-Palestinian kinship" (Rickford 2019, 53), *and* the Black "subject" is a sentient tool, its ontology hollowed out, its future "social death."

A powerful short video titled "When I See Them, I See Us" (Black-Palestinian Solidarity) released October 14, 2015, renders visible a renewed Black-Palestinian solidarity. Each participant in the video holds up signs carrying messages including "Gaza stands with Baltimore," "I remember: Deir Yassin, Greensboro, Gaza, Charleston," and "solidarity from Ferguson to Palestine." This video puts on display the ways in which

the onslaught on Black and Palestinian lives is rife with a discourse of victim-blaming that softens the edge of systematic violence and illuminates the dehumanization process. [It] is a message to the world as much as it is a commitment among ourselves that we will struggle with and for one another. No one is free until we all are free.[11]

Black lives matter opens to Palestinian lives matter. What BLM and Palestinian activists are seeking to rectify is the systemic devalorization of Black and Palestinian lives. Gaza and Baltimore/Ferguson are compared.

This video contravenes the tenets of Afropessimism. It violates the movement's first commandment, "Thou shalt not make false comparisons." Beware of "the ruse of analogy," as Frank Wilderson puts it (2010, 35); learn to "differentiate between Blacks and all others" (Wilderson 2016, 5). To be sure, any parallel between American Blacks and Palestinians in the Occupied Territories must be drawn with interpretive nuance so as to avoid overgeneralizations about racial arrangements and socioeconomic conditions that are by no means identical. For Wilderson, however, there is an incommensurability between Blacks and Palestinians that no hermeneutical care could ever bridge. He cautions against the tendency to see a common struggle between Blacks and Palestinians, as if they are objecting to the same thing:

> Comparisons such as these are based on an empirical comparison of cops killing a Black youth in Ferguson and IDF forces killing Palestinian youths in the West Bank and in Gaza. If we use our eyes the two phenomena have a lot in common. It stands to reason, by extension, revolutionaries in Palestine, such as the largely secular and Marxist Front for the Liberation of Palestine, and revolutionaries in the U.S., such as the largely secular and Marxist Black Liberation Army, could be seen as fighting different factions of the same enemy (capitalism and colonialism), in different countries. But this is not the case. (2020, 243–44)

Palestinians and Blacks are not fighting the same fight. Worse. More than a question of incommensurability, affirming blackness is fundamentally at odds with the Palestinian cause: "Ferguson is not Palestine. Ferguson is a threat to Palestine, a threat far greater than that of Israel's occupying army" (Wilderson 2020, 244). This is a startling observation, which if true, invalidates the dream of a Black-Palestinian solidarity.

What compels the suspicion of Afropessimism is the underlying antiblackness informing any attachment to the "human." To be invested in humanity is to be anti-Black. Prior critical frameworks fail to attest to the historico-ontological specificity of antiblackness. With a Marxist focus on political economy, there is a visible remedy to the worker's exploitation and alienation (better working conditions, the destruction of capitalism). But in the case of antiblackness no such relief is available. Living under constant suspicion, "perpetual onticide" (Warren 2018, 129), subjected to "gratuitous violence" (Wilderson 2010, 11), Black people find themselves in a state of permanent alienation. Afropessimists are keen to displace (Sexton 2019, 103) political economy with libidinal economy, underscoring the extent to which antiblackness "naturally" springs from society's collective unconscious. Explaining further the mechanisms and logic of antiblackness, Afropessimists define the notion of libidinal economy as

> the economy, or distribution and arrangement, of desire and identification, of energies, concerns, points of attention, anxieties, pleasures, appetites, revulsions, and phobias—the whole structure of psychic and emotional life—that are unconscious and invisible but that have a visible effect on the world, including the money economy. (Wilderson et al. 2017, 7 n. 1)

Simply put, the libidinal economy regulates the production and circulation of antiblackness.

The problem of blackness lies, then, in the collective unconscious of Palestinians (and other non-Black people). What makes Blacks a threat greater than the Zionist regime is that blackness terrifies Palestinians at the core ontological level.[12] Ferguson—as a project of Black resistance—is antithetical to the Palestinian cause. Ferguson challenges Palestinian reliance on the human, the Black struggle against civil society being irreconcilable with the Palestinian struggle for (human) recognition, since the latter is predicated on antiblackness. Wilderson offers an anecdote about his disillusionment with Black-Palestinian solidarity: "Eradication of the generative mechanisms of Black suffering is not in the interest of Palestinians and Israelis, as my shocking encounter with my friend Sameer, on a placid hillside, suggests; because his anti-Black phobia mobilizes the fantasy of belonging that the Israeli state might otherwise strip him of. For him to secure his status as a relational being (if only in his unconscious), his unconscious must labor to maintain the Black as a genealogical isolate. 'The shame and humiliation runs even deeper if the Israeli soldier was an Ethiopian Jew'" (2020, 251–52). One can definitely see how Sameer's words troubled him. For Wilderson, his Palestinian friend's observation attests to Palestinian antiblackness. Wilderson registers a legitimate objection: who gets to decide who belongs to Palestine? And yet there is something unsatisfactory about his gloss of his friend's statement. Wilderson offers a simple causal

explanation: the libidinal economy of Palestinians, their collective unconscious, is shot through with antiblackness. His comment about the Ethiopian
Jew is proof of that antiblackness. It is as simple as that. Wilderson does not
consider that it might be the Ethiopian Jew's complicity with settler colonialism that is provoking his friend's reaction. As a newcomer, an outsider, the
Ethiopian Jew possesses absolute power over the land's indigenous population. In Wilderson's recounting, the Ethiopian Jew is made to appear as a passive subject, or even a victim—it is true that white Israelis lure African Jews
to come to Israel to do their "dirty work" (2020, 12). He is a victim who just
happens to be an IDF soldier as well. Love thy neighbor, love thy Palestinian,
falls on deaf ears. In performing his military duties, the Ethiopian Jew fully
identifies with the nation-state, declining the refusenik option. Is this decision really beyond reproach? Indeed, we might ask Wilderson: Are Black
soldiers enforcing the Occupation any less objectionable than white soldiers
enforcing the Occupation? Are Black police officers any less responsible than
white police officers for perpetuating and legitimizing antiblackness in the
United States?

Black exceptionalism clouds Wilderson's judgment. Being Palestinian can
only point to a failure to attest to the condition of Blacks. There is no recognition for Blacks, but Blacks are needed for others to be recognized, to be
redeemed and folded back into the plenitude of humanity.[13] To be human
means that I am not a slave/Black. In seeking to disturb this definition of
the human, Black activism represents a bigger problem for Palestinians than
political Zionists eager to annex more Palestinian land. Human redemption
remains a possibility, however remote, for Palestinians regardless of Israeli
mistreatment.

To be sure, Wilderson does not claim to speak for BLM or the Ferguson
activists (one of the iconic Ferguson images is that of a protester holding a
sign that reads, "We are human too" [Bloch 2015]), but he did run workshops
for BLM in at least two major cities, New York and Los Angeles. As part of
his political education, Wilderson stresses the dual projects of Black activism, with the concept of "Two Trains Running (Side by Side)" (Wilderson
2016, 18). One train means you adopt a pragmatic approach; you focus, for
example, on reforming the police and reducing its brutalization of Black
bodies; with the other train, you question the very justification of civil society. You are no longer content in simply treating the symptoms (police brutality as flare-ups), you are looking for ways to destroy the system, actively
taking on its necropolitics (policing and the use of violence are not about

managing or disciplining of Black people, but about punishing or killing them for *being* Black [Wilderson 2016, 15]), what unconsciously generates antiblackness and designates Blacks as "absolute contaminant" (Wilderson 2016, 14) to white purity. In other words, the liberal push for police reform is no longer seen as sufficient. The American script—which typically contrasts rogue officers with "the majority of men and women in law enforcement who take pride in doing their tough job, the right way, every day"[14] (Obama's inadequate response to Floyd's murder)—is faltering, losing credibility by the minute. White people are waking up to the fact that the problem is not the brutality of the police but the police force itself—whence the urgent call to defund the police.[15] White liberals, in particular, are struggling with this call. What does it mean for them? They were enjoying hating the haters (Trump and his supporters, the alt-right and the Charlottesville protestors, etc.), but can they hate the police—police officers are figures of authority that white liberals have been taught to trust, admire, and respect all their lives?

Wilderson's workshops target Black youth. The "learning goal" of his Afropessimist teachings is to instill an antagonistic attitude in Black bodies, spark in them an indocile will when it comes to American civil society and its police: "What we're trying to do now is to infuse an antagonistic orientation in Black people who are white-collar people in college so that their intellectual skills can be enhanced by the orientation that is felt by Black people in the ghetto" (Wilderson 2016, 18). Blacks are not in a *conflict* that can be resolved. Antiblackness indexes a fundamental *antagonism* between Blacks and non-Blacks. Cultivating an antagonistic will in Blacks is, then, one of the major pedagogical goals of Afropessimism. His teachings are a provocation to politicize the world, to question why politics has become toothless, reduced to a question of access: "How do we make our terrain more hospitable to immigrants?. . . How to bring more people into civil society as opposed to why civil society has no right to exist" (Wilderson 2016, 11–12). This is reminiscent of Žižek's point about the refugee crisis: in the postpolitical age, multiculturalists can only imagine a response to the crisis that works from within the system, failing to ask, why has the system a right to exist?

BLM endorses this side of Afropessimism without, at the same time, endorsing its separatist ideology. Unlike Wilderson, BLM activists did not hesitate to back the Palestinian cause, incorporating statements into its platform condemning the ongoing Israeli genocide of the Palestinian people, even characterizing Israel as an apartheid state, and boldly supporting BDS, the Boycott, Divestment, and Sanctions movement against Israel. BLM made this life-affirming decision, fully cognizant of its ramifications at home. For example, disgraced Harvard Law professor Alan Dershowitz was one of the first to accuse BLM of anti-Semitism for "singling Israel out and falsely accusing it of 'genocide,'" which, he claims, "can be explained in no other way than blatant hatred of Jews and their state" (2016). Since BLM does not pay sufficient attention to the human rights abuses of Syria, Saudi Arabia, Turkey, China, and others, Dershowitz, as with other staunch apologists of Israel, interprets the focus on Israel as evidence of anti-Semitism. A fact that Dershowitz conveniently omits is that unlike the other nations with dismal human rights record, only Israel purports to be a democracy. Who would confuse Turkey or China with a democracy? If Israel's claim to democracy is contested—say by exposing its apartheid logic, as BLM did—the counter-charge of anti-Semitism almost invariably follows (as we saw in chapter 2, a global Left that takes up the Palestinian question as a universal cause is bound to be on the receiving end of dubious anti-Semitic charges).

While Žižek is highly critical of the accusation that BDS is anti-Semitic, he does express some concerns about the movement:

> While I fully support these goals [the end of the Occupation, removal of the wall in the West Bank, full equality for Palestinian living in Israel], my reluctance towards BDS was based on two main reasons. One, in the current situation when anti-Semitism really is alive in Europe, it's dangerous to play with the idea of blacklisting. Two, why should we not also boycott China for what the Chinese state is doing to Uyghurs. Of course, the cynical response from my BDS friends is that such tactics would not work on China but may work against Israel. But are they for real? Such reasoning implies weird ethics: punish the relatively weak, not the really bad. (2020g, 172)

The first point is a bit odd. Blacklisting is not qualitatively different from any substantial critique of Israel—isolating its practices, drawing attention to its oppressive operations—which, unfortunately, always runs the risk of being co-opted and misused by actual anti-Semites. On the second point, there is a way of framing the problem in less cynical terms: China's abuse is transparent to its citizens and the rest of the world, whereas Israel's is often explained away by Western powers (every nation has a right to defend itself, and the like). A better argument would be why not boycott the United States—why not impose sanctions based on its war crimes in Iraq and Afghanistan and for its mistreatment of Blacks, Native Americans, asylum seekers, and so on? Most of the world may be blind to America's founding violence—the crimes of racial slavery and indigenous genocide, but Israel's is still happening (Žižek 2008, 117). The world is its witness. BDS is trying to forestall Israel's naturalization of its violence, embodied in its will to annex Palestinian land. BDS's struggle for justice is a universal one (this is a point well understood by BLM)—if it proves effective against Israel, Western nations will have much too fear: the taste of justice can be contagious.

BLM survived the unfounded but politically crippling accusation of anti-Semitism;[16] its solidarity with the Palestinian people never wavered. But what about BLM's relation to Afropessimism? Is BLM's solidarity with Palestinians a minor divergence from the principles of Afropessimism? Or does it speak to a fundamental difference in the ways each envisions the future of blackness? Perhaps it is not overstatement to say that how we understand the significance of this divergence will determine the viability and desirability of BLM as a universal project. If BLM begins with an affirmation that black lives matter, Afropessimism gives an ontological explanation for why they don't.

For Afropessimists, the invisibility of Black trauma persists, and without its acknowledgment, solidarity coalitions are dead on arrival. To make this point, Wilderson elaborates on the ontological devastation of the transatlantic slave trade. The Jews have their Shoah (the Hebrew word for "catastrophe"), Blacks have their Maafa (a Swahili term that means "great disaster," "calamity," or "terrible occurrence"). The two traumas are incomparable: "Jews went into Auschwitz and came out as Jews, Africans went into the ships and came out as Blacks. The former is a Human holocaust; the latter is a Human *and* a metaphysical holocaust. That is why it makes little sense to attempt analogy: the Jews have the Dead (the *Muselmann*) among them; the Dead have the Blacks among them" (Wilderson 2010, 38). Blacks stand alone in the world. Their neighbors are the dead. Why? Because unlike other marginalized groups, Blacks were/are never afforded any of the privileges of humanity. Accordingly, the possibility of redress only exists for non-Blacks:

> Blacks do not function as political subjects; instead, our flesh and energies are instrumentalized for postcolonial, immigrant, feminist, LGBTQ, transgender, and workers' agendas. These so-called allies are never authorized by Black agendas predicated on Black ethical dilemmas. A Black radical agenda is terrifying to most people on the Left—think Bernie Sanders—because it emanates from a condition of suffering for which there is no

imaginable strategy for redress—no narrative of social, political, or national redemption. (Wilderson 2020, 15)

Unlike Black people, Palestinians are never denied the pleasure of redemption, never discouraged from entertaining a just solution to their predicament. They can imagine a Palestinian state, a return to a "prior plenitude,"
to a "spatial place that was lost" (Wilderson 2018, 58). For Blacks, diaspora
means something completely different.[17] Orlando Patterson describes the
condition of diasporic Blacks as "social death."[18] Jared Sexton insists that social death is ungeneralizable: "It is indexed to slavery and it does not travel"
(Sexton 2011, 21). Cross-racial coalitions ignore the fact of antiblackness,
too eager to make analogies with Blacks, "render[ing] equivalent slavery and
other forms of oppression" (Sexton 2008, 293 n. 9).

With Afropessimism, then, the prospects a universal politics are
jettisoned along the analogies that subtend the project. At the same time,
Sexton gestures to an alternative form of solidarity grounded in "*radical
opposition*" (2010, 48). Solidarity is a genuine option if the "structural position of the black" is not assumed to be an "afterthought" but something
foregrounded in the antiracist struggle: "The whole range of positions
within the racial formation is most fully understood from this vantage
point" (2010, 48). In elaborating on this point, Sexton differentiates between "the vantage of black existence" and "the views of black people"
(2010, 56 n. 75). He adds: "The two will likely overlap, but they are not
identical. A sensibility derived from attention to the structural position
of the category of blackness is likely to be produced by people designated
or self-identified as black, but it will neither be exclusive to nor inherent
in their intellectual practice" (2010, 56 n. 75). He clarifies that this is not
"a totalizing gesture," but is akin to the "slave" "embod[ying] what Slavoj
Žižek would call the 'universal particular': not another particular group
among others, but 'a singularity of the social structure' that 'relate(s) to
the totality,' a point of identification with constitutive—not contingent—
exclusion" (2010, 56 n. 75). Solidarity is possibility when and only when
the cross-racial coalition adopts the "vantage of black existence" and
engages "black existence [as] the truth of the racial formation" (2010, 56
n. 75).[19] Sexton likens taking up the vantage point of Black existence in
matters of racial formation to adopting feminist and queer interpretive
lenses when it comes to "the range of gender and sexual variance under
patriarchal and heteronormative regimes" (2010, 48).

We might say that what Sexton is describing here is Black people as candidates for the part of no-part. Blacks are formally citizens (included in the "set" of American society), but live a "shadowy existence" (Žižek 2000b, 313) devalued by, and excluded from, white civil society. In this formulation, the separatist character of Afropessimism is minimized given that the lived experience of antiblackness is *not* in and of itself sufficient to elevate Blacks into the position of the "concrete universal" or the part of no-part. Blacks, after all, must *adopt* the "vantage of black existence." "Black" functions as the subjectivization of the part of no-part; the injustice suffered by Blacks is raised and staged as "the ultimate test of universality" (Žižek 1998, 989).

The video "When I See Them, I See Us" must be read in this context, in light of the part of no-part. This is neither an abstraction of their shared positive humanity nor a narcissistic reduction of the Other's trauma to one's own: the Maafa to the Nakba (the Arabic term for "catastrophe") and vice versa. Their oppositional alliance is predicated not on identification (an identitarian logic) but on a common struggle for emancipation, not on a "shared analogy of oppression" but on "shared principles of liberation" (Kelley 2019, 73). History is not destiny. What they perceive in each other's position is precisely their "actual universality": "Actual universality is not the deep feeling that above all differences, different civilisations share the same basic values, etc.; *actual universality appears (actualises itself) as the experience of negativity, of the inadequacy-to-itself, of a particular identity*" (Žižek 2008, 157). Blacks and Palestinians have been narrated by their respective racist civil society. But understanding that their humanity as non-all enables them to weaken the attachment to a racialized and exploited identity and pursue the emancipatory, "worldmaking" project of Black-Palestinian solidarity (Kelley 2019).

BLM is a miracle. It renders the impossible possible: an antiracist critique that does not follow the postpolitical path of identity politics. The movement became an event, "giv[ing] rise to a commitment of the collective subject to a new universal emancipatory project, and thereby sets in motion the patient work of restructuring society" (Žižek 2014b, 180). BLM's preoccupation with anti-Black violence never authorized a separatist ontology, an ontological equivalent of the narrow Black nationalism of the 1960s. Nor did it play into the hands of liberal democrats. BLM's activists courageously declined the ideological rewards of the system: more recognition, more access to civil society (as long as you play by the rules of the system). They didn't present themselves as *an* injured identity but rather insisted on the movement's universal message—its call for justice is *open to all*—puncturing the horizon of American politics, countering the lures of identity politics with a call for transnational solidarity. BLM's message is universalist, or it is nothing at all.

BLM's platform showcases the struggle for social justice—the ceaseless struggle against "the interlinked systems of white supremacy, imperialism, capitalism and patriarchy." BLM not only shook white civil society; it also unsettled America's Black elite and their complicity with a system that devastates racial minorities. In the words of Cornel West,

> The emergence of the Black Lives Matter momentum is a marvelous new militancy that is [among] the early signs of the shattering of the neo-liberal sleepwalking in Black America. This emergence exposes the spiritual rot and moral cowardice of too much of Black leadership—political, intellectual and religious. The myopic careerism and chronic narcissism that prevented any serious critique of Obama's neo-liberalism are now out in the open, owing to the courageous young people who stood in the face of military tanks in order to show their love of those shot down by unaccountable police under a Black president, Black attorney general and Black homeland security cabinet member. (West 2016)

Whereas the Black elite "opted for symbolic crumbs" (West 2016), settling for neoliberalism's ready-made rewards, BLM sought a different route, casting intervention as a project of emancipation. BLM understood that the plight of Blacks is universal and universalizable, part and parcel of an anti-imperialist struggle, alerting us that global capitalism is in the process of deworlding the world. Capitalism divides to racialize. Don't be fooled by big companies' support of BLM (Amazon, McDonald's, Walmart, among others). In its neoliberal mode, capitalism is responsible for the "*Becoming Black of the world*," as Mbembe puts it (2017, 6), where only the obscenely wealthy are spared from blackening—from instrumentalization and animalization—from a capitalist logic that bestows luxury to the 1 percent and dishes out misery to the rest, producing a never-ending stock of new slaves.

A Transnational Plea for #MeToo

As with the spark that ignited #BlackLivesMatter, the #MeToo hashtag triggered by actress Alyssa Milano—after allegations of sexual harassment and assault by Hollywood producer Harvey Weinstein, she said: "If you've been sexually harassed or assaulted write 'me too' as a reply to this tweet" (@Alyssa_Milano, October 15, 2017)—galvanized victims to call out their abusers and tormentors (the French translation of #MeToo, #balancetonporc, or "call out your pig," renders this even more explicit). And yet #MeToo was mired in controversy early on for its unacknowledged repetition of an earlier "Me Too" movement organized in 2007 by Black grassroots activist Tarana Burke. This earlier movement sought to help female victims of sexual harassment and assault in underprivileged racial communities. After seeing Milano's tweet, Burke said that she felt overwhelmed with panic, "a sense of dread, because something that was part of my life's work was going to be co-opted and taken from me and used for a purpose that I hadn't originally intended" (Garcia 2017). If Burke's movement focused on women of color, the most vulnerable of women, #MeToo placed privileged white women of Hollywood—basically, female celebrities[20]—at the center of the movement, generating mass-media interest (though it was never clear if the public interest in the coverage stemmed from people's sense of social outrage over abusive powerful men or from the stories' sensational content—in other words, were people moved by sexual injustice or by sex?). In Me Too and #MeToo, the women are on the receiving end of sexual violence—harassment or rape.[21] This is a fact that should not be forgotten. We must not conflate the "event" of #MeToo, the euphoric force of its "rallying cry" (Khomami 2017), its deroutinizing of misogyny as usual, with its mediatic reception—the latter surely affects the former, but it should not determine it, exhaust its virtuality or what the movement can be or become.

In her introduction to *Where Freedom Starts: Sex Power Violence #MeToo*, Jessie Kindig frames #MeToo as emerging at a moment when disenchantment with law enforcement, with the legal structures of redress and protection, ran high among women: "The weapons we have to protect our bodies and our rights are not good enough, for they sit within a legal framework which doesn't recognize the undisciplined nature of desire and sex nor the systemic violence of capitalism, white supremacy, patriarchy" (2018, 20). Poised as an event, #MeToo, we might say, was "something shocking, out of joint that appears to happen all of a sudden and interrupts the usual flow of things; something that emerges seemingly out of nowhere, without discernible causes, an appearance without solid being as its foundation" (Žižek 2014b, 2). Sexual harassment and sexual violence are unfortunately nothing new, and yet #MeToo did jolt the general (mostly male) public out of its numbing indifference, its feminist slumber, so to speak, exposing the "dark underside" of liberal democracy, setting in motion a revolutionary desire for transformative change beyond the system's assurances and promises of "equality and mutual respect" (Žižek 2018a, 153).

But the whiteness of #MeToo, at least in its inception, did eclipse the movement's evental character, minimizing the shared character of the struggle, stalling its potential for collective political action, with many Black activists dismissively designating #MeToo's digital activism as a white feminist movement: a feminism mostly concerned with protecting the identity of white, economically privileged women. Who comes to represent the face of #MeToo is first and foremost a political question, for "which agent stands for the totality of struggle as its exemplary case is never a neutral fact" (Žižek 2020h, 196). Is this a fair criticism of the movement? Yes and no. By focusing attention on individual testimonies via the use of the hashtag, the movement ran the risk of "disavowing the socioeconomic and cultural structures shaping our lives" (Rottenberg 2017; see also 2018) welcoming, in turn, a whitewashed, depoliticized mode of activism—earning it the oxymoronic label of "neoliberal feminism" (a feminism not so much invested in critiquing male-dominated structures of power as in fortifying one's symbolic ego and promoting a narrative of *personal* struggle and overcoming). The focus is on "individual bogeymen" and not "power and privilege" (Adetiba and Burke 2018, 27). No one is untouchable, but the system itself is redeemable: the system without its nasty symptoms (Weinstein and Trump). Not engaging capitalism would be a limitation of the movement. Capitalism breads inequality, and inequality, unequally distributed by gender, facilitates sexual harassment and abuse. Without altering the system in any significant way, the backlash is certainly to come, with women scapegoated for whatever mild legislative reforms get implemented.

Moreover, #MeToo's emphasis on "consent" simplifies the situation of harassment quite a bit. Radical feminists like Andrea Dworkin and Catherine McKinnon had already drawn attention to the use and abuse of consent, how coercion never simply disappears when consent is given.[22] Žižek develops this critique further, stressing how a contract mindset "downplay[s] the complexity of sexual interaction" (2018b, 153). The idea of contractual sex is analogous to the contract between workers and capitalists. There is a "structural weakness" (Žižek 2020h, 205) that invalidates any objective compliance with the contract. Even if the capitalist pays the worker what they agreed to, "There is exploitation since the worker is a commodity which produces surplus-value, i.e., more value than its own value" (Žižek 2020h, 205). The contract obfuscates the absence of actual equality. Verbal agreement in sexual matters may then be the latest ruse of coercion. A sexual contract is not the next emancipatory step to take. It traps you in the illusion of control and symmetry. Worse, Žižek perceives in some of the partisans of #MeToo an attempt at "revenge," exploiting this structural asymmetry for their own advantage, "ruthlessly using structural weakness as a means of its own empowerment" (Žižek 2020h, 206). The personal is not simply political; the personal overrides the political. Western liberal ideology allows for the relative empowerment of the structurally weak and vulnerable (to personalize their struggle against patriarchal domination) as long as the questions that they raise do not seriously disrupt the flow of capital (Žižek 2018a, 153).

At the same time, we must proceed carefully here and not engage in a form of victim blaming: for not saying enough about the impact of the anonymous structures of male domination on women from underprivileged communities, for treating their victimization as an opportunity for profit and empowerment. The point of the debate is to assess the universal potential of #MeToo. Does the movement *disturb the underground of the unspoken underpinnings of our sexual lives?*[23] Is #MeToo's "revolutionary upheaval" (Žižek 2018a, 7) going to translate into a mass movement? Is its feminism *open to all?* #MeToo, at times, takes it for granted that the victim or survivor of sexual violence is already positioned as someone who counts and, of course, counting here does not immunize you from sexual predators. Unlike Burke's version, #MeToo foregrounds the efforts of "wealthier women, whiter women, women with more access to power," which, "while necessary and laudable, are by no means the cutting edge of this struggle" (Kindig 2018, 19). But is #MeToo completely at fault here? Aren't the movement's shortcomings also connected to its reception?

It is not an exaggeration to say that mainstream media outlets dulled the "cutting edge" of #MeToo, almost from the start. They transformed the event of resisting sexual harassment into a spectacle of individual suffering, transfixing the *image* of harassment at the level of subjective violence, the type of violence that is "performed by a clearly identifiable agent . . . [and] is seen as a perturbation of the 'normal,' peaceful state of things" (Žižek 2008, 1–2). Sexual harassment is clearly an instance of subjective violence, but it is also much more. To remain at this level of analysis is to fall prey to the ideological pull of subjective violence. As Žižek puts it, "There is something inherently mystifying in a direct confrontation with [violence]: the overpowering horror of violent acts and empathy with the victims inexorably function as a lure which prevents us from thinking" (2008, 3–4). Subjective violence is engrossing, always at risk of becoming titillating fodder for entertainment (masquerading as news), a voyeuristic indulgence in the other's suffering. "While attention to violence against women may be sparked by anger and a desire for redress," Jacqueline Rose astutely adds, "it might also be feeding vicariously off the forms of perversion that fuel the violence in the first place" (2018). Moral outrage slides into obscene enjoyment. Consuming subjective violence reproduces sexual violence.

A transnational plea for #MeToo would interrupt this consumerist hunger. It would turn #MeToo's critical energy toward harassment as an instance of objective violence (in its symbolic and systemic forms), toward a patriarchal global system that produces men and instills in them an aura[24] of invisibility and sovereignty (I can harass with impunity). To transnationalize #MeToo, to make its feminism universal, emancipatory for all, the movement must trouble its own positionality, and take on the politico-hermeneutic challenge to "read up the ladder of privilege," as Chandra Talpade Mohanty puts it (2003, 231). To adhere to this injunction would be to place marginalized women of color—society's parts of no-part[25]—at the center of #MeToo.

If in media culture, the abuses of patriarchy are relegated to examples of subjective violence, a universal politics frames patriarchy as a problem of objective violence. Patriarchy is a form of social organization in which power is attributed exclusively to men; patriarchy's hegemony, its power to reproduce itself, however, is not absolute, nor is it a constant feature of history. It undergoes a significant change after the rise of capitalism. The capitalist ethos deworlded the world of patriarchy, wreaking havoc with its system of power. Žižek credits Marx and Engels for their observation that patriarchy is no longer a "hegemonic position,"

> Marx and Engels wrote more than 150 years ago, in the first chapter of *The Communist Manifesto*: "The bourgeoisie, wherever it has got the upper hand, has put an end to all feudal, *patriarchal*, idyllic relations." Such an insight is still ignored by those leftist cultural theorists who focus their critique on patriarchal ideology and practice. Is it not time to start wondering about the fact that the critique of patriarchal "phallogocentrism" and so forth was elevated into the main question at the very historical moment—ours—when patriarchy definitively lost its hegemonic role, when it was progressively swept away by the market individualism of rights? (2010b, 103–4)

Capitalism, from its neoliberal fetish of the market (everyone is a Homo economicus) to the "becoming black of the world" (everyone is becoming instrumentalized and animalized), has severely weakened the previous authority of patriarchy. At the same time, patriarchy is clearly enjoying a second life under capitalism, functioning as an ideology that nurtures and inculcates a hyper-masculinity, masculinity dangerously "out of control" (Rose 2018),[26] that elevates and *falsely* universalizes the male perspective, engendering a misogynist horizon within which women are a priori sexually violable, and men given license to dominate women, to engage in sexual harassment, where harassment is the harasser's right, his ultimate male privilege. To insist on the hegemony of patriarchy, to focus on patriarchy in isolation, away from the system of capitalism, away from the socioeconomic and cultural structures conditioning our existence and relation to others, is to neoliberalize feminism, to imagine a feminism winning the struggle against patriarchal domination without having to alter society's economic coordinates, bracketing, as it were, the struggle against exploitation. Again, is this feminism open to all?

With an eye for symbolic violence, a universal politics pays attention to the ways girls and women, living in a patriarchal universe of meaning, are habitually interpellated as sexual instruments, intimate objects, ready-at-hand for sexual harassment or coercion. The #NotYourHabibti hashtag by Palestinian-American woman Yasmeen Mjalli, which creatively translates #MeToo as "not your sweetheart," exposes and disrupts patriarchy's soft power, its fake proximity or assumption of intimacy, under the guise of the inoffensive word "sweetheart." Language creates disparities between men and women (one is a desiring subject, the locus of agency, the other a reified object, awaiting/dreading male affection), sustaining a sense of inferiority among women.

In *The Second Sex*, Simone de Beauvoir meticulously accounted for the ways women are *produced* as the "second sex," as inferior beings: "When an individual or a group of individuals is kept in a situation of inferiority, the fact is that he or they *are* inferior. But the scope of the verb *to be* must be understood; bad faith means giving it a substantive value, when in fact it has the sense of the Hegelian dynamic: *to be* is to have become, to have been made as one manifests oneself" (2010, 12). Beauvoir's observation about the inferiority of women clearly jars with what one would expect of a feminist to say. We could imagine a "minor" liberal edit to Beauvoir's statement: this is how misogynists interpret and judge women, not how they really *are* (see Žižek 2008, 72). But this is exactly what Beauvoir is not saying. Refuting patriarchy, resisting misogyny, is not an idealist struggle, waged at the level of ideas. The label of inferiority is not merely a subjective judgment on the part of the sexist that liberals can dismiss simply by claiming it is not true, that women, in fact, are equal to men. The leftist remedy to symbolic violence is not a liberal feminism at the level of ideas. A feminist struggle cannot limit itself to demystifying ideas, to claiming that women are equal (ontologically) and inferiorized (ontically) and that people living under the yoke of patriarchy just fail to see that they are (Žižek 2008, 73). Patriarchy wields a "performative efficiency" (Žižek 2008, 72). It is more than interpretation of what women are; patriarchy is "an interpretation that determines the very being and social existence of the interpreted subjects" (Žižek 2008, 72).

Beauvoir follows the preceding words by gesturing to what the next step might look like: "Yes, women in general *are* today inferior to men; that is, their situation provides them with fewer possibilities: the question is whether this state of affairs must be perpetuated" (2010, 12). The surest way to remain stuck in the position of inferiority is to somehow buy into feminine identity. To change the patriarchal state of affairs requires a universalist intervention.[27] It is here that Mohanty's intervention in feminist debates is most relevant. How to challenge and transform "this state of affairs" does not follow a ready-made recipe, or rather, the recipe itself calls for specificity: "Within a tightly integrated capitalist system, the particular standpoint of poor indigenous and Third World/South women provides the most inclusive viewing of systemic power" (Mohanty 2003, 232). Feminists in general must learn "to read up the ladder of privilege" (although this is a lesson that is less familiar to the feminists of the global North, with #MeToo serving as a reminder). Universality is not embodied in society's elite—an identity politics masquerading as universal (pretending to speak for all women). Universality is to be found in society's least privileged, starting at the bottom of the ladder of privilege—or in the register of this book, the part of no-part. Such an approach avoids "ethnocentric universality," what we've been calling "abstract universalism," a mode of Western thinking that posits "women as a coherent, already constituted group that is placed in kinship, legal, and other structures, defines Third World women as subjects outside social relations, instead of looking at the way women are constituted through these very structures" (Mohanty 2003, 40). Mohanty lambasts this kind of identitarian feminism, which construes Third World women as always already oppressed, in need of rescue due to their cultural backwardness (according, of course, to Western standards). This form of easy universalism also generates Robin Morgan's concept of "global sisterhood" (1984), which homogenizes women and "seems predicated on the erasure of the history and effects of contemporary imperialism" (Mohanty 2003, 110–11). A global feminism that excludes the effects of (neo)imperialism is a feminism akin to the neoliberal kind. Both feminisms ignore or cover over the plight of the women who stand for the parts of no-part.

If one of the ideological tricks of patriarchy is to naturalize its mode of domination, circulating cultural fantasies of masculine control over a feminine/feminized body, patriarchy is all too willing to collaborate with whiteness and settler colonialism.[28] Operation Protective Edge, the 2014 Israel-Gaza war, is a case in point. Here patriarchy infiltrates itself in the "hyper-masculinization" (Lentin 2018, 126) of Israeli Jews and its feminization of Gazans. Consider this obscene Israeli reaction posted on Facebook by a female teenager, Talya Shilok Edry, who has more than one thousand followers: "'What an orgasm to see the Israeli Defense Forces bomb buildings in Gaza with children and families at the same time. Boom boom'" (Strickland 2014). Or this post addressed to Prime Minister Netanyahu, which reached a broad audience on Israeli social media, displaying "a veiled woman labeled 'Gaza,' naked from the waist down, holding a message: 'Bibi, finish inside this time! Signed, citizens in favor of a ground assault'" (Shalhoub-Kevorkian, Ihmoud, and Dahir-Nashif 2014). Watching the massacre of Palestinians is like watching a snuff film. Palestinians are ventriloquized, perversely interpellated in this rape fantasy, starring Netanyahu as the patriarch, the rapist-in-chief.

Do Western feminists care about another Gaza war? Does their resistance to patriarchy cover Israel's hyper-masculinization of its Jewish citizens, along with its circulation of rape metaphors[29]? Is solidarity between Western feminism and Third World feminism possible? While critical of Western feminism, Mohanty does not give up on the emancipatory force of feminist struggle. The possibility of "feminist solidarity" (Mohanty 2003, 3)—a feminism across boundaries—must not be ruled out, since without it the struggle against global capitalism can only be hindered. Differences are not to be fetishized, categorized, or ontologized, but carefully compared; they are to serve as the basis for a shared universal project of emancipation:[30]

> In knowing differences and particularities, we can better see the connections and commonalities because no border or boundary is ever complete or rigidly determining. The challenge is to see how differences allow us to explain the connections and border crossings better and more accurately, how

specifying difference allows us to theorize universal concerns more fully. (Mohanty 2003, 226)

What feminist solidarity must adhere to, though, is a serious engagement with the global South, which, as Boaventura de Sousa Santos understands it, "is not a geographical concept, even though the great majority of its populations live in countries of the Southern hemisphere," but instead "a metaphor for the human suffering caused by capitalism and colonialism on the global level, as well as for the resistance to overcoming or minimising such suffering" (2016, 18). The global South is where the parts of no-part emerge, where we witness "*the very site of political universality*" (Žižek 2000b, 313). The relation between the global North and the global South must be based on "common differences," grounded in "mutuality, accountability, and the recognition of common interests as the basis for relationships among diverse communities" (Mohanty 2003, 225, 7). Feminist solidarity is a *global* solidarity of the exploited and oppressed of the global South in its geographical and figurative sense. They are "the 'nothing,' not counted in the order" (Žižek 1998, 988). When they speak, they "are the people, we are all, against others who stand only for their particular privileged interest" (Žižek 1998, 988). The "poor indigenous and Third World/South women"—which gives Mbembe's "becoming black of the world" a gendered dimension—stand for social justice and for universality as such: "If we pay attention to and think from the space of some of the most disenfranchised communities of women in the world, we are most likely to envision a just and democratic society capable of treating all its citizens fairly" (Mohanty 2003, 231).[31]

#MeToo can read up the ladder of privilege by foregrounding the experiences of "invisible" Native American women, who, in the United States, have the highest rate of sexual violence (Pember 2019). Another way of reading up the ladder of privilege is for white feminists to question their demand "to believe women" (#BelieveWomen),[32] to suspend due process, and acknowledge the history of racial violence in the United States behind Black men being wrongfully accused by white women (let us not forget how in 1955 accused fourteen-year-old Emmett Till was falsely accused of sexually harassing a white woman in a Mississippi store, leading to his horrific lynching), which helps to explain the reluctance of some Black women to give #MeToo a blanket endorsement. As Ashwini Tambe observes: "The dynamics of #MeToo, in which due process has been reversed—with accusers' words taken more seriously than those of the accused—is a familiar problem in Black communities. Maybe some Black women want no part of this dynamic" (2018, 200). This is a point of difficult negotiation since it brings the full weight of an intersectional reality to bear on #MeToo. Black women, as Kimberlé Crenshaw (1991) powerfully explained, are also caught in a double bind—should I call out my Black sexual harasser/victimizer? Or should I protect / not betray my community and remain silent? No feminism worthy of the name should ignore this heart-wrenching predicament.

When white feminists object to patriarchy, their objection often eschews questions of race/racism, and thus they are prone to repeat society's systemic violence. They forget that "white people are not simply 'protected' by the police, they *are* the police" (Wilderson 2010, 82). The label "Karen" names and makes visible the social phenomenon of middle-aged white women who function as the police, "the policewomen of all human behavior" (Miller 2019), displaying their particular white privilege in monitoring the behavior of "suspicious" Black men, eagerly dispatching the actual police to assist. And even if white women and feminists are not actively engaged in the policing of Black bodies, they remain complicit with the matrix of racism when they exclude or remain indifferent to the plight of nonwhite, disenfranchised women: only the beneficiaries of global capitalism—the economically powerful but not invulnerable white women of the global North—can freely register their complaint against patriarchy or sexual harassment. The future of #MeToo serves as a test case for thinking the viability of feminist solidarity—a universal politics by another name.

The Liberatory Dimensions of Political Islam

Islamophobia has been integral to the construction of Western identity, dating back to at least the Crusades (eleventh century) and the Spanish Inquisition (fifteenth-sixteenth centuries), and continuing today in the wake of 9/11, the "War on Terror," and the rise of anti-immigrant neopopulism. Edward Said (1979) sees it as integral to the armory of Orientalist discourse, evidenced, for example, in French philologist Ernest Renan's famous words at his 1862 inaugural lecture at the Collège de France—"The Muslim is in the profoundest contempt of education, science, [and] everything that constitutes the European spirit" (1883, 3)—or the nineteenth-century German historian Leopold von Ranke's declaration that Islam is the "antithesis" of Christian Europe (quoted in Sardar 1999, 50). Such anti-Muslim sentiment is plainly manifest today—in former NATO secretary general Willy Claes's statement that Islamic fundamentalism is "at least as dangerous as Communism was" (quoted in Mosley 1995), or more recently in Trump's and Orbàn's anti-immigrant/refugee policies. In many ways, the latter policies actualize Samuel's Huntington's thesis (1997) about the inherent cultural difference between the West and the Islamic world, and the inexorable "clash" that allegedly ensues between them. In fact, what is remarkable is that, despite the neopopulist disdain of "multiculturalism," neopopulist regimes share—and push to an extreme—precisely a late-capitalist multiculturalist viewpoint (implied in Huntington's thesis): others will be tolerated, but only insofar as they are kept at a distance—contained, isolated, anesthetized; we will interact with them, but only to the extent that their differences (precisely what makes them unique) are diluted or cleansed; other cultures are equal to ours, but we must nonetheless protect ourselves from them.

Meanwhile, during the last few decades, the "Muslim world," for its part, has witnessed the rise of "Islamism": groups—ranging from political parties/movements (e.g., Jamaat-e-Islami, Hamas, Ennahda)[33] to "fundamentalist terrorist" organizations (al-Qaeda, Al-Shabaab, Boko Haram, Islamic State, etc.)—which more often than not tend to reject all things Western, advocating a return to a romanticized Islam (modeled on Prophet Mohammed's founding of an Islamic community in Medina in the early seventh century), and seeking to impose (a degree of) Sharia law.[34] Although often portrayed as regressive and anti-modern, such groups are more accurately to be understood as thoroughly modern. That is, they are a response, first, to the social dislocation wrought by contemporary global capitalism: inequality, poverty, unemployment, cultural estrangement (e.g., in the face of the Hollywoodization of the world) are the breeding grounds for disaffection and alienation, particularly by younger people. It is Islamism's promise of a better (Islamic) world that helps heal such wounds. And second, the rise of Islamism is a response to the upsurge of corrupt and/or authoritarian regimes in many parts of the "Muslim world" (e.g., Saudi Arabia, Kuwait, Pakistan, northern Nigeria). Islamism is thus a (misdirected) response to a lack of political accountability and public debate (i.e., postpolitics). When postpolitics replaces politics, the remaining political outlet is most often ethnic and religious struggle.

But of course, both these—liberal multiculturalism and the Islamic resurgence—are not to be seen as separate but two sides of the same coin. While they may portray each other as the adversary/enemy, both equally feed off a vicious cycle of othering. This is perhaps most visible in the common forms of demonization deployed by both Islamofascists and Western anti-immigrant racists (us-them, civilized-barbaric, pure-corrupt, moral-permissive, etc.). But ultimately, this is a false and mystifying conflict, each binary pole generating and presupposing the other. Instead, both sides are to be seen as symptomatic of the antagonisms of today's (still mostly) Western-dominated global capitalist order.

For one thing, several of the "fundamentalist"/"terrorist" groups that the West rails against are in fact Western creations, often initially supported to suit short-term geopolitical interests (e.g., British promotion of the Saudi Wahhabis [after World War I] and Egyptian Muslim Brotherhood [during World War II] as part of a divide-and-rule strategy; US backing of the Taliban to counter the Soviet invasion of Afghanistan in the 1980s; Israeli support of Hamas in the 1980s to undermine the PLO). Moreover, the United States and Europe have a long history of championing totalitarian regimes, especially in the Middle East (Saudi Arabia, the Gulf States, Egypt, Iran under the shah, etc.): it is not implausible, in fact, to suggest that the West is (and has been) invested in these countries remaining undemocratic so that they can be counted on for their geopolitical support, and perhaps especially their oil reserves. Western economic interests thus trump Middle Eastern political well-being, with Islamic religious resurgence as a resulting symptom.

What should not be missed here is that, despite the outward "Islamic" character of (post)politics in the Middle East, it is a region that has been fully integrated into global capitalism. Can one imagine more capitalistic countries than Saudi Arabia or Kuwait, for example, with their immense wealth and ultramodern cityscapes, but also their sizable social inequality/hierarchy and high dependence on exploited migrant labor? Even Iran's "Islamic democracy" cannot hide anymore that its ruling elites (ayatollahs, Islamic Guards) are "market-oriented capitalists" with significant control over the economy (industry, trade, land/real estate) (Rahnema 2009). Ethno-religious conflicts are the only form of struggle that fit the frame of such an unequal and postpolitical capitalist global order, in the Middle East as else-where: as chapter 1 underlined, the universalism of global capital allows and tolerates only the particularity of cultures (i.e., multiculturalism), which are ultimately unthreatening, and in fact easily adaptable, to the system. Hence, if there is any civilizational "clash" today, it concerns the conflicting ways in which different groups cope with the antagonisms of global capitalism (and its accompanying postpolitics), increasingly in the form of culturalized politics. So rather than focusing only on (depoliticized notions of) Islam, one needs to focus on the relationships between the socioeconomic and geopolitical factors operating in the background. It is in this sense that "Jihad and McWorld are two sides of the same coin: Jihad is already McJihad" (Žižek 2002b, 187).

Universal politics provides a way of breaking through the purported deadlock between the West and Islam: it means, as we have been arguing, reconceptualizing this "deadlock" not as an essence that forever divides the one from the other (i.e., as a "clash of civilizations"), but as a negativity that both sides always already share and would hence need to face/embrace. The idea therefore would be to engage in an emancipatory politics from both within and without. To quote Žižek on this point: "This is why a crucial task of those fighting for emancipation today is to move beyond mere respect for others towards a positive emancipatory Leitkultur that alone can sustain an authentic coexistence and immixing of different cultures. Our axiom should be that the struggle against Western neocolonialism as well as the struggle against fundamentalism . . . [are components] of one and the same universal struggle" (2014d).

Part of this struggle involves an unrelenting critique of liberal multicultural "tolerance" (in the West as much as the rest), which despite all pretenses, prioritizes dominant white European culture (or in such countries as India, dominant Hindu culture), while patronizingly "tolerating" others (see Iqtidar and Sarkar 2018). Here, Muslim culture is fixed and stereotyped, most often reduced to a religious category, thereby ignoring the dynamic, diverse, and indeed secular mix that makes up the "Muslim world" (both outside and inside the "West"). What is most often missing is a properly politicized view of Muslim culture (or indeed culture writ large), in which political-economic antagonisms play a key role: thus, violence against women is not the result of some pathological religious practice, but most often imbricated with unequal state property/inheritance laws (and their lack of enforcement) and/or male domination in the advancing cash economy (Visweswaran 1994, 510; Salhi 2013).

A universal politics worthy of its name cannot, as a result, engage in a purely "cultural politics" that avoids the key question of the politicization of the economy; this would merely play into the hands of postpolitical global capitalism, which, as underlined already, seeks to keep culture and economy apart. Linking the two spheres is precisely what enables universality: seeing the antagonisms of culture/identity (struggles of representation, violence against women, queer rights, racialization) as intimately linked to the antagonisms of global capitalism (socioeconomic and spatial inequality, environmental catastrophe) is what opens the door to shared struggle. It helps establish bonds of solidarity between those who struggle for justice in the West and those who participate in the same struggle in the "Muslim world" (and elsewhere).

Perhaps those of us Westerners engaging in universalizing struggles can learn from the political vitality and truculence of the "Muslim world": at a time when engagement, energy, and commitment to change the system are often so fickle in the West, the Islamic resurgence, despite often being misdirected, can teach us something about a refusal to be so easily co-opted and seduced by Western hegemony. The challenge, though, is to channel such "rage" to the right target, that is, to make it anti-systemic rather than anti-symptomatic.

Yet the struggle for a universal politics also implies a self-critique from within the "Muslim world" (as suggested by the notion of a "Political Islam").[35] For, if Orientalism/Islamophobia commits the error of essentializing Islam, so does Islamism: it fixates on one set of meanings—a "real" Islam or the "true" Muslim woman—which translates into an attempt to contain, control, or hierarchize the Other, particularly women. Politicizing Islam means seeing it not as a collection of clearly definable values or "customs," but rather a contested terrain of lived practices and contingent interpretations. Making place for the secular, in particular, remains a significant challenge, especially given that much of the "Muslim world" is secular, albeit increasingly stifled by the Islamic revival.

Of course some of this work of self-critique is already being done, by Muslim activists/scholars (and their allies) in the Third World as much as in the West. The move here has been to try to reinvent Islam for the present, to retrieve a disavowed emancipatory horizon. Already in the early part of the twentieth century, Hegelian-influenced philosopher and poet Muhammad Iqbal, seized upon such Quranic notions as *qiyas* (reason) and *ijtihad* (textual interpretation) to foreground practices of independent and reasoned explication of Islamic texts. Inspired by Turkey's then-emerging republican form of government, his clear intent was to wrest politico-religious power away from the clerics toward the creation of an elected assembly of laypersons/citizens: "The growth of republican spirit and the gradual formation of legislative assemblies in Muslim lands constitute a great step in advance. The transfer of power of *Ijtihad* from individual representatives of schools to a Muslim legislative assembly . . . is the only form *Ijma* [collective deliberation] can take in modern times" (1986, 138; see also 1964). For him, not only does Islam prioritize equality and social justice, but it needs to also be "reconstructed" and democratized in favor of difference, debate, and disagreement (see Cwikowski 2021; Kurzman 1998).

More recently, activist-scholars have highlighted the role of feminism in Islam (e.g., Badran 2009). Of note here are the activities of such organizations as Women Living under Muslims Laws to fight against Sharia, while also reinterpreting Muslim legal texts for the defense of women's' rights (http://www.wluml.org; see also Hélie-Lucas 1994). Also worth mentioning is the "Progressive Islam" group (Safi 2003), which carries out a critique of both Islam and the West by foregrounding questions of social justice, gender equality, and pluralism.

Countless other collective efforts could also be cited;[36] yet a significant weakness is that they often lapse into a liberal critique, limiting themselves to the sphere of ethical values and civil-political rights, while refraining from any meaningful confrontation with global capitalism (see Zimeri 2015, 264–65). Any politicization of Islam worthy of its name would need to break through not just Islamism's theological obscurantism or the grip of Sharia but also the shackles of global capital. The demand for *égaliberté*, after all, is a demand for egalitarian justice in terms of not just the civil, political, and individual but also the socioeconomic and collective, particularly as the latter affect the subaltern (equal pay, the removal of feudal ties that still grip much of the rural sector in such countries as Pakistan and Afghanistan, land rights for indigenous communities and the landless, housing for the urban poor, access to health and education for women and girls, etc.). And it is fighting for the latter that is the greatest challenge today, as we have been repeatedly underlining, implying not an easy or smooth politics, but a difficult, struggling, and messy universality to enact a radical rupture in the system.

In order for such a radical break to happen, though, what is needed, and sorely missing, in the "Muslim world" as much as anywhere, is an organized (secular?)[37] Left. This is not entirely surprising, given that, in many places, the Left has been made to systematically disappear by right-wing authoritarian regimes with active support from Western governments (e.g., the toppling of Afghanistan's Communist regime in the 1980s engineered by the United States and Pakistan, among others; Indonesia's Communist purge in the 1960s with aid from the CIA; the US- and British-engineered coup in 1953 to install the shah and eliminate the democratically elected leftist

Mosaddegh government). It is the lack of left mobilization, in fact, that is at least in part to account for the rise of Islamic resurgence, the latter successfully occupying the political vacuum and tapping into popular "rage." Let us quote Žižek at length in this regard:

> The recent vicissitudes of Muslim fundamentalism confirm Walter Benjamin's old insight that "every rise of Fascism bears witness to a failed revolution": the rise of Fascism is the Left's failure, but simultaneously a proof that there was revolutionary potential, dissatisfaction, which the Left was not able to mobilize. And does the same not hold for today's so-called "Islamo-Fascism"? Is the rise of radical Islamism not exactly correlative to the disappearance of the secular Left in Muslim countries? When, back in the Spring of 2009, [the] Taliban took over the Swat valley in Pakistan, [the] *New York Times* reported that they engineered "a class revolt that exploits profound fissures between a small group of wealthy landlords and their landless tenants." If, however, by "taking advantage" of the farmers' plight, [t]he Taliban are "raising alarm about the risks to Pakistan, which remains largely feudal," what prevents liberal democrats in Pakistan as well as the US from similarly "tak[ing] advantage" of this plight and try[ing] to help the landless farmers? The sad implication of this fact is that the feudal forces in Pakistan are the "natural ally" of the liberal democracy. (2015a)

There are, of course, exceptions here, including, for example, the primary role played by the Tunisian General Labor Union in the 2010–11 "Jasmine Revolution" that overthrew Ben Ali and ushered in a new democratic regime.[38]

But the recent tribulations of the Left notwithstanding, there is undoubtedly genuine liberatory potential in political Islam, as we have been highlighting, so that one doesn't have to go back to seventh-century Medina to find a "good" Islam: it exists right here, right now, even if its universalist underpinnings remain to be realized on a large scale. This is to say that political Islam's future remains uncertain, especially in the absence of a left upswing to help lead and drive it. As Žižek puts it once again: "Instead of celebrating the greatness of true Islam against its misuse by fundamentalist terrorists, or of bemoaning the fact that, of all great religions, Islam is the one most resistant to modernization, one should rather conceive this resistance as an open chance: it does not necessarily lead to 'Islamo-Fascism,' it can also be articulated into a Socialist project" (2004b, 48–49; see also 2009b).[39]

Bolivia under Morales: A Universalist State?

Evo Morales was elected president in 2006 as part of Latin America's "pink tide," which saw a series of left-wing governments come to power in the region (Bolivia, Venezuela, Ecuador, Uruguay, and Argentina). He became South America's first indigenous government leader since the end of Spanish colonial rule in 1825, heading the Movimiento al Socialismo (Movement toward Socialism, or MAS), which had been created in the 1980s to represent the interests of the indigenous-campesino sectors of the country. Indeed, although over 80 percent of Bolivia's population is of indigenous origin or mestizo (mixed), until the arrival of Morales, they had been reduced to a silent majority, dominated by a small elite (mostly white).[40] One of the first priorities of the Morales regime, as a result, was the development of a new constitution (promulgated in 2009) recognizing the multiethnic nature of the country and forefronting the plurality of indigenous communities (the country's name was changed, accordingly, from "Republic of Bolivia" to "Plurinational State of Bolivia").

Under Morales (who served as president from 2006 to 2019), Bolivia made some remarkable strides, especially in favor of the country's most downtrodden. Socioeconomic policy shifted unimpeachably from a mainly neoliberal market-led model to a state-led development model. To be sure, the MAS regime created a social safety net (e.g., minimum wage increases) and an array of social programs (health, education, communications) that managed to reduce extreme poverty rates by over a half, while also engaging in (a degree of) land reform to the advantage of the poor indigenous-campesino sector. The state lent support, as well, to an indigenous-initiated program of Buen Vivir (Living Well),[41] drawing on an indigenous-decolonial cosmovision and aiming at more inclusive and equitable development. A not insignificant success, in this regard, was the regime's unprecedented resistance to, if not defiance of, the neoliberal debt and structural adjustment programs of the World Bank and IMF, culminating in the government's 2017 declaration of "total independence from international money lending organizations" (Telesur 2017).

But Morales's administration also displayed several weaknesses and vulnerabilities. While the first part of his rule (2006 to 2011) was characterized by a politically innovative, indigenous-inspired, "post-neoliberal" turn, the latter part (2012–19) increasingly depended on natural resource extraction (and revenue), thereby compromising to some extent commitments to indigenous self-determination. Indeed, the state's much-lauded nationalization of the hydrocarbon industry (oil and gas), while expanding government regulation and deriving greater financial benefits for the country, did not substantially change multinational corporate control of production. Natural resource wealth (lithium, steel, gold, zinc, etc.), moreover, was mostly left in the hands of transnational capital. The regime thus began to renege (at least to a degree) on questions of indigenous land and environmental rights, causing tensions and rifts with indigenous movements across the country (see Webber 2017b, 2017a; Wolff 2019).

At the end of his term, it is likely Morales's inability to adequately satisfy either his supporters or his political adversaries that contributed to his downfall following the disputed 2019 presidential elections: indigenous groups generally backed him but, given what some saw as his government's relative cozying up to the business sector and economic elites, were not as enthusiastic about him as they previously had been; while business and landed elites, despite not having lost as much as they could have under Morales, were quick to push for regime change. In the end, as the security forces and military sided with the ruling elites (thus engineering, for all intents and purposes, a coup), Morales resigned and fled to Mexico. He was briefly replaced by a right-wing (and by all accounts, white religious supremacist) caretaker government, but then returned to Bolivia following new elections in late 2020, which saw a MAS victory under the leadership of Luis Arce.[42]

The weaknesses of the Morales regime notwithstanding, what is remarkable is that he was able to deftly balance for thirteen years a fight *for* indigenous rights (including negotiating conflicts among indigenous groups) with a fight *against* business and conservative elites (especially those displaced from power). This required difficult, skillful, and patient work, particularly given the challenge of addressing the problems of one of the poorest countries in Latin America while facing fierce national and transnational opposition to such policies as land reform and the nationalization of hydrocarbons. As Žižek (2019d) states:

> The reign of Morales was not the usual story of the radical Left in power which screws things up, economically and politically, generating poverty and trying to maintain its power through authoritarian measures. A proof of the non-authoritarian character of the Morales reign is that he didn't purge the army and police or his opponents (which is why they turned against him). . . . Morales and his followers were, of course, not perfect,

they made mistakes.... [But the] result was nothing short of a miracle: the economy thrived, the poverty rate fell, healthcare improved, while all the democratic institutions so dear to liberals continued to function.

Crucial for our purposes, though, is that the Morales regime was one of the very few (arguably along with Venezuela under Chávez, Nepal under the Maoists, Ecuador under Correa)[43] that put the country's subaltern first (indigenous groups and the socioeconomically most poor and marginalized). It is precisely this identification of power with those most socially excluded that qualifies it with a claim to egalitarian universality. For, as we have been suggesting, the abject position of the excluded is symptomatic of what is wrong with the system yet what allows it to function. And indeed, in Bolivia, it is the indigenous, poor, and landless who have enabled the country's elite to thrive over decades, if not centuries: absent their racial subalternity and socioeconomic oppression, the system would not have been able to reproduce itself. They thus occupy the position of singular universality, directly embodying the truth of Bolivian society.

Žižek contends that, by wielding power in favor of the part of no-part, regimes such as that of Morales or Chávez actualize a modern-day form of what he calls "the dictatorship of the proletariat." He has in mind here, not a Soviet-style authoritarianism, but on the contrary, a regime that always maintains a preeminent link with "the dispossessed . . . although [it] still respects the democratic electoral process, it is clear that [its] fundamental commitment and source of legitimation is not there, but in the privileged relationship with the poor. This is the 'dictatorship of the proletariat' in the form of democracy" (2008a, 379, 427). Here the predominant link between the state and the subaltern needs to be both bottom-up and top-down for it to be a meaningful democratic dictatorship of the proletariat.

The challenge, though, is the political organization of/by the subaltern so that it can move from "de-structured" mass to revolutionary political agent. In Bolivia, this was precisely the role played by the MAS as Morales ascended to power in 2006: it managed to galvanize the rage and frustration of indigenous groups, workers, and the poor (including, for example, miners, teachers, the landless, and the urban poor), becoming, as it were, the leader-coordinator of a collection of diverse social movements (Zegada 2011; Harten 2011). Far from being sidelined, indigeneity became a key part of the MAS platform, but what brought together the disparate groups was precisely their shared subalternity: despite tensions and internal differences, the MAS (and Morales) played an important role in helping these groups traverse their particularities by constructing a shared agenda (e.g., demand for indigenous self-determination, higher minimum wages, land redistribution, healthcare)—which is to say, a universality.

But the challenge, at the same time, is for the state not to pretend to act for all while serving the ruling elites (in the usual liberal democratic or populist manner), but to maintain its close links to the part of no-part. This implies a radical reshaping of the relationship of the state with its base: "We effectively have the 'dictatorship of the proletariat' only when the State itself is radically transformed, relying on new forms of popular participation" (Douzinas and Žižek 2010, 220). Such was precisely the case with the Morales regime: at least during the 2006–11 period (if not after, at least to an extent), the MAS continued to function as a facilitative-catalyzing party, exercising power in a non-statal fashion (i.e., through direct mobilization of its wide infrastructure of subaltern support) rather than relying exclusively on the country's liberal-democratic framework. The Bolivian state-as-party thus operated as a site for the mobilization of a new kind of politics: "Is this not the predicament of the Morales government in Bolivia . . . ? [It] came to power through 'fair' democratic elections, not through insurrection, but once in power, [it] exerted it in a way which was (partially, at least) 'non-statal': directly mobilizing [its] grassroots supporters and bypassing the party-state representative network" (Žižek 2009a, 155).

It is for this reason that indigeneity became integral to the Bolivian state under Morales: indigenous rights were not bestowed by the state (in response to civil society pressures) in a top-down manner that leaves intact the powers that be (i.e., multicultural protection of civil rights, yet no guarantee of collective land or socioeconomic rights), but were politicized from below from the start: they were incorporated into state policy without compromising questions of land reform, better access to education and health for women, higher minimum wage rates, and greater indigenous involvement in extractive industry regulation. Indigeneity was thus the result not of some postpolitical "integration" but intense and ongoing democratic struggle, disagreement, and debate. While MAS acted in support of indigenous groups as political coordinator, there was enough critical distance between the two for indigenous groups to maintain their heterogeneity. It is this critical distance/heterogeneity that prevented the Morales regime from becoming an authoritarian one-party state. And it is also this critical distance that, ironically, contributed to an extent to his downfall: as the state began to compromise on its commitments (at least as perceived by some of its base), to relent on greater regulation of transnational capital, it began to loosen its links with (if not alienate) the grassroots, thus resulting in reduced electoral support for the regime in the 2019 elections (and ultimately, the coup that followed).

The Morales administration thus gives us a glimpse into what a universal state-based politics might look like. The state, after all, is the site of a key social deadlock—class antagonism, and while liberal/social democratic states across the globe without exception have ended up siding with ruling elites to address this deadlock, thereby maintaining and reproducing the system, the Bolivian state under Morales managed to upend such a logic. Although of course not without limitations, it is a state that, for the most part, identified with the symptom, not the cause, that is, the excluded social element. In this sense, it was not a run-of-the-mill social democratic state: the usual (liberal) state form was restructured, to make it, not one in which the proletariat replaced socioeconomic elites to become the ruling class, but one in which non-statal relationships were forged and maintained with the proletarian subject. In other words, in the Bolivian case, the state-subaltern link was not "organic" or taken for granted (which would have implied a one-party state, as mentioned earlier) but at least temporarily operative and well functioning, yet always in question. The out-of-jointedness of the excluded thus informed state policy, but also ensured subaltern groups their political integrity, that is, their ability to engage in the properly political through litigation. Ultimately, of course, such a state-subaltern link was not powerful enough to withstand various elite neoliberal pressures, leading to the Morales regime's compromises with capital and subsequent downfall. But the example remains, pointing to the possibilities of a universalist state.

Most importantly, though, what made the Morales regime universal was its struggle for *égaliberté*. Its political objective was to fight for the part of no-part, that is, to plainly address social antagonism (racial and socioeconomic injustice) for the benefit of—and from the partial perspective of—the excluded. It may not have succeeded in accomplishing its objectives, but its universality lay in decidedly taking sides, that is, in endorsing a particular position. Yet because this was not just any position, but that of the excluded, it meant that by addressing *their* demand for *égaliberté*, it was addressing everyone's; by confronting racial and social injustice, it was confronting a social antagonism that cut across the entire social body. Such is indeed the paradoxical nature of (negative) universality: backing a particular disposition, yet in so doing, addressing a gap that affects us all.

The European Union: A (Flawed) Model for Transnational Governance?

Although initially formed as a customs union between six countries in 1957, the European Union (EU) was established in 1979 comprising twelve countries, gradually expanding to the present twenty-seven member states (twenty-eight before Brexit, the UK being the first country to leave). Along the way, several key measures were implemented, including the establishment of a single market with a standardized system of laws, common policies in trade and agriculture, an "open borders" policy (no passport control for member states' citizens), common justice/rights-related legislation (as well as a Court of Justice), an elected European Parliament, and a nineteen-member monetary union (the Eurozone). Without a doubt, to date the EU has proven to be the most effective and long-standing socioeconomic union in the world, bringing unprecedented wealth and trading opportunities to its member states, and setting global precedents for progressive common social, labor, and environmental standards.

But today, the EU faces a series of mounting crises (including the refugee crisis mentioned earlier). Wedded as it is to a capitalist market system, it has become victim to growing inequalities, in particular a spatial unevenness that pits the wealthy and powerful northern states (especially Germany) with the growingly indebted southern states (especially Greece and Spain). Noteworthy here has been the recent fate of Greece, which succumbed to a severe EU-imposed structural adjustment program, the result of years of ineptitude and corruption by the Greek state, in combination with greedy and irresponsible lending by European banks. It is to address this debt crisis and socioeconomic deadlock—massive social spending cuts, high unemployment and homelessness, widespread rioting—that the country's radical-left Syriza government came to power in 2015, trying but ultimately failing to stand up to the authority and inflexibility of EU bureaucrats, political leaders, and banks.

Neoliberal structural adjustment programs like the one imposed on Greece have, to be sure, an unmistakable libidinally charged disciplinary dimension, not dissimilar to those imposed by the World Bank / IMF on Third World countries, under which the latter are brought to account, often in humiliating ways (see Kapoor 2020, 109–12; 2008, 33): "Imagine a vicious teacher who gives to his pupils impossible tasks, and then sadistically jeers when he sees their anxiety and panic. The true goal of lending money to the debtor is not to get the debt reimbursed with a profit, but the indefinite continuation of the debt, keeping the debtor in permanent dependency and subordination" (Žižek 2015; Žižek and Horvat 2015, 10).

An equally troubling trend has been the EU's penchant for creating a new global investment and trading regime, which further escalates its embrace of the global capitalist system. With World Trade Organization negotiations stalled (due to the rise of the BRICS and their refusal to acquiesce to Western demands), the EU and the United States appear to be sidestepping multilateral negotiation in favor of individual and regional "mega-trade agreements," which effectively are "by invitation only." Many of these—the Transatlantic Trade and Investment Partnership (TTIP), the Trans-Pacific Partnership (TPP), and the Trade in Services Agreement—have been secretly negotiated. Worryingly, they not only aim at opening up export markets for multinationals, but also pose a threat to democracy: "Nowhere is this clearer than in the case of Investor-State Dispute Settlements (ISDS) [incorporated into both TTIP and TPP], which allow companies to sue governments if their policies cause a loss of profits. Simply put, this means that unelected transnational corporations can dictate the policies of democratically elected governments" (Žižek 2016b).

All of this—socioeconomic disruption, technocratic inertia and inflexibility, lack of accountability of leaders—has created widespread popular unease and frustration across the EU. Austerity measures may well have allowed capitalism (especially finance capital) to broadly flourish across the continent, but they have also engendered large-scale social instability and loss. In countries such as Greece, Spain, and France (as well as the UK during the Brexit debacle), popular rage against the European economic and bureaucratic establishment has been palpable, as witnessed over the last few years by recurring demonstrations, protest movements, and strikes (e.g., the Yellow Vests, the rise of Podemos, Vox, and Golden Dawn). Such instability has, to be sure, been fertile ground for the ascension of new forms of nationalism and extreme-right politics.

Thus, while the European political space used to be dominated by parties of the center-left and center-right, what is now emerging across the continent (with regional variations) are right-of-center parties that stand for global capitalism (as well as social/gender/gay rights); and opposing it mostly right-wing anti-immigrant populist parties, supported on the fringes by neofascist and racist groups. It is the latter, much more than left parties, that have successfully advocated for the protection of working-class interests, often on the basis of nationalist, anti-EU, and anti-immigrant/refugee sentiment. The low point of such a political crisis was of course the 2016 Brexit referendum, which brought together on the "winning" side a mix of a few left anti-imperialists but mostly right-wing populist-nationalists, the latter fueled once again by working-class rage and anti-immigrant fearmongering. At the heart of their "leave" campaign was an ardent desire to withdraw from what many viewed as Brussels's bureaucratic control (seen as compromising British sovereignty).

Yet this choice between a prying Brussels technocracy and a virulent nationalist, anti-immigrant populism is a false one, successfully pedaled (via a politics of fear) by both the EU establishment and the Right to cover over the growing gap between political institutions and popular rage in Europe (as elsewhere). It is a gap that, for the likes of Žižek, the Left can, and needs to, equally address (as it has by Bernie Sanders in the United States, for example) in an attempt to construct a different type of Europe—a more socially just, democratic, and indeed universalist Europe (see also Varoufakis 2019).[44]

Žižek lays out three lines of argumentation in this regard. First, he claims that Europe has something important to offer the world—its modern emancipatory tradition, including feminism, workers' rights, and the welfare state (1998, 1009). He readily admits this is a Eurocentric position; but his is not a run-of-the-mill kind that papers over European colonial history, seeing the continent as the flagbearer of liberal democracy and human rights. Instead, he acknowledges his inescapable European background and carries out a critique of many of its legacies (colonialism, liberalism, racism, the Holocaust, exploitation, misogyny, etc.), stating that "if the European legacy is to be effectively defended, then the first move should be a thorough self-criticism . . . there is no room for self-satisfied arrogance" (2004b, 35). He is even unafraid of characterizing his native Slovenia as a "shitty country" for this reason (Žižek 2016a at 27:40). But nonetheless, he insists on defending and reinvigorating such left-European legacies as radical egalitarianism, universal emancipation, and justice. In this connection, he reminds those who are too quick to engage in critiques of Eurocentrism that the very conceptual tools they use are part of (what these same critics identify as) the European philosophical tradition, evidence precisely of these tools' subversive universality (see chapter 3).[45]

But of course, for Žižek, Europe must first live up to its own emancipatory legacy. This is especially the case as the EU moves toward greater technocratic governance, paralleling capitalism's current favoring of the postpolitical and authoritarian to make way for a more efficient and smooth global production process. Late market capitalism, it seems, is less and less able to afford even bourgeois democracy. The challenge for the Left, then, is to struggle for the democratic (re)politicization of Europe: "Will we be able to invent a new mode of repoliticization, questioning the undisputed reign of global capital? Only such a repoliticization of our predicament can break the vicious cycle of liberal globalization destined to engender the most regressive forms of [right-wing racist and] fundamentalist hatred" (Žižek 1998, 1000). This means not just appealing to "freedom and democracy," but moving beyond liberal democracy to be able to radically rethink both democratic governance and ways of combating (the excesses of) capitalism.

Žižek's second (related) line of reasoning in favor of a left-universalist Europe concerns the potentially progressive role it can play in current global politics: "For many years, I have pleaded for a renewed 'leftist Eurocentrism.' To put it bluntly: do we want to live in a world in which the only choice is between the American civilization and the emerging Chinese authoritarian-capitalist one? If the answer is no, then the true alternative is Europe. The Third World cannot generate a strong enough resistance to the ideology of the American Dream; in the *present* constellation, only Europe can do that" (2004b, 32–33). The idea here is for a Europe, armed with its social democratic-egalitarian legacy and socioeconomic power, to counter the neocolonial and postpolitical directions of global capitalism; that is, for Europe to stand for something politically "traumatic" and "antagonistic," as Vighi and Feldner put it, to act as a "viable leftist alternative to American [and increasingly Chinese] hegemony" (2006, 345). Here the danger to guard against will be for such a progressive Europe not to repeat its past mistakes by engaging in new forms of racism and neocolonialism in its defense/pursuit of (global) egalitarian justice.

Finally, what a left-universalist Europe points to is transnational governance—a key priority in our globalized world (as our sections on climate change and Covid-19 also contend). Not only does the EU allow for the imposition of standards on such things as women's rights, antiracism, and environmental and labor codes, but more than ever it is proof of the success of multilateral cooperation to establish executive power at a supranational level: "I remain convinced that our only hope is to act trans-nationally—only in this way do we have a chance to constrain global capitalism. The nation-state is not the right instrument to confront the refugee crisis, global warming, and other truly pressing issues. So instead of opposing Eurocrats on behalf of national interests, let's try to form an all-European left" (Žižek 2016b). Arguably, such a left Europe is what can prevent the EU from becoming another organ of capital and ensure the better regulation (or demise) of capital mobility—dismantling trade "agreements" such as the TTIP, for example, which, as argued earlier, present a real threat to popular sovereignty. Transnational governance, in this sense, need not necessarily weaken the nation-state; it may also act a bulwark against encroachments on such things as local culture or social and health programming.

This is why Brexit is ultimately a wrong turn in the current global conjuncture: instead of severing ties with Brussels to "restore" British sovereignty, the goal should have been to bring Brussels better to account. Now, exiting the EU, rather than strengthening national sovereignty, will further dismantle it by exposing Britain to a more radical submission to global capital. Žižek avers in this regard that the "British attitude, of leaving the EU to its fate, is the logic of the wrong era in an age of global problems: ecology, biotechnology, intellectual property. Britain all alone will be even more vulnerable, exposed to the pressure of international capital without any of the protections" (2016e). As we have been claiming, the global capitalist order cannot be (and to date has not been) defeated with local or national resistance; what we need instead is an even more combative universalism, or what we've been calling universality, in the form of transnational governance bodies such as the EU.

Perhaps the idea of a leftist transnationalism is pie in the sky, but the fact is that Europe is in crisis, and if the Right can successfully exploit it (and has!), so can the Left. The future of Europe, in this sense, is an open question; it can turn toward a retrograde nostalgia for European "greatness," or it can equally open up a space for a radically alternative vision. Here, we leave you once again with Žižek's words:

> Although crises are painful and dangerous, they are the terrain on which battles have to be waged and won. Is there not a struggle also in heaven, is the heaven also not divided—and does the ongoing confusion not offer a unique chance to react to the need for a radical change in a more appropriate way, with a project that will break the vicious cycle of EU technocracy and nationalist populism? The true division of our heaven is not between anemic technocracy and nationalist passions, but between their vicious cycle and a new pan-European project which will addresses the true challenges that humanity confronts today. (2016c)

Against Market Solutions: The Politics of Covid-19

In Mathieu Kassovitz's *La Haine* (1995), Hubert recounts, more than once, a story about a man who falls from the roof of a skyscraper and, to reassure himself on the way down, repeats over and over: "*Jusqu'ici tout va bien* [So far, so good]." But, we are told, "It's not the fall that matters, it's the landing." The social and political implications of this individual's story is rendered explicit by the end the film, when it becomes the story of a society falling, heading for the same crash-landing insofar as it is preoccupied exclusively with the fall. Doesn't *La Haine*'s story capture the current predicament of Covid-19? Isn't every society in the process of falling? And who is uttering "So far, so good" other than the "inner voice of liberal democracy" (Sharma and Sharma 2000, 105) the reassuring, authoritative voice of politicians, pundits, and medical experts invested in the virtues of private industry, in the ideological fantasy of free-market solutions to pandemics? In Lacanian terms, these reassuring speakers occupy the position of today's "subject supposed to know" (*sujet supposé savoir*).

In the analytic session, the "subject supposed to know," argues Lacan, does not refer to the analyst as such but rather marks his function in the treatment, registering the patient's view of the analyst as a representation of absolute certainty who holds knowledge of the patient's secret meaning or unconscious desire (disclosing what had been hidden, what lay behind the speaker's words): the analyst "is supposed to know that from which no one can escape, as soon as he formulates it—quite simply, signification" (1977, 233). Without the idea of the "subject supposed to know," transference would be impossible. Transference is predicated on the patient's (mis)identification of the analyst as a "subject supposed to know." Endowed with "a certain infallibility" (Lacan 1977, 234), the analyst is purported to penetrate the depths of his patient's unconscious desire, deciphering at will the meaning of the latter's hidden secrets and symptoms.

The psychoanalytic scene is governed by a radically different hermeneutical logic. Rather than feeding the analyst's phantasmatic status, the analytic session ironically seeks to *de-suppose* the analyst. The analyst eschews the hermeneutic powers readily attributed to him by the transference: "He is not God for his patient" (Lacan 1977, 230). The analyst takes a different path, guiding the patient, through free association, to take stock of the idea that *there is no ultimate authority*. As Jason Glynos observes, "The whole psychoanalytic operation is aimed at deflating the analyst's own status as

Subject-Supposed-to-Know by making the patient him- or herself *do the work*, only intervening so as to facilitate the subject's confrontation with his or her truth, namely, that there is no universal symbolic Guarantee" (2002, 60).

Žižek has made productive use of the "subject supposed to know," expanding its critical reach. In accessing America's racist libidinal economy, Žižek coins his own formulation of the "subject supposed to loot and rape." Žižek turns to the aftermath of Hurricane Katrina, when the stories about Black criminality circulated like a virus. The "subject supposed to loot and rape" reflects the workings of ideology, and the enjoyment racists felt from having their speculation and paranoia about blackness "confirmed." If the "subject supposed to know" refers to the function of the analyst rather than the analyst as such, the "subject supposed to loot and rape" does not stand for Black subjects and what they have actually done or not (evidence-based suspicion) but symbolizes instead the phantasmatically projected Black body, that is, the unconscious mechanisms at play in the racialization of Blacks through their identification with barbarity (Žižek 2008c, 99–100).

We can detect a variant of "the subject supposed to loot and rape" in discourse early in the Covid-19 pandemic. Donald Trump, in an attempt to deflect responsibility for his handling of the health crisis, tried to appease his populist base by framing the coronavirus as a "Chinese virus," a "Chinese plague," or a "foreign virus." Trump's calculated words engendered a "subject supposed to infect," an external enemy wreaking havoc on the United States and the other Western nations. Simultaneously, the Trump administration fully embraced the president's assumed authority as the helmsman and commander in chief. True, a genuine aura of incompetence and ignorance of the law dogged the Trump administration from the beginning (from its Muslim ban to its family separation policy to the Ukraine fiasco, and so on)—and the coronavirus is no exception. And yet Trump's responses to the pandemic became increasingly sober in tone and predictable. Basically, he started to behave as would a president of any liberal-capitalist state. The federal government in the United States implemented, as did most of the world's governments, strict guidelines (quarantines and travel bans) to curtail the spread of the coronavirus and protect human life.

In his polemical commentaries on such moves during the pandemic, Giorgio Agamben warns of the dangers of enhanced social control and its intolerable regulation of life: "The control exercised through video cameras and now, as has been proposed, through cell phones, far exceeds any form of control that was exercised under totalitarian regimes such as Fascism or Nazism" (2020c). Agamben laments a society that "no longer believes in anything but bare life" (2020a). He asks, "What is a society that has no value other than survival?" (2020a). What is happening in the name of security is the normalization of the state of exception at the cost of sacrificing our shared humanity (2020b). In contrast to Hardt and Negri's life-affirming biopolitics, discussed in chapter 3, Agamben's version is decidedly more pessimistic. On Agamben's account, biopolitics manages life by reducing it to its biological condition, emptied of its social, political, human, and affective traits. Our political life—a life oriented toward the idea of happiness and how to live well—is becoming less relevant, less important to us. It is shrinking: what matters first and foremost is not the good life, but biological life, mere existence.

Biopolitics proves more effective in its deployment of martial rhetoric than outright xenophobia. If Trump's effort to recycle the racist trope of the "yellow threat" failed to gain wide appeal (beyond his staunch, racist base), his biopolitical intervention was better received. Trump's and other leaders' "war on the coronavirus" produced a more insidious enemy—not a foreign enemy (the "Chinese" virus, which could have been contained via travel bans), but a mutated enemy, an enemy dwelling within our midst, turning my neighbor into a potential source of infection: "Fear thy neighbor" is substituted for "Love thy neighbor." As Agamben states, "It is not surprising that for the virus one speaks of war. The emergency measures obligate us in fact to life in conditions of curfew. But a war with an invisible enemy that can lurk in every other person is the most absurd of wars. It is, in reality, a civil war. The enemy is not outside, it is within us" (2020a).

But what Agamben's negative biopolitics ignores is the actual threat of Covid-19. Agamben reads the coronavirus much too myopically; his paranoia transforms the global menace of the virus into an instance of fake news, implying that states are treating the epidemic as a mere pretext for biopolitical expansion: more surveillance and control over their human population. And while many of the leftist objections to Agamben seek to rein in the philosopher's immoderate pessimism (pointing out, for instance, that coronavirus is not like the seasonal flu, since there is no vaccine for this new disease and its mortality rate is much higher), Žižek's intervention is less sentimentalist and cuts deeper, revealing the limits of the biopolitical paradigm (the immanent fear of reducing human life to bare life). Informing Žižek's critique is the Lacanian insight that "*il n'y a pas de grand Autre*" (2020h, 167). Politics begins with a *no!* Žižek's Lacanian politics takes the big Other's nonexistence—and thus the contingency of the socioeconomic established order—as axiomatic: the Symbolic is incomplete or non-all; it could be otherwise—whence the necessity of critique, of insisting on the *gap* between what *is* and the ontological lack that bolsters it.

Agamben's negative biopolitics by contrast operates primarily at the level of the Symbolic, fueling a "politics of fear . . . fear of immigrants, fear of crime, fear of godless sexual depravity, fear of the excessive state itself, with its burden of high taxation, fear of ecological catastrophe, fear of harassment" (Žižek 2008, 40–41), and we can add to the list a fear of pandemics. Again, as we saw in chapter 3, this makes the biopolitical paradigm postpolitical in its orientation (it is "a politics which renounces the very constitutive dimension of the political" [Žižek 2008, 40]) and for that reason ill-equipped to take on the challenges of Covid-19. With Agamben's account of biopolitics, then, we get a moral response to Covid-19 and a moral resistance to the state's mismanagement of life, its elimination of political life or reduction of complex human life to biological existence. With Žižek's emphasis on economic exploitation, we get a political response to Covid-19 and a political resistance to the state's market-friendly solutions.

Aside from neglecting the actual threat of the virus, Agamben also fails to appreciate the positive collective response that Covid-19 has ignited: "The threat of viral infection has also given a tremendous boost to new forms of local and global solidarity, and it has made more starkly clear the need for control over power itself" (Žižek 2020b, 75).[46] The coronavirus clearly disabled the world's population—hitting racial minorities and the socioeconomically vulnerable most heavily[47]—but it also enabled a rethinking of global health, community, and humanity: "It is through our effort to save humanity from self-destruction that we are creating a new humanity" (Žižek 2020b, 105). Many of the measures undertaken as part of the response to the pandemic would have been unthinkable only a year ago, especially given the hegemony of neoliberal economics: state intervention to limit, if not suspend, the market, commandeer resources (transportation, infrastructure), and even mobilize industry to produce medical supplies (masks, ventilators, etc.) in order to protect citizens; the increasing realization of the pressing need for universal healthcare coverage for all, particularly the most marginalized, and renewed consideration of the provision of a "universal basic income" in some countries; despite Trump's effort to terminate US support for the WHO, efforts by many other world leaders toward global cooperation to coordinate a common response to the present crisis and prevent future ones; and a growing sense of the commons (of nature, knowledge), increasingly threatened by viral pandemics, and more generally by inadequately regulated neoliberal capitalism (industrial farming, bioengineering, environmental encroachments in the name of profit and power, etc.). Indeed, the pandemic crisis has opened a horizon under which the question of the commons *can* be posed anew, a horizon under which we can raise questions about the common good, about what belongs to all of us in common, about how we share resources, spaces, risks, and ultimately life together, about what belongs to the public versus private property owners.

But countering this desire for the commons—for global justice and solidarity with the excluded of neoliberal capitalism—is the government's willingness, if not eagerness, to occupy the position of the "subject supposed to know." Unlike the Lacanian analyst who seeks to de-suppose himself in the analytic session, making the analysand come to grips with the painful realization that the big Other does not exist, the government works to uphold its authority by guiding us through the pandemic, projecting a brighter future that is more or less a reproduction of the status quo—that is, a reproduction of how life operated prior to the "event" of the coronavirus. The solution to Covid-19, and to future pandemics, we thus hear, ought to come primarily from private industry. This sort of claim is emanating not only from pro-free market enthusiasts (Republican and Democratic politicians alike, not to mention pro-business mainstream media) but from Dr. Anthony Fauci, director of the National Institute of Allergy and Infectious Diseases. More than any government figure, Dr. Fauci stands in for the capitalist big Other—perpetuating the ideological fantasy of a capitalism with a human face, a capitalism that cares for the health of its citizens. In an interview with *The Daily Show* host Trevor Noah, Dr. Fauci follows a neoliberal script for how to deal with pandemics:

> Things are implemented at the state and local level, that's the way this country works so well. The federal government is a facilitator, it's a supplier, it's a supporter and that's the way things should be going, and that's what we're starting to see now as we're catching up on things that weren't done so well at the beginning. We now have many, many more tests. The private industry is getting involved. The government is not making the tests. The private industry is. . . . So it really is a marriage between the federal government as the facilitator and supporter of where the real action is, at the state and local level. (Fauci 2020)

While Dr. Fauci's answer was prompted by Trevor Noah's question about how the United States can work together as a unit to effectively tackle the coronavirus, his answer clearly exceeded his expertise in infectious diseases. "In science," as Žižek writes, "there is no big Other, no subject on which we can fully rely, *who can be unequivocally presumed to know*. There are different conclusions, as well as different proposals about what to do, advocated by serious epidemiologists" (Žižek 2020b, 135, emphasis added). Nevertheless, Dr. Fauci effortlessly slides from epidemiologist to biopolitician, an authority invested in the protection of (capitalist) life. His answer is comforting; it clearly outlines the role of all the parties involved: the federal government, the states, and private industry. Dr. Fauci knows what we need (an understanding of how the coronavirus spreads) *and* what we desire (a reassurance that the system knows what it is doing, that it knows what we should do).

The purported "marriage" between the federal government and the states (with private industry supplying a helping hand to the states—*the private sector is making the tests, not the government*) effectively legitimizes the role of the market in matters of national and global health. If Americans, in healthcare discussions (due in large part to Bernie Sanders, who made Medicare for all the major policy issue in his presidential runs), were beginning to take seriously the idea that healthcare is a human right rather than a profit-making industry,[48] Dr. Fauci readily forecloses this line of inquiry when he minimizes the role of the federal government in the response to the pandemic. If the "adult in the room" (Heer 2020) (this is the way many progressives and liberals refer to him, since he embodied the voice of reason on the Trump team) praises private industry—that is, market solutions—for its work in containing Covid-19, why should we look elsewhere for answers? *So far, so good*. Dr. Fauci, the subject supposed to know, reassures us that our current pandemic—our global fall—is fixable from *within*. Why should we be suspicious of the stock market? Why should we doubt, for instance, Big Pharma's commitment to finding cures for infectious diseases (even though their economic concerns about low profits and liability have limited their ventures in this area in the past) (Posner 2020)?

We can take a look at a recent example. Dr. Peter Jay Hotez and his team at Texas Children's Hospital Center for Vaccine Development engineered a potential vaccine for one of the strains of coronavirus several years ago. Unfortunately, the project faltered after the team failed to raise the necessary funds for human trials. We might expect now that companies would be lining up to support the project. But even during this pandemic, Big Pharma showed lukewarm interest. As Hotez shared with NBC News on March 5, "We've had some conversations with big pharma companies in recent weeks about our vaccine, and literally one said, 'Well, we're holding back to see if this thing comes back year after year' " (Bee 2020). A cost-benefit logic overrides any ethical or political obligation to secure a vaccine for the well-being of the global community.[49]

To return to Dr. Fauci's marriage metaphor, such a representation of the federal government's relationship with the states distracts us from another marriage, the troubled marriage between democracy and capitalism. The idea of a "capitalism with a human face" is, after all, predicated on the stability of this marriage. But for Žižek this marriage has been deteriorating for some time now. His message is the opposite of Dr. Fauci's: "We have to learn to think outside the coordinates of the stock market and profit and simply find another way to produce and allocate the necessary resources" (Žižek 2020b, 90–91). Driven by an insatiable will to privatize and corporatize, neoliberalism has all but severed the link between the two. Functioning like a virus, infiltrating all facets of public life, neoliberalism has transformed liberal-democratic citizens into "entrepreneurial actors in every sphere of life" (Brown 2005, 42). Its logic is to depoliticize by reducing political matters to questions of individual responsibility. But, in the case of Covid-19, "Such a focus on individual responsibility, necessary as it is, functions as ideology the moment it serves to obfuscate the big question of how to change our entire economic and social system" (Žižek 2020b, 88).

Neoliberalism's hegemony seems to make a divorce between democracy and capitalism a fait accompli. And yet, as suggested earlier, we can detect a weakening of neoliberalism's hold in the recent policies taken, even by the Trump administration. American-style capitalism, purified under the age of neoliberalism, is faltering and misbehaving, acting in ways deeply at odds with its free-market ethos: "As the saying goes: in a crisis we are all Socialists. Even Trump is now considering a form of Universal Basic Income—a check for $1,000 to every adult citizen. Trillions will be spent violating all conventional market rules" (Žižek 2020b, 93). We are, in this respect, living in exceptional times, a time governed by exceptions to neoliberal capitalism. But what exactly follows from neoliberalism's apparent retreat? Is it socialism to come? If so, what kind of socialism will it be? Žižek asks:

Will this enforced Socialism be the Socialism for the rich as it was with the bailing out of the banks in 2008 while millions of ordinary people lost their small savings? Will the epidemic be reduced to another chapter in the long sad story of what Naomi Klein called "disaster capitalism," or will a new better balanced, if perhaps more modest, world order emerge from it? (Žižek 2020b, 93–94)

What is at stake here are two versions of socialism: a socialism of the postpolitical era and a socialism triggered by politics as such, a taste of the contingent, a dissatisfaction with liberal democracy's "subjects supposed to know." The former traffics in rescue packages that benefit corporate elites more than citizens. The latter seeks to render the *impossible possible*, treating Covid-19 precisely as an "event." We share here Rocco Ronchi's perspective in emphasizing the full force of the term "event":

> If it is true that the virus displays the characteristic of an event . . . , then it must also possess its "virtue." Events are such not because they "happen" or, at least, not only because of this. Events are not "facts." Unlike simple facts, events possess a "virtue," a force, a property, a *vis*, that is, they do something. For this reason, an event is always traumatic to the point we may say that if there is no trauma there is no event, that if there is no trauma, literally nothing has happened. What exactly do events do? Events produce transformations that prior to their taking place were not even possible. In fact, they only begin to be "after" the event has taken place. In short, an event is such because it generates "real" possibility. The "virtue" of an event thus consists in rendering operational methods possible, methods that "before" were simply impossible, unthinkable. (2020)

The shepherds of global capitalism—the transnational political and social elites—are eager to de-eventalize the event of Covid-19, to return matters back to normal, even to create *nostalgia* for a pre-quarantine capitalism, which is, of course, predicated on obscuring the traumatic Real of capital, "the systemic contradiction that the pandemic did not cause but certainly accelerated" (Vighi 2020). In stark opposition, a universal politics must actively reconfigure the terms of the debate, and decline the blackmail of a choice between liberal capitalism or the Gulag (if you are not for liberal democracy, your position leads to the Gulag [or the Holocaust]).[50]

It is undeniable that Covid-19 shocked the market, deroutinized our way of life, and generated exceptional measures across the world, but it is we— as a global community—who must decide which exceptions we want to be permanently adopted.[51] The stakes couldn't be higher. Covid-19 should not be isolated but seen as symptomatic of structural global problems. As Žižek notes, "We are not dealing only with viral threats—other catastrophes are looming on the horizon or already taking place: droughts, heatwaves, killer storms, the list is long. In all these cases, the answer is not panic but the hard and urgent work to establish some kind of efficient global coordination" (2020b, 42). For the less than nothing, Covid-19 discloses a different world, a world that is not strictly speaking unsettled, but always already ravaged: "The fact that Covid almost brought the world to a standstill at a time when many more people were dying of pollution, hunger, and similar things, clearly indicates this phantasmatic dimension. We tend to forget that there are people—refugees, those caught in a civil war—for whom the Covid pandemic is a negligible minor trouble" (Žižek 2020e). Dealing with "the pandemic of poverty" (Žižek 2020e) is a precondition for containing the spread of the coronavirus. Vulnerability to the virus must be politicized. We are *not* all in the same boat—the economically and racially privileged have lifelines available to them that are simply unavailable to the excluded of global capitalism. Indeed, another lesson of COVID-19 is that despite the assurances from Western leaders that the pandemic is a global concern and that the vaccines should be shared with the world's most vulnerable peoples (remember the global reaction of protest to the Trump administration's early attempt to secure exclusive rights to the vaccine from the German pharmaceutical company CureVac), we are seeing a clear hierarchy to the immunization. Wealthy nations are the first to be served the vaccine. Tribal nationalism overrides a politics of the commons. Moreover, such a logic tends to continue operating inside the nation as well, creating similar exclusions domestically. The United States and France, for example, are struggling to administer the vaccine to a broad population; Israel receives media praise for its highly successful rollout, for having the highest per capita inoculation rate in the world, but this bar is only achieved by excluding Palestinians in the Occupied Territories from the calculation. These Palestinians are not eligible for vaccination, though Israeli settlers are—a clear example of Jewish privilege that Israel attempts to counter by claiming that under the Oslo Accords, the "powers and responsibilities in the sphere of health in the West Bank and the Gaza Strip" fall on the "Palestinian side," ignoring that international law dictates that it is the obligation of the occupying power to immunize the occupied in times of pandemics. What is farcically tragic about all of this is Israel's shameless evocation of the Oslo Accords when it has systematically violated the spirit and the letter of that agreement from the start (Harb 2021). Tribal nationalism and neoliberalism complement each other in the eclipsing of the political, in the foreclosure of the commons.

Žižek also cites Latour's apt description of Covid-19 as "dress rehearsal" for the catastrophe of climate change, while cognizant of the fact that in the case of the looming ecological crisis, it is humanity that occupies the position of the virus. Latour, however, qualifies this statement by adding that "this does not apply to all humans, just those who make war on us without declaring war on us" (2020). Whereas Latour's foes are a group of people whose policies or practices are killing all of us, Žižek returns to the system itself as the agent of our foreseeable demise: "The agency which 'makes war on us without declaring war on us' is not just a group of people but the existing global socio-economic system—in short, the existing global order in which we all (the entirety of humanity) participate" (Žižek 2020b, 112). There is no system without its nasty symptoms (corporate polluters, fossil fuel investors, etc.).

Working from within the basic coordinates set by neoliberal capitalism (and yes, neoliberalism will likely return, blaming the viral crisis on excessive regulations, crony capitalism, and a failure to truly abide by free-market principles), adhering to its "subjects supposed to know," will do little to attenuate the next pandemic. Worse, market expansions—environmental encroachments in the name of profit and power—got us into our current predicament in the first place: they bear a large responsibility for zoonotic disease, having created the prime conditions for the spread of infection from wildlife to humans (Žižek 2020b, 88–89).[52] Market solutions to viral pandemics should thus give us pause, if not strike us as cruel and deadly fantasies.

No, Wall Street will not save us. On the contrary, market solutions ensure that our fall will end in a crash landing. Neoliberalism is predicated on the myth that capitalism is the engine of innovation. Competition drives creativity—and we, the consumers, ultimately benefit. Big Pharma will not protect us. The law of profit will only make us more vulnerable to loss and suffering. What could prevent such catastrophes, however, is what we might call a "de-neoliberalization of the mind." This is not an aspirational goal, but a first step in the struggle, in this demystifying process, in liberating oneself from the internalized, controlling image of Homo economicus, will be to usher in a new sense of the commons, the stuff of solidarity: becoming subjects who "care about the commons—the commons of nature, of knowledge—which are threatened by the system" (Žižek 2012d, 83) and, of course, by viral pandemics. A commitment to the commons is unamenable to liberal capitalism; it rails against "the very basic features of the society in which we live" (Žižek 2020b, 41). Such a renewed commitment would provide the grounds for increased international cooperation and organizing against neoliberalism, stimulating solidarity and resistance. If politics begins with a no, its negativity can only be sustained by an uncompromised and uncompromising passion for the commons.

Conclusion

We have examined eight examples in this chapter (and two others in chapters 2 and 3) that reflect, on the one hand, what we see as some of the key sites of struggle/antagonism across the globe today, and on the other, how we envision a universal politics might play out in each case. Needless to say, there are no easy answers or formulas for addressing any such cases, and this is why we have not hesitated to underline their weaknesses, failings, challenges, and/or internal divisions or debates. We readily admit that all of them are defective exemplars of universality; they point to conditions of possibility but fall short. A negative universal politics, after all, aims at facing and working through our deadlocks, which always already confront us, even after "success." There is no triumph after victory, only more work, more struggle, more failure. "Success"—if at all—is only temporary, and idealism is always flawed and fleeting. Hence the abiding need to engage in politics.

The shared deadlock faced by all our cases is of course that created by our global capitalist order. Part of the challenge of a universal politics is precisely keeping an eye on this target, given the overwhelming ideological tendency today to focus on the symptom (climate "change," refugee "crisis," patriarchy, etc.) rather than the cause (market-created inequalities, unevenness, environmental destruction). The insidiousness of neoliberal capitalist universalism is that it manifests in multifarious ways—police racism and brutality as the embodiment of state violence aimed at protecting and reproducing the status quo; anti-immigrant racism as a displacement of popular revolt against austerity; Islamophobia to justify brutalizing Palestinians or invading Iraq and Afghanistan to take over their oil and gas fields; and so forth—making it difficult to connect the dots. Systemic contradictions always manifest in specific ways, and the test of a universal politics, as we have been claiming, is bringing out the universal-antagonistic dimension of each particular.

What grounds a universal politics, as well as giving it its emancipatory orientation, is the part of no-part: the universal reveals itself, after all, through what is missing, in what is abjected or doesn't belong. All of our case studies have aimed at forefronting the latter: the socioeconomically dispossessed, the migrant/refugee, the racialized Black or indigenous woman, and so forth. It is they who make evident the failures, inequities, and cruelties of the system; hence their attendant universal call for *égaliberté*. For, without the ethico-political identification with the part of no-part, without an understanding that it is the underlying social antagonism—the social division between the included and excluded—that makes the global capitalist order possible, a universal politics loses its radical edge, descending into more of the same. The example of the celebrification of #MeToo discussed earlier is a good case in point, in which the powerful take up an important social cause, resulting in the privileging of the already privileged—a "pseudo-radicalization, which fits the existing power relations much better than a modest reformist proposal" (Žižek 1999, 230). It is only when the call for *égaliberté* is issued by the part of no-part that it becomes an "impossible" demand—one that requires reconfiguring, rather than tweaking or reforming, the system.

But finally we must address perhaps the greatest challenge of a universal politics: the coordination and joining of struggles. For, if capitalist globalization is indeed our political-economic adversary, then it requires a truly universal response. As Žižek rightly notes, "We need to do more than simply organize a multitude of sites of resistance against capitalism. There is a basic necessity to translate this resistance into a more global project—otherwise we will merely be creating regulatory instances that control only the worst excesses of capitalism" (2004c, 149). This is why anticapitalism is not just one among multiple struggles but, as each of our case studies points out, plays a centrally structuring role (in fact, the very multiplicity of struggles around the globe today is made possible—and constrained by—the universalism of capitalist globalization). The task ahead nonetheless lies in finding ways of aligning multiple sites of resistance. The establishment of a universalist state (inspired by the likes of the Bolivian state under Morales) or progressive transnational bodies such as a repoliticized EU or a World Environmental Organization, as we have argued, is a significant possibility here, enabling the better regulation of multinationals and capital mobility. But at a more localized level, our contention is that a negative universal politics paves the way for political alignment by enabling solidarity across sites on the basis not of positive identities—which most often divide people along class, social, and

North-South lines—but of shared antagonisms. We get insights into what such a politics might look like when, as discussed earlier, BLM activists refuse to be co-opted by the establishment or tow the left–Democratic Party line by daring to espouse the cause of Palestinians and speaking out against Israeli colonialism and apartheid. This is not just run-of-the-mill cross-group alliance making; it is taking a firm and potentially perilous stand against domination and for *égaliberté* for Blacks as much as Palestinians, which is to say, *for all.*

Conclusion
After the System
The Challenges of a Universal Politics

"What comes after the system?" is a question that cannot be neglected but to which we can give no ready-made answer. What follows is precisely not pro-pelled by any law (of history, of economics, etc.). If Covid-19 has managed to revive a sense of the commons, a commitment to a world no longer driven by a cruel market logic, the world that it has opened up is still precariously in the making. Its futurity is at risk; the "impossible possible" is at stake. An organizational structure beyond the contours of the existing system is what a universal politics is fighting for. We know that the system, though weakened, is poised for a rally, an afterlife of its choosing. Its motto is clear enough: trust in the marketplace. This capitalism to come—it is already here—will be even crueler, or as cruel as before, just to more people. It is a neoliberal capitalism that cuts its ideological losses with democracy. Freed from its origins, it can assume and embrace its intrinsic barbarism: "the becoming black of the world," the making useful and disposable (useful because disposable) of a larger amount of the world's population.

The challenges of a universal politics are double: first, to block the system's revival, the return to its exploitive and naturalizing machinery; second, to gesture to a life after the system, a life that is more just and egalitarian, but not without lack or alienation (a difficult pill for the Left to swallow—given its dream or fantasies of direct democracy, unalienated labor, and harmonious coexistence). A universal politics also faces challenges of its own. How does it sustain its struggle? What comes after the system has everything to do with its imagined evental sites of global resistance (many of which we analyzed in chapter 4). Against the cultural Left, Žižek reiterates the primacy of class struggle: "One should . . . insist on the difference between class struggle and other struggles (anti-racist, feminist, etc.) which aim at a peaceful coexist-ence of different groups and whose ultimate expression is identity politics" (2020, 12). David Harvey likewise excludes race and gender as relevant or intrinsic preoccupations in the struggle against capitalism: "Although they

CLASS REDUCTIONISM
AGAIN

Universal Politics. Ilan Kapoor and Zahi Zalloua, Oxford University Press. © Oxford University Press 2022.
DOI: 10.1093/oso/9780197607619.003.0005

[gender and race] are omnipresent within capitalism they are not specific to the form of circulation and accumulation that constitutes the economic engine of capitalism" (2014, 7–8). Exploitation is capitalism's most effective naturalized violence, a systemic violence experienced by most of the world, and yet rarely recognized as a form of violence, or a form of violence that you can do something about: *We know that capitalism is bad, ruthless even, but we don't believe anything else is better. Capitalism or the Gulag? We choose the former each time.*

At the same time, Žižek, unlike Harvey, does not treat racial or gender domination reductively as mere epiphenomena. The problem is not so much with concerns for race or gender as with identity politics—how responses to racism and patriarchy, as potential evental sites (BLM and #MeToo, respectively), are contained by a postpolitical framework that encourages the expression of their grievances through the toothless language of identity politics. But as we saw in chapter 4, identity politics is not destiny. A universal politics is predicated on alternative modes of critique. It does not treat racism, for instance, as a fake problem, a distraction, or an inessential concern but rather as a critical factor in the survival of capitalism. The task here is to politicize racism: to take up race as a universal concern. Indeed, as Todd McGowan points out, "Any attempt to forge universal equality has to take racism into account" (2020, 183). Racism is not a natural phenomenon, without mediation, provoked by the encounter with a different race, a racial Other. Rather, "Race is the child of racism, not the father," as Ta-Nehisi Coates succinctly formulates it (2015, 7; see also Zalloua 2020). Racism is an ideological problem that attests to the hegemony of the postpolitical, a world construed to be without antagonism and with solvable conflicts. The opposite is true: "The political (the space of litigation in which the excluded can protest the wrong or injustice done to them) foreclosed from the Symbolic then returns in the Real in the guise of new forms of racism" (Žižek 1998, 997). Addressing racism as a problem of intolerance misfires. It is not about the coexistence of different racial identities. *Racism is a constitutive problem of the system.* This is why an antiracist movement must be anticapitalist, if the goal of the struggle is not to exact minimal concession from the system in term of recognition and reward, but actually to change the coordinates of one's social existence. And conversely, an anticapitalist movement that brackets race/racism from an analysis will fail in its project, precisely by failing to mobilize the indignant rage of racialized bodies against the racist system.

To paraphrase Walter Benjamin, every sanctioned identity politics is a sign of a failed revolution.

A universal politics that ignores these sites of protest would do so to the detriment of its emancipatory project. The violent antiracist demonstrations in Ferguson and Minneapolis serve as powerful examples. Sparked by the 2014 murder of Michael Brown, and reignited by that of George Floyd in 2020, BLM protests signal a breakdown in society's symbolic order. "No longer perceived as the agent of law, of the legal order," the police ironically became "just another violent social agent," at odds with "the predominant social order" (Žižek 2016g, 253). This denaturalization of the police force produced an explosion of "abstract negativity," from the "untying" of social ties (Žižek 2016g, 253). This untying holds political promise, designating "a zero-level that opens up the space for political intervention" (Žižek 2016g, 253; reminiscent of the discussion of *Joker* in chapter 3). Rather than dismiss this rage or passionate struggle against racial domination as a distraction from politics, a movement away from exploitation, Žižek elevates it as a "pre-political condition of politics" (Žižek 2016g, 253).

A universal politics cannot denigrate the affective appeal of the antiracist movement, nor should it compromise on its cognitive critique. It must engage in both: "Cold analysis and passionate struggle not only do not exclude each other, they need each other" (Žižek 2020g, 51). If Harvey errs in adopting too narrow an economic focus, sidelining the fact of antiblackness, the cultural Left errs in its fetishization of nonviolence, failing to attend to black anger and dissatisfaction. The cultural Left purports to support black dissident voices against right-wing populists, but what it really wants is a decaffeinated BLM. Liberals are eager to fold BLM's anger into a reformist agenda: multicultural tolerance as the ultimate antidote to racist prejudices. From their perspective, the "violent excess" of the protests is in principle avoidable. They fail to appreciate its real meaning: "a reaction to the fact that liberal, peaceful and gradual political change has not worked and systemic racism persists in the US. What emerges in violent protest is an anger that cannot be adequately represented in our political space" (Žižek 2020a). The virtual radicalization of that anger is what terrifies the cultural Left and establishment Right alike. Blaming Trump and the rise of the alt-right for antiblackness conveniently forgets that BLM came into existence during the "golden age" of the Obama presidency. Another cultural war fought within the coordinates of the present system will not yield true change. An antiracism worthy of its name still awaits. A universal politics thus cannot and must not denigrate sites of *workerism?* (handwritten note in left margin)

resistance that do not align *immediately* with the workers' struggle. Quite the contrary, it takes as axiomatic the shift from *one* revolutionary agent to "proletarian *positions*": "an explosive combination of different agents" is the path for a "new emancipatory politics" (Žižek 2009a, 92).

The challenge, as chapter 4 stressed, is how to unify these proletarian positions around a *common struggle*. Today's problems are something that, like it or not, we share. The refugee crisis is not simply Europe's problem or America's; Covid-19 is a global health problem; the apartheid logic of global capitalism cannot be effectively countered by an anti-globalist view, a populist ethos, a fetishization of national sovereignty or of one's precolonial cultural roots. A passion for the commons revives the stakes of politics. The commons is a counter-logic to the system's privatization and division of the world, to its allocation of individuals to predetermined subject positions and its shrinking of collective or public goods. And while focusing on the part of no-part, a given order's constitutive outsiders, we should think along the lines of Fred Moten and Stefano Harney's notion of the "undercommons" (2013), the commons of the excluded / the excluded of the commons.

Not unlike Mohanty's call "to read up the ladder of privilege," a universal politics fights for the commons from the perspective of the undercommons, "black people, indigenous peoples, queers and poor people" (Halberstam 2013, 6). As Jack Halberstam surmises, the undercommons "cannot be satisfied with the recognition and acknowledgement generated by the very system that denies a) that anything was ever broken and b) that we deserved to be the broken part" (2013, 6). A universal politics challenges the system's sovereignty, its capacity to decide who matters and who doesn't, who gets recognized and falls by the wayside (and is cruelly blamed for their own exclusion). It takes as the embodiment of the concrete universal those "less than nothing," the refugees, the *real* neighbors, the undercommons, those who belong to global capitalism's "geo-social class" (Žižek 2020c; see also Latour and Schultz 2019)—individuals exploited not only "in what they are doing" (the classic Marxist worker) but also "in their very existence, . . . exploited via the material conditions of their life: their access to clean water and air, their health, their safety" (Žižek 2020c)—all who have been dispossessed of being, disprivileged or excluded by society's laws and norms, residing outside the liberal and humanist umbrella. They embody the universal that a universal politics is fighting for.

The challenge for the part of no-part, as for all of us for that matter, is not to fall into the trap of approaching the violations of (colonial) power as a victim—which only empowers the violator to either ignore or further repress you or benevolently "right" the wrongs done to you in the form of minority rights protection or identity recognition—but to use the violation as an occasion to confront your *own* alienation. Violations disrupt one's "organic" unity with one's social context or community, and while violent and disorienting, they provide one with the opportunity to extract oneself from such a context, to come to terms with one's non-coincidence with oneself. So rather than resorting to victimhood, ressentiment, or a search for authenticity and pride (which only strengthen the hand of multicultural/identity politics, as we have seen), the point is to use the violation to become a political agent of universality—by facing one's own antagonisms, joining forces with those who are moved to do the same, and struggling to reconfigure together the system that made the violation possible in the first place.

If subaltern voices are to be made visible in a fashion that parts ways with the cultural Left's humanist playbook of empathetic imaginings, a new revolutionary grammar is needed. Indeed such a grammar requires constructing new bonds of solidarity, based not on common enemies or goals but, as just underlined, loss and peril. It is shared trauma (exploitation, dispossession, alienation, oppression) that enables political groups to forge alliances, but as chapter 4 emphasized, universal emancipation also means giving up a degree of privilege/enjoyment, especially on the part of the included. It is the curbing of enjoyment, after all, that underlies a politics of egalitarian justice, since the point is not to aspire to the lifestyle of the privileged, but to reconfigure the system to minimize "privilege" (i.e., social inequalities). This is particularly the case in our current environmental crisis, which increasingly demands making do without new wealth creation (e.g., public transit instead of personal automobiles, computers using recycled rather than new materials, etc.). As Eisenstein and McGowan state, everyone "claims to want solidarity, but few want to pay the price for it. It does not require hatred of an enemy or the willingness to kill for the collective but the self-inflicted violence of the rupture. The solidarity that forms in the rupture is a solidarity without ground because the bond that exists is nothing but the shared absence of ground" (2012, 94). Without self-violence, without the will to unplug from the system and its rewards, critique will only ever be the *semblance* of critique, reform without transformation.

A new revolutionary grammar also begins with a cold defense of hopelessness. One of the system's most effective tricks is the cruel lie of reform. Hope gives life to the system, prolonging its brutal existence. It breeds nostalgia. The system—with a new president, a new prime minister, and so on—will be redeemed. Liberal democracy can get a reboot. It can still deliver on its emancipatory promises. Hopelessness interrupts this postpolitical calculus. Without this sense of hopelessness, we would never demand something qualitatively different. Politics as such would be inexistent. Hopelessness opens onto pessimism, onto a critical and skeptical hermeneutics. Pessimism is a political doing; it embodies an active and vigilant disposition vis-à-vis power. We might recall here Foucault's insistence that power doesn't mean "that everything is bad," but rather "that everything is dangerous" (1983, 231–32). And more importantly, what follows from this apprehension is not despair or apathy (power is all there is; there is no outside-power), but a resolve to confront any configuration of power identified as dangerous by adopting what Foucault suggestively terms "a hyper- and pessimistic activism" (1983, 232). In Lacanese, power is non-all. Žižek repeats this kind of "hyper- and pessimistic activism" when he stresses the lack of transcendence *from within*. The antidote to the "slow death" (Berlant 2011, 102) of quotidian life is decidedly not reform but revolution. Against the liberal model of incremental change, the experience of change without change, a universal politics affirms the sober vision that there is no light at the end of the tunnel; on the contrary, as Žižek puts it, if there is a light, what we are actually seeing is another train bearing down on us (2017a, xi–xii). In this respect, "the courage of hopelessness" is counterintuitively "the height of optimism" (Agamben 2014).

A pessimistic orientation does not seek accommodations with the system. We share the goal of the undercommons, which "is not to end the troubles but to end the world that created those particular troubles as the ones that must be opposed" (Halberstam 2013, 9). Moten and Harney don't play the liberal game of reform; they are constantly reframing the problems at hand. What questions we ask are crucial—for bad questions yield worse answers, ones that compound the problem. On prison abolition, their intervention is decisive and reconfigures the coordinates of the debate: for them, it is "not so much the abolition of prisons but the abolition of a society that could have prisons, that could have slavery" (Moten and Harney 2013, 42). How do you abolish a society? How do you fight state power? Is anti-statism, ethical (that is, nonviolent) anarchism, the only solution? Is it a solution? Or do you dare to seize power, as with the example of Morales? A universal politics takes these questions to heart. For this reason, its skeptical negativity is put into the service of a more virtuous end: locating antagonisms, rather than settling for conflicts or pseudo-struggles. Its challenge is to sustain the antagonistic logic of class struggle, and avoid the comfort of static oppositions. The cultural Left has its enemies (Trump, Putin, Le Pen, Erdoğan, Modi, Duterte, Netanyahu, Orbán, Bolsonaro, Suu Kyi, MBS, etc.)—and, conversely, notorious leaders blame liberal media, demonizing bad press with the "enemy of the people" charge—but nothing really changes; the basic features or coordinates of the current society remain the same. Worse, the liberal capitalist system is legitimized (only in a free democracy can you, as a citizen, criticize tyrants abroad and, more importantly, express your outrage at the president, politicians, or state power without the fear of retribution) and the cultural Left is tacitly compensated for playing by the rules—for practicing non-antagonistic politics, for forgoing class insurgency and not engaging in class war (Žižek 2020f)—rewarded with "libidinal profit" (Žižek 1997b, 47), with what Lacan calls a "surplus-enjoyment" (2007, 147), an enjoyment-in-sacrifice. That is to say, cultural leftists, with their "Beautiful Souls" intact, enjoy not being a racist, a misogynist, a transphobe, an ableist, and so on. Hating the haters, the morally repulsive, the fascists of the world, is indeed an endless source of libidinal satisfaction for "woke" liberals. But what changes does it actually produce?

A universal politics is not only preoccupied with events and evental sites but also with the *aftermath* of the event. The question *What comes after the system?* is intimately tied to *What comes after the event?* Indeed, it is not an exaggeration to say that what matters more is what takes place after the traumatic eruption of the event, after the disruption of the symbolic order. The excitement of negativity can give a false sense of victory. Strikes and other mass movements are capable of shutting down a whole system. But what comes next? As Žižek rightly cautions, "The success of a revolution should not be measured by the sublime awe of its ecstatic moments, but by the changes the big Event leaves at the level of the everyday, the day after the insurrection" (2009a, 154). Fidelity to the event is the ultimate challenge of politics. After making the impossible possible, a universal politics must be alert to the system's backlash, its capacity to strike back or co-opt. The advances brought about by events can be undone; de-eventalization is an immanent possibility. And here again the greatest threat to universal politics does not come from the populist Right but from the liberal Left, whose complicity with the system, its willingness to compromise (capitalism must be saved!), is a bigger obstacle to building an emancipatory movement, to forging a common project.

But a universal politics must not make false promises either: after capitalism comes plenitude, the absence of alienation, and communal harmony: postpolitical 2.0. No. Antagonism is a constitutive element of our being. We are strangers, neighbors, and even enemies to ourselves:

> To grasp the notion of antagonism, in its most radical dimension, we should *invert* the relationship between the two terms: it is not the external enemy who is preventing me from achieving identity with myself, but every identity is already in itself blocked, marked by an impossibility, and the external enemy is simply the small piece, the rest of reality upon which we "project" or "externalize" this intrinsic, immanent impossibility. (Žižek 1990, 252)

Post-capitalism will not be envy-free, ressentiment-free. A more just society predicated on the disavowal of symbolic castration (lack), envy, or ressentiment is a recipe for failure of the worse kind. Liberalism serves as a cautionary tale. The liberal Rawlsian fantasy of a just society is that of a system without its undeserved privileges, a system that is not rigged, where our lower position in society is "tolerated" (Žižek 2008c, 88) on condition that there is a robust welfare net to take care of society's least fortunate, and on condition that our lower status reflects our natural inequality rather than inherited hierarchies. For Rawls, our inequality would be fully "justified," and no one else would be to blame. But for Žižek this "just society" would only "create conditions for an uncontrolled explosion of *ressentiment*" (Žižek 2008c, 88; see also Žižek 2016h, 285–86).

The anti-Rawlsian model is not any more appealing. It renounces any direct involvement in the system, capitalizing instead on people's refusal to accept their inferior lot as just and their inclination to be persuaded by the "'irrationality' of the market": "The fact that capitalism is not 'just' is thus a key feature of what makes it acceptable" (Žižek 2008c, 89). Capitalism is as capricious as Fortuna. Its actions cannot be predicted, only painfully accepted. Either way, the system survives. Ressentiment effortlessly translates into the racialized scapegoating of foreigners who are envied for stealing our enjoyment (the cause for our suffering is displaced and mystified), or we accept our miserable lot as beyond our control and responsibility, giving up, in turn, the option of class struggle (which would actually deal with the cause of our suffering).

In theorizing post-capitalism—in thinking about what comes after the system—a universal politics cannot downplay "the power of envy"

(Derbyshire 2009) or engage in a fetishistic disavowal of envy. We know very well that envy is part of human nature, but we believe in utopia, that a just society will be freed of envy, that envy is really a capitalist problem. Envy is to be avowed, acknowledged as a constitutive element of human existence. To be clear: this is not to naturalize or justify envy. Quite the contrary, the avowal of envy enjoins us to politically confront it, to de-individualize envy's hold on us—and not to transcend it (dreaming of a prelapsarian mode of plenitude, attaining the ideal of completion) nor acquiesce to its presence (normalizing its social manifestations, legitimizing the fear of Others—the "theft of enjoyment"). Envy registers first and foremost an ontological dissat-isfaction, a "glitch" in us, that the current system is all too keen to exploit and manipulate. And this insight must not be lost on a universal politics.

The unavoidable implication is that the struggle for emancipation is a never-ending one—it always fails; it always falls short of its objective. Reaching a destination inevitably brings with it killjoys and spoilers, making for new struggles. But this should come as no surprise since universality, after all, is about the very absence of meaning—impossible to reach, possess, or fully realize. *Struggle, struggle again, struggle better.*

Notes

Chapter 1

1. Note that we differ here from Wilson and Swyngedouw (2014) in seeing postpolitics as characteristic not just of capitalist liberal democracies but of contemporary global capitalism. In other words, we see a postpolitical continuum between authoritarian capitalism and capitalist liberal democracy.
2. Hegel writes, for instance, that the "sickness of the animal is the birth of the spirit" (quoted in McGowan 2019, 36), implying that it is the emergence of an ailment/limitation that gives rise to human subjectivity.
3. A precursor to the "Black is beautiful" movement, the Negritude movement was championed by mainly French-speaking African-Caribbean writers during the 1930s– 1950s (Senghor, Césaire, Damas) who, in response to European colonial domination and racism, sought refuge in African/Black life, often constructing a glorified past in a bid to valorize African/Black heritage and pride.
4. Note that we are mobilizing Fanon here not simply to support our argument but to point out that the idea of negativity / antagonism / the unconscious (which both undergirds and undoes consciousness, racism, culture) is a key preoccupation of his, too.
5. For Žižek the reason the Other's enjoyment (excessive pleasure that overwhelms and outmaneuvers reason) is intolerable to one is because one can't relate it to one's own: it is intrusive, mysterious, unmanageable, and so "to resolve this deadlock . . . the subject projects its *jouissance* onto an Other" (2015d).
6. This is sometimes translated as "part with no part." Other possible denotations are the "subaltern" (Gramsci), "wretched of the earth" (Fanon), "excluded" (Žižek), and "proletariat" (Marx). The last of these tends to restrict itself to the working class, while the remaining terms are more reflective of contemporary global capitalism, under which marginalization happens on the basis of not just class but broader patterns of socioeconomic and political exclusion (on the basis of gender, racialization, disability, sexuality, etc.). What all terms point to, however, is systemically induced exclusion.
7. A single revolutionary assault is unfeasible if not impossible. Instead, as Žižek suggests, "We can begin . . . by measures which appear modest but nonetheless undermine the foundations of the existing system like a patient subterranean digging of a mole" (2018a)—for example, demanding better state oversight of multinationals or a limit/ end to financial speculation.

Chapter 2

1. Alain Badiou makes a similar observation about the universality underpinning a certain Jewish tradition: "From the apostle Paul to Trotsky, including Spinoza, Marx and Freud, Jewish communitarianism has only underpinned creative universalism in so far as there have been new points of rupture with it. It is clear that today's equivalent of Paul's religious rupture with established Judaism, of Spinoza's rationalist rupture with the Synagogue, or of Marx's political rupture with the bourgeois integration of a part of his community of origin, is a subjective rupture with the State of Israel, not with its empirical existence, which is neither more nor less impure than that of all states, but with its exclusive identitarian claim to be a Jewish state, and with the way it draws incessant privileges from this claim, especially when it comes to trampling underfoot what serves us as international law" (2006, 162).

2. Balibar distinguishes "ultrasubjective violence" (which "requires that individuals and groups be represented as incarnations of evil, diabolical powers that threaten the subject from within and have to be eliminated at all costs, up to and including self-destruction") from "ultraobjective violence," defined as a "kind of cruelty [that] calls for treating masses of human beings as things or useless remnants" (2015, 52).

3. While the origins of binationalism are to be found in the writings of early European Zionist intellectuals (including Martin Buber, Judah Magnes, and Arthur Ruppin), it was Edward Said who almost singlehandedly reinvigorated the universalist idea of a binational state. Said argued against the separatist logic of the two-state solution and in favor of coexistence, acknowledging that "the lives of Jews have become more and more enmeshed with those of non-Jews" (Said 1999) and embracing existential entanglement as a way out of this seemingly intractable situation.

4. This is in many ways the tragic lesson of post-apartheid South Africa. It successfully freed the black majority from white minority rule, but it left the capitalist infrastructure for the most part untouched—making South African still one of the most unequal nations in the world. See Clarno 2017. Overcoming the sedimented belief that capitalism is the *only game in town* requires a collective effort, a "revolutionary solidarity"—when "the repressed, the exploited and suffering, the 'parts of no-part' of every culture . . . come together in a shared struggle" (Žižek 2008c, 157).

5. "One should, perhaps, rehabilitate Marx's (implicit) distinction between the working class (an 'objective' social category, a topic of sociological study) and the proletariat (a certain subjective position—the class 'for itself,' the embodiment of social negativity, to use an old and rather unfortunate expression)" (Žižek 2002b, 336).

6. For Lacan, the primal father of Freud's *Totem and Taboo* exemplifies the masculine logic. The father—who enjoyed all women at will, "achieving complete satisfaction" (Žižek 1991, 123)—had to be killed for the symbolic order to emerge; but his exceptional subject position persists in the cultural imaginary, pointing to the ideal of pure enjoyment.

7. Admitting antagonism may well be foreign to liberal democrats inclined toward a belief in the postpolitical, but it is second nature to conservatives *and* reactionaries alike,

as reflected in their embrace of the "clash of civilizations" discourse. Conservatives cling to a phantasmatic past under threat from without (Islam) and within (a cultural Left that appeases anti-Western voices). Reactionaries do more of the same, only in a cruder fashion. They are less inclined to hide their racism—openly endorsing the West's cultural superiority—unwilling to question its values, to fully acknowledge its complicity with colonialism and slavery (and its legacies in contemporary times). Both argue that the problem lies squarely in the non-European, who has not only taken advantage of European generosity, but also corrupted the very relation between host and guest: "For the first time in the history of immigration, the ones being welcomed are denying the host, whichever country it may be, the possibility of acting as a host" (Finkielkraut 2013a, 115, our translation). Finkielkraut's reactionary commitment to the tradition of the Enlightenment—emblematized in the Republican ideal of *laïcité*—barely masks his rabid xenophobia.

8. Finkielkraut is by no means alone in making this association between the Left and anti-Western forces. Pierre-André Taguieff, for example, points out the shared anticapitalist sentiment of both Islam and Marxism. The Left's hatred of capitalism distorts the politics of the Middle East, creating the false impression that Israel is the enemy, while an "intrinsically good Palestinian—the innocent victim par excellence," is engaged in a "'just liberation struggle'" (2004, 67). Pascal Bruckner follows in similar ideological footsteps, pitting the West and Israel against the East and Israel's Arab neighbors: "It is wrong to declare that the West is guilty simply because it exists, as if it were an insult to creation, a cosmic catastrophe, a monstrosity to be wiped off the face of the earth. The question of Israel is fundamental in this regard. Through non-recognition of the Jewish state, the entire Western World is held to be illegitimate" (1986, 127).

9. Benhabib's response to *l'affaire du foulard* converges more with that of Balibar. Although Balibar was not in support of the ban, which he considers evidence of "an exclusionary discourse" (2017b), he rejected an anti-universalist framing of the argument: a defense of the *foulard* meant that you're for the resistance against colonialism, for Muslim difference against Eurocentric universalism (Enns 2005, 377).

Chapter 3

1. Of course, Foucault has a materialist analysis of discursive practices, but that is not the same as political economy. See Negri 2017 and Olssen 2006.

2. See also Marchart 2007, who looks approvingly on Laclau's approach to the political (because it enables a productive articulation between political subjects despite groundlessness) but ignores Žižek's equally productive notion of negative universality.

3. There is a further problem here: L&M's vision of a plural society composed of multiple "subject positions" appears to assume a master position from which one can distinguish one from the other, which runs counter to their notion of a contingent universality.

4. Meillassoux differentiates between two forms of correlationism: a weak version and a strong one. Weak correlationism rules out knowledge of the noumenal real, of the in-itself, yet without dismissing its thinkability. Strong correlationism excludes the possibility of even its thinkability: "According to Kant, we know a priori that the thing-in-itself is non-contradictory and that it actually exists. By way of contrast, the strong model of correlationism maintains not only that it is illegitimate to claim that we can know the in-itself, but also that it is illegitimate to claim that we can at least think it" (2008, 35).

5. "For the last few decades, at least in the humanities, big ontological questions—What is reality? What is the nature of the universe?—were considered too naive. It was meaningless to ask for objective truth. This prohibition on asking the big questions partly accounts for the explosion of popular science books. You read Stephen Hawking's books as a way to ask these fundamental, metaphysical questions. I think that era of relativism, where science was just another product of knowledge, is ending. We philosophers should join scientists asking those big metaphysical questions about quantum physics, about reality" (Else 2010, 29).

6. In this formulation, one hears Foucault's anti-identitarian cry of protest, "Do not ask me who I am and do not ask me to remain the same" (2014, 17).

7. Capitalism presents itself as most welcoming of queer sexualities, "tend[ing] to replace the standard normative heterosexuality with a proliferation of unstable shifting identities and/or orientations" (Žižek 2008a, 435).

8. "The problem with this [queer] vision of a new fluid subjectivity is not that it is utopian but that it is already predominant—yet another case of the hegemonic ideology presenting itself as subversive and transgressive of the existing order" (Žižek 2017a, 190–91).

9. Žižek defines the ego ideal as "the agency whose gaze I try to impress with my ego image, the big Other who watches over me and impels me to give my best" (2006a, 80).

10. Although Mignolo employs the term "universality," we are denoting it as "universalism" (since he means it as "abstract universalism") to distinguish it from our notion of negative universality.

11. Mignolo borrows the notion of "delinking" from Samir Amin (1990). But while the latter sees it as a primarily political-economic delinking from the global capitalist system, the former sees it as a "de-linking from the rhetoric of modernity and the logic of coloniality" (Mignolo 2010, 317).

12. Although Mignolo (2015) claims that Franz Hinkelhammert and Enrique Dussel came up with term "pluriverse," Kimberly Hutchings (2019, 115) points out the notion comes to us from William James (who wrote about the "multiverse" in 1895).

13. A rare instance of such critique is when Mignolo cites "Islamic fundamentalism" as an abstract universal, along with Christianity, liberalism, and Marxism (2010, 354).

14. It should be noted that Escobar has been taken to task by several critics (Kiely 1999; Pieterse 2000; Storey 2000; Kapoor 2008, 52–53) for the same romanticizing tendencies. Kiely, for example, sees Escobar's post-development theory as the "last refuge of the noble savage," emphasizing how it celebrates the local while downplaying such problems as internal disagreements, gender violence, exploitation, or inequality.

15. See Castro-Gomez 2008; Coronil 2008; Mignolo 2011, 2–24; and Mignolo and Escobar 2010 for a review of the work done by the MCD group.

16. Michaelsen and Shershow are incredulous at Mignolo's claim that Amerindian signification systems escape logocentrism (Mignolo 2003, 319), suggesting that such a view "springs from a kind of nostalgia for some unadulterated Amerindian 'voice' imagined as not yet disturbed in the plenitude of its self-presence and self-possession . . . [Mignolo] insists that Amerindians did have writing, yet imagines the writing they had as one that escapes all of writing's problems and that exists in the form of an untamed 'voice' not yet contaminated by the letter" (Michaelsen and Shershow 2007, 43–44).

17. It is for this reason that we take issue with Linda Alcoff, who, while critical of parts of Mignolo's decolonial epistemology, looks favorably on his goal of delinking. For her, the fact that "Western epistemology's internal complexity is somehow able to co-exist" with European colonialism buttresses Mignolo's advocacy of delinking (Alcoff 2007, 91). But like Mignolo, she is wrong to assume that critical counter-discourses "coexist" with hegemonic ones on a level playing field; they are engaged in an (often losing) battle with hegemony. So like Mignolo, she conflates *hegemonic* European thought with European thought writ large.

18. See also Jimmy Casas Klausen (2019, 868), who claims that Mignolo has an impoverished and caricatured view of power: "What Mignolo offers is a quasi-conspiratorial view of the world divided into the few 'controlling and managing' and the many 'being managed and controlled.'"

19. The Gramscian notion of hegemony (Gramsci 2000, 306–7) refers to the construction of mass consent.

20. Given the colonial matrix of power, the decolonial subaltern can denaturalize, hybridize, or creatively deflect the hegemony, but it cannot supersede or transcend it so as to create a radically different space in the way that Mignolo expressly indicates. It should also be noted in this regard that while Mignolo most often asserts a radical decolonial alterity, he does occasionally waiver, as witnessed by the earlier quoted statement of his, "The reason of the master is absorbed by the slave," enabling the subaltern to incorporate "another reason to his or her own" (2012, 157), which suggests some form of negotiation with colonial hegemony. But even here, notice that it is the master's reason that is incorporated into the slave's (rather than the reverse), which again appears as a convenient refusal of the (continuing) dominance of coloniality and a misreading of the notion of hegemony. See also Alcoff 2007, 98–99, on this point.

21. We are certainly no apologists of the liberal state, which can be coercive and beholden to elite interests, but do believe that a universalist state, which puts the part of no-part first (as exemplified, at least to some extent, by the Bolivian state under Morales; see chapter 4), is worth defending.

22. Mignolo presumably sees "communal nodes" as devising universal programs through cooperative and communal practices/institutions. Yet even were these successful internally, it seems unrealistic that small autonomous regions would be able to continually defend against powerful multinationals or unfriendly nation-states; some kind of effective regional or transnational authority would still be needed to fulfill such

202 NOTES

functions. Perhaps Mignolo also envisions cooperation between nodes (this dimension can be surmised based on the logic of decolonial arguments, but once again remains sorely undeveloped). At times, he comes close to such a view, declaring, for example, that "what different people in spatial and temporal locales have in common is the colonial wound" (Mignolo and González García 2006, 42). This echoes our own argument about the Real-as-universal as the basis of political solidarity (see chapter 1), but remains unexplained and untheorized in Mignolo's work, likely because of his general aversion to universality.

23. As Homi Bhabha pointedly observes, "Migrants, refugees, and nomads don't merely circulate. They need to settle, claim asylum or nationality, demand housing and education, assert their economic and cultural rights, and come to be legally represented within legal jurisdictions" (2003, 347).

24. Highly critical of Deleuze's positive reception and growing influence among the "anti-global Left," Žižek points to "those aspects of Deleuzianism that, while masquerading as radical chic, effectively transform Deleuze into an ideologist of today's 'digital capitalism'" (2012a, xi, xii).

25. "Our hypothesis is that decision-making and assembly do not require centralized rule but instead can be accomplished together by the multitude, democratically" (Hardt and Negri 2017, xiv).

26. Jim Geraghty from the *National Review* states he "worried that a certain segment of America's angry, paranoid, emotionally unstable young men will watch Joaquin Phoenix descending into madness and a desire to get back at society by hurting as many people as possible and exclaim, 'finally, somebody understands me!'" (2019).

27. Matthew Rozsa (2020) from *Salon* indicts the film for its trafficking with examples of white male rage: "One symptom of white male rage is the feeling of entitlement thwarted, the concept that because you are a white man, the things you want naturally ought to be given to you. Fleck benefits from the presumption that he deserves success, that his desire to be regarded as a great comedian is legitimate because of his position of social privilege." Richard Brody (2019) from the *New Yorker* laments how "*Joker* is an intensely racialized movie, a drama awash in racial iconography that is so prevalent in the film, so provocative, and so unexamined as to be bewildering."

28. Of course, we must extend the adventures with capitalism outside America; seeing the situation in its full despair involves provincializing the American example. Most recently, Covid-19 serves as a reminder that health is a global matter. Is there a market solution to pandemics? Are nation-states looking to score geopolitical points (rather than securing international cooperation) any better at resolving crises?

29. Žižek credits Agamben for this formulation; see Agamben 2014.

30. For the virtual Joker of emancipatory ressentiment (he also remains as much of a stranger to a liberal audience as did the actual Joker on the screen), physical violence is not the first or only option. He learns that an effective form of anti-violence can be very violent. This is the next unrealized step that *Joker* suggests to the audience, a next step we are entrusted to take up: "An additional change of subjective stance is to be accomplished if we are to pass from Joker's outbursts to becoming the one able to

'stand and fight and focus your attention on the nonviolent power you hold in your hands every single day.' When you become aware of this power you can renounce brutal bodily violence. The paradox is that you become truly violent, in the sense of posing a threat to the existing system, only when you renounce physical violence" (Žižek 2019a).

31. The film is ambiguous about Wayne being the father of Arthur. Wayne denies any involvement with Penny and tells him that he is not the father, and also that Arthur himself is adopted. This information is later collaborated in Penny Fleck's medical folder. At the same time, it is clear that Wayne's reach in Gotham is practically unlimited, so it is not unlikely that he had the documents doctored (especially given that we see on the back of a photograph of a younger Penny the initials TM).

Chapter 4

1. See also Žižek 2011, 329. There is likely a close link between the rise of disaster capitalism and the rise of neopopulism, both equally based on a politics of fear, and both emerging in the wake of the breakdown of the global liberal consensus.

2. Right-wing, neopopulist governments and political parties (e.g., in Hungary, India, Britain, Italy) have fanned the flames of xenophobia, often pitting the working class against refugees.

3. Admittedly, several of the Arab Spring popular uprisings were unsuccessful in defeating authoritarianism (in Egypt's case, the regime that has succeeded Mubarak's is arguably even more authoritarian), underlining the many real perils of revolution. Still, few would have predicted the uprising in Tunisia in 2010–11 or its subsequent spread across the region.

4. Žižek stands firmly against the authoritarian communist examples of the Soviet Union, China, or North Korea. Instead he argues for a reinvention of communism based on such ideas as collective decision-making and the commons.

5. This 2015 agreement is often seen as a "lowest common denominator" accord, not only for specifying low emission reduction targets but also making these targets a matter of commitment rather than legal enforcement.

6. It should be noted that Žižek is not uncritical of Thunberg, for example accusing her (and Bernie Sanders) of not being radical enough in connecting the climate crisis to other global problems such as antiracism and Covid-19: "One should insist on the basic unity of the three domains: epidemics explode as part of our unbalanced relationship with our natural environs, they are not just a health problem; antiracist protests were also given the additional boost by the fact that racial minorities are much more threatened by the epidemics than the white majority which can afford self-isolation and better medical care" (2020d). It is Thunberg's climate change *leadership* that helps point to what a universalist political leadership might look like, which does not necessarily mean that Thunberg's overall political platform is consistent with a radical Žižekian politics.

7. Consider as well the Far Right's opportunistic call to close borders, which capitalizes on the pandemic by scapegoating refugees, blaming them for the spread of the coronavirus in its European cities (Scott and Overly 2020).

8. Compounding the problem is the subject's disavowal of the unruliness of its own enjoyment, or jouissance: "The ultimate incompatibility is not between mine and other's *jouissance*, but between myself and my own *jouissance*, which forever remains an ex-timate intruder" (Žižek 2016d, 75). It is this constitutive impasse that is phantasmatically displaced onto the refugee, creating, in turn, a hostile relationality to the Other: "It is to resolve this deadlock that the subject projects the core of its *jouissance* onto an Other, attributing to this Other full access to a consistent *jouissance*. Such a constellation cannot but give rise to jealousy: in jealousy, the subject creates or imagines a paradise (a utopia of full *jouissance*) from which he is excluded" (Žižek 2016d, 75). Anti-immigrants fantasize about the refugees enjoying the wealth and the privileges of the Western world without any of the sacrifices: they get to keep the mysterious ways of their culture without suffering the alienation of modern life.

9. Though the Yellow Vests are exerting pressure on Emmanuel Macron, asking him to put into practice "impossible" policies, they are still operating from within the system (as if it could deliver on their economic demands): "In all the explosion of demands and expressions of dissatisfaction, it is clear the protesters don't really know what they want; they don't have a vision of a society they want, just a mixture of demands that are impossible to be met within the system, although they address them to the system. This feature is crucial: their demands express their interests rooted in the existing system" (Žižek 2020g, 252).

10. BLM is responding, and contributing, to an emerging divide in the Democratic Party. An unqualified support of Israel is no longer a given, especially with the younger generation of voters. Bernie Sanders, who represents the progressive wing on the political stage, has been the most prominent critic of Israel. In the 2020 Democratic presidential primary debate in Charleston, South Carolina, Sanders ruffled some liberal feathers when he referred to Netanyahu as a "reactionary racist." There is a danger, however, in overreading the force of the comment, since what he uttered right after it paints a far less critical intervention: "I happen to believe that what our foreign policy in the Mideast should be about is absolutely protecting the independence and security of Israel. But you cannot ignore the suffering of the Palestinian people." Netanyahu is the problem, not political Zionism. Netanyahu is the problem, not the illegal settlements, and so on. Sanders's acknowledgment of Palestinian suffering—though brave when set against the backdrop of the more cowardly Democratic candidates—recycles a vision of Occupation with a human face (the fantasy of liberal Zionism). Sanders's lack of support for BDS further attests to his reluctance to fully support a universalist critique of Israel. Democrat leaders (from Susan Rice to Chuck Schumer) may be unified in their objection to Israel's West Bank annexation (enjoying their performance of public outrage), but they remain utterly silent (aside from the meaningless and toothless proclamations that *new* settlements are not conducive for peace) on the existence of the illegal settlements. The question of annexation alarms the supporters of Israel because it makes it that much harder to defend a "separate-but-unequal" ideology (Tamari 2020), and discloses the utter sham of the

two-state solution, which still pacifies liberals, since it gives them an ideal that can allow them to fetishistically disavow the brutality of Israeli Occupation: *yes, I know Israel's racial treatment of Palestinians is harsh, but I believe in nonviolence and the two-state solution* (the latter serves as an alibi against the charge of racism—how can I be a racist if I support Palestinian indigeneity?). Moreover, annexation is now an option only because the world powers—namely the United States—refused to do anything about the settlements and Israel's apartheid logic. If Democrat leaders want to take a genuine antiracist stance (and not limit their antiracism to their [geo]political foes), where is their call to immediately dismantle the settlements—a bare minimum for anyone committed to a just resolution to the Occupation? When Israel is aggressively moving forward in its annexation—under the cover of the United States, whose veto power on the United Nation Security Council rules out the possibility of international pressure in the form of sanctions against Israel—BDS increasingly appears as the only viable global response to Israel's racist segregation politics, which explains why the movement and any individuals or organizations (such as the American Studies Association) who supports it are frequently subjected to "lawfare," frivolous lawsuits, meant to deplete you emotionally and financially, as well as to discredit and margin-alize you in the academic community (see USACBI 2020).

11. Jadaliyya Reports, "Black, Palestinian artists and activists affirm solidarity in new video," 14 Oct 2015, https://www.jadaliyya.com/Details/32588/Black,-Palestinian-Artists-and-Activists-Affirm-Solidarity-in-New-Video. Patrisse Cullors comments on her experience visiting Occupied Palestine as part of BLM delegation: "It was probably the most profound trip of my life. It was really intense, walking through the streets of East Jerusalem, Ramallah, and throughout the West Bank. I remember walking with a Palestinian woman who asked me, 'How are you feeling?' I said to her, essentially, 'I've only felt this way when I visited a prison.' I think it was important for us to let Palestinian people know, just like Malcolm did, and like the Panthers did, that we are in solidarity with their struggle against occupation and also that the #BlackLivesMatter movement is most definitely not going to align itself with the state of Israel. It was important to show that" (Heatherton 2016, 85–86).

12. For Wilderson, the divide between Blacks and Palestinians is metaphysical, that is, insurmountable. Any attempt on the Palestinian side to understand the plights of Blacks is cynically dismissed as inauthentic. *Pace* Wilderson, the Arabs for Black Lives Collective foregrounds the question of antiblackness in its struggle for global justice. See https://www.mpowerchange.org/culture-blog/arabs-for-black-lives.

13. "Without the presence of a being who is, ab initio, barred from redemption (a being that is generally dishonored, natally alienated, and open to naked violence), history and narrative would lack their touchstones of cohesion" (Wilderson 2020, 226).

14. https://twitter.com/barackobama/status/1266400635429310466.

15. There is a parallel realization among US progressives calling for defunding the Israeli military complex.

16. After the Floyd tragedy, Morton Klein, the head of the Zionist Organization of America, urged the Southern Poverty Law Center on Twitter (June 6, 2020) to place "Black Lives Matter on their list of hate groups," adding that "BLM is a Jew-hating,

white-hating, Israel-hating, conservative Black-hating, violence-promoting, dangerous Soros-funded extremist group of haters" (Abunimah 2020).

17. "'Homeland' cannot be reconciled with 'Africa,' in part, because Africa is a continent, and the word homeland implies a cartographic scale smaller and more intimate than a continent. The 1948 Palestinian exodus, also known as the Nakba, dispersed a people from a homeland, not a continent" (Wilderson et al. 2016, 18).

18. "Slavery . . . is a highly symbolized domain of human experience. While all aspects of the relationship are symbolized, there is an overwhelming concentration of the profound natal alienation of the slave. The reason for this is not hard to discern: it was the slave's isolation, his strangeness that made him most valuable to the master, but it was his very strangeness that most threatened the community. . . . On the cognitive and mythic level, one dominant theme emerges, which lends an unusually loaded meaning to the act of natal alienation: this is the social death of the slave" (Patterson 1982, 38).

19. A cross-racial coalition worthy of its name takes up mass incarceration as a paradigmatic case of injustice, revealing how Blacks are treated as socially and legally insignificant, "meant to be warehoused and die" (Wilderson 2003, 238).

20. Rosalind Gill and Shani Orgad point to the women in the workforce who have not been at the forefront of #MeToo: "Women in sectors such as health and social work, wholesale and retail, administration, accommodation and food services, manufacturing and hospitality—in which female employment is concentrated—have been conspicuously absent from the majority of the discussion" (2018, 1319).

21. In the #MeToo movement, men, though in far small numbers, are also included among the victims of sexual harassment and violence.

22. As Ashwini Tambe argues, "Coercion . . . should be defined by more than just whether someone says yes or no. It hinges on whether one has power over that other person such that they might interpret a request as force—or even as a threat. If s/he faces negative consequences for saying no to a sexual advance, then that sexual advance is coercive" (2018, 201). See also Rose 2018.

23. We are alluding to Žižek's adaptation of the following line from book 7 of Virgil's *Aeneid*, "If I cannot bend the higher powers, I will move the infernal regions [*flectere si nequeo superos, Acheronta movebo*]": "Dare to disturb the underground of the unspoken underpinnings of our everyday lives" (Žižek 2008, 168). Freud makes the quotation from Virgil the epigraph to his first edition of *The Interpretation of Dreams* (*Freud* 1953–74, ix).

24. But as Jacqueline Rose points out, "Harassment is ruthless, but it also has a desperation about it, as if the harasser knows at some level that his cruelty, like all human cruelty, has its source in a fraudulent boast" (2018).

25. Jamil Khader also relates Mohanty's emphasis on transnational struggle to Žižek's deployment of the part of no-part. See Khader 2013, 20.

26. Rose does not subscribe to the radical feminist view of "masculinity as perfectly and violently in control of itself" (2018). Rose considers the roots of toxic masculinity in childhood trauma, in the trauma of sexuality. For psychoanalysis, what makes sexuality traumatic are not only the instances of sexual abuse. Rather, it is

the fact of sexuality that discloses our fundamental disjointedness, lack of wholeness and control: "Sexuality is lawless or it is nothing, not least because of its
rootedness in our unconscious lives, where all sexual certainties come to grief"
(2018). We are indeed terrified of this truth, that "in the unconscious we are not
men or women but always, and in endlessly shifting combinations, neither or both"
(2018). Unwilling or unable to come to terms with this traumatic sexual past,
men project this internal strangeness, this tortuous pain onto others, turning to
power, adopting a toxic masculinity as a remedy, a way for them to re-establish
self-mastery through a domination of women. "This doesn't exempt harassers in
any way," Rose adds, "but it does allow (some) men a glimpse of their own im-
perfection. It opens up a gap between men who won't tolerate any challenge to
their authority and those for whom such authority is nothing to be proud of, not
least because they understand that power is always exercised at somebody else's
expense" (2018). Toxic masculinity is not destiny; it can be de-reified. Rose's psychoanalytic supplement helps in the universalist fight against sexual domination insofar as it works to weaken patriarchy's psychic hold on men by unsettling
and contesting its phantasmatic appeal and false promises. In a similar but non-
psychoanalytic vein, Burke pleads for "restorative justice and transformative justice," for caring about male perpetrators (and not simply writing them off) in the
process of defending women: "If we're ever going to heal in our community, we
have to heal the perpetrators [help them work through their own childhood sexual
abuse] and heal the survivors, or else it's just a continuous cycle" (2018, 31).

27. As McGowan correctly notes, Beauvoir stresses the ambivalence of feminine identity. While yielding some benefits, it does trap you within the patriarchal system: "If
identity is oppressive, it nonetheless provides recognition from a social authority. But
it is for this reason that identity cannot be emancipatory. Identity remains within the
domain of the social authority that recognizes it and is thus dependent through and
through. For Beauvoir, valuing the particular identity of the feminine is not a way of
fighting sexism but the ultimate acquiescence to it. Beauvoir understands that identity is an ideological trap that the feminist must avoid" (2020, 19).

28. Though capitalism dethroned patriarchy as the new hegemony, the former's
inequality-producing system is ripe for the latter's naturalization of these differences,
justifying, in turn, society's asymmetrical divisions along gender lines.

29. The threat of rape is also used literally as a way of taming the anti-colonial struggle
against the Occupation. Palestinian feminists Nadera Shalhoub-Kevorkian, Sarah
Ihmoud, and Suhad Dahir-Nashif document the permissibility of this idea, the fact
that it is uttered without shame or backlash: "On 1 July, just after discovery of the
bodies of three Jewish settler youth who had gone missing in the occupied West Bank,
Israeli professor Mordechai Kedar of the Begin-Sadat Center for Strategic Studies
remarked on public radio: 'the only deterrent for . . . those who kidnapped the [Israeli]
children and killed them, the only way to deter them is their knowledge that either
their sister or their mother will be raped if they are caught . . . this is the culture of the
Middle East.' His comments suggested that raping Palestinian women was the only
deterrent to Palestinian resistance and 'terrorism'" (2014).

30. Feminist solidarity cannot be based on liberal or white tolerance, which, as Audre Lorde stresses, is "the grossest kind of reformism." For difference to open onto a universal project, it "must not be merely tolerated, but seen as a fund of necessary polarities between which our creativity can spark like a dialectic" (1984, 111).

31. We can put Mohanty's notion of "common differences" in dialogue with Catherine Malabou's idea of a "minimal concept" of woman. Malabou formulates a "minimal essence" of woman based on women's shared exposure to violence—of being "dominated sexually, symbolically, socially, economically, and culturally," of being denied their own essence (2011, 93, 92). It is negativity (its negation by patriarchy, for example) rather than any positive attribute that defines "woman." Mohanty (like Žižek) turn this negative essence of woman into a transnational political project, looking to what in women's material condition universalizes their plight, what opens them up to the world, that is, what transforms their concrete example into a concrete universality.

32. Susan Faludi points out the dangers of all conflating #BelieveWomen with #BelieveAllWomen. The former is a feminist intervention, the latter a right-wing act of trolling. Faludi is rightly critical of #BelieveAllWomen, since it misapprehends the situation, distorting the message of #BelieveWomen, which seeks to question the doubts cast on the legitimacy and credibility of a woman's speech in the eyes of the Law. In this sense, women's words have not mattered (as much as those of [white] men). It is one thing to say that a woman's word matters and another to say that only a woman's word matters, which is the way the right wing counters the feminist claim. If you don't support *all* women (that is, women who accuse Democratic politicians), then you are a leftist hypocrite. But as Faludi argues, this right-wing claim misconstrues the feminist point: "The ultimate hypocrisy would be a women's movement that rallies behind the banner of reductive hashtags about what every woman thinks. Feminism was birthed out of a desire that women be treated as individuals, not as a cookie-cutter ideal or a faceless stereotype" (Faludi 2020). A universal politics fully endorses the critical edge behind the feminist version of the hashtag. To argue for the right of women to be believed is a universalist plea: what applies to women—as the parts of no-part—applies to those who have been structurally excluded from mattering, such as Black men and queer and transgender people of color.

33. Between 1988 and 2016 Tunisia's Ennahada movement/party was a pointedly Islamist one, committed to the Islamization of Tunisian society, but in 2016 it decided to renounce much of its religious platform to focus more exclusively on electoral politics.

34. Sharia laws most often aim at regulating behavior; inculcating such values as honor, piety, and modesty; and imposing notions of the "proper" or "virtuous" female. Women frequently end up as the main target of such laws.

35. We are distinguishing between "Islamism," under which Islam-as-religion is made into political ideology, and "political Islam," by which we mean the site of disagreement, debate, and antagonism in the "Muslim world" (which includes the struggle for the secular). Implied here is also a distinction between Islam-as-religion and Islamic/Muslim culture, which is not reducible to the religious. Needless to say, none of these are distinct categories, each with porous and overlapping boundaries. In this regard, we are well aware that our view of political Islam is a reconceptualization of the term,

which is most often associated with the idea of Islam as a basis for ordering society. We are, in a way, turning the idea around: seeing politics—the site for addressing social antagonism—as the basis for (dis)ordering Muslim society(ies); hence the implication that the struggle for the secular (or at least the non-religious) is integral to political Islam. Our thanks to Anne-Marie Cwikowski for pushing us to clarify this point.

36. There are, for example, progressive elements even within the ranks of the Islamic clergy (e.g., Iran's Grand Ayatollah Saanei, who has spoken in favor of women's equality, even pronouncing on the prospect of loosening clerical control of the Iranian political regime, although stopping short of coming out as a full-fledged dissident) (Ghosh 2015). See also Devji 2008 and Li 2019; each in their own way sees in some forms of jihadist militancy an appeal to a global/universalist "humanity."

37. Many left groups and parties, in the "Muslim world" as elsewhere, have tended toward the "secular" (with all the baggage that goes along with that; see Asad 2003), but there is no reason a religious group/party could not also espouse a left political-economic agenda (e.g., Sudan's Islamic Socialist Party or Iran's Islamic Labour Party).

38. The left "victory" in Tunisia is mixed, though, decidedly helping to usher in a new regime, yet a compromised liberal democratic one, not a meaningfully left one (see Kapoor 2020, ch. 9).

39. It should be noted that there is a certain ambivalence in Žižek's work on the question of Islam. In his political commentaries, like the ones just quoted, he speaks favorably of Islam's political potential. Yet, in his theoretical exegeses, Islam tends to come across less favorably, especially in relation to Christianity: he champions the latter, because for him, it yields to atheism, in light of its ultimate assertion of the death of God as represented by the crucifixion; whereas Islam, according to him, arriving as it does in the wake of Christianity, ends up disavowing the crucifixion and reasserting the power and omnipotence of God (see Žižek 2013, 114; 2003; Žižek and Milbank 2009; Žižek and Gunjević 2012, 64ff.; Zimeri 2015). The relationship between these two positions is left unclear, including whether Žižek thinks the lack of adequate space for atheism and the secular in Islam is an inherent obstacle to its politicization/universalization (a position that would conflict with his political commentaries on Islam).

40. The indigenous communities in the Americas (North and South) are the survivors of an unspeakable genocide by Spanish and British colonization (1492 to the mid-twentieth century), during which it is estimated that some one hundred million people died / were exterminated (hence referred to as the "Indigenous Holocaust") (Smith 2017, 11–12).

41. There were no doubt tensions between the state-led vision of Buen Vivir, which tended to compromise to a degree with the country's extractive sector (e.g., by relaxing environmental regulation) and the country's indigenous movements, which have seen Buen Vivir as a broader political program for self-determination and territoriality (see Merino 2016; Ranta 2016).

42. The interim president who replaced Morales, Jeanine Añez, declared on her ascent to power that "the Bible has re-entered the [government] palace" (Collyns 2019). Note that the Organization of American States (largely US-funded) appears to have also played a role in Morales's ouster by, as it turns out, falsely claiming that the first round

of the presidential vote, which Morales was officially declared to have won, had been rigged. Commentators believe this claim was seized upon by Bolivian right-wing groups and used as an excuse to obtain army support for the coup (Kurmanaev and Trigo 2020).

43. The cases of the Indian states of Kerala and Bengal may also be cited here, each one having been governed almost without interruption since the late 1950s and 1970s, respectively, by a democratically elected communist government. Kerala, in particular, is often heralded as a successful "model" of equitable development (although not without many of its own social problems), especially relative to the sea of inequality in the rest of the country.

44. There are several other prominent visions of Europe, including that of Habermas (2012), who sees it as the paradigm of a cosmopolitical community, and Derrida (1992), who suggests a Europe always beyond itself, open and unpredictable.

45. One should also not forget that critiques of Eurocentrism are fashionable among the likes of Putin, Erdoğan, and Mahathir, who, as purveyors of an increasingly authoritarian capitalism, are keen to dispense with questions of democracy and egalitarian justice.

46. Covid-19 indirectly intensified the public outrage of police brutality, sowing the seeds of solidarity. Undistracted by sports or other recreational activities, thrust into mass unemployment, and conscious of their own vulnerability to death through disease, people in the United States and around the world were interpellated as witnesses to this gross racial injustice.

47. As Keeanga-Yamahtta Taylor notes, "Coronavirus has scythed its way through Black communities, highlighting and accelerating the ingrained social inequities that have made African-Americans the most vulnerable to the disease" (2020). The intense focus on the global viral threat ironically obfuscates the pandemic of poverty, the "invisible" systemic violence suffered by the poor. In the United States, "Trump's economic politics centered around dismantling the welfare state are, to a large extent, responsible for the fact that many poorly paid workers find themselves in such a dire situation that, for them, poverty is a greater threat than the virus" (Žižek 2020b, 121–22).

48. Judith Butler radicalizes further Sanders's view, asking us to move beyond the rhetoric of human rights and consider healthcare "a social obligation, one that follows from living in society with one another" (2020).

49. Any medication related to Covid-19 is also subject to almost automatic price gouging. Take, for example, the drug remdesivir, which is said to reduce the recovery time for Covid-19 patients by a significant four days. Big Pharma company Gilead announced that it plans to charge each privately insured citizen in the United States $3,120 for a five-day treatment, despite the fact that remdesivir was developed in part with taxpayer money, and that the total cost to produce the drug is less than $10 (Rabin-Havt 2020). One can surely imagine more "generous" companies selling their product for modest profit (and subsequently marketing their largesse). These would be the exception to the system that keeps the fantasy of a capitalism with a human heart alive. Gilead is not a case of an unusually greedy capitalism; it is capitalism at

work, emblematic of a system that treats wealth-making—or submission to the logic of profit (it is, after all, each company's fiduciary duty to its shareholders)—as the supreme good, prioritizing profit maximization over all other *social* goods (such as health and dignity).

50. "The moment one shows a minimal sign of engaging in political projects that aim to seriously challenge the existing order, the answer is immediately: 'Benevolent as it is, this will necessarily end in a new Gulag'" (Butler, Laclau, and Žižek 2000, 217).

51. The institutionalization of "social distancing" risks quickening and homogenizing the move toward online education in schools and universities, depoliticizing higher education by making it serve more efficiently the "demands" of society as conditioned and imagined by the neoliberal market.

52. Similarly, David Quammen, author of *Spillover: Animal Infections and the Next Human Pandemic*, asserts, quite insightfully, that "we invade tropical forests and other wild landscapes, which harbor so many species of animals and plants—and within those creatures, so many unknown viruses. We cut the trees; we kill the animals or cage them and send them to markets. We disrupt ecosystems, and we shake viruses loose from their natural hosts. When that happens, they need a new host. Often, we are it" (2020).

References

"2015 Black Solidarity Statement with Palestine." http://www.blackforpalestine.com/read-the-statement.html/

Abunimah, Ali. 2020. "Israel Lobby Sees Black Lives Matter as Major Strategic Threat." *Electronic Intifada*, June 8. https://electronicintifada.net/blogs/ali-abunimah/israel-lobby-sees-black-lives-matter-major-strategic-threat.

Adalah (The Legal Center for Arab Minority Rights in Israel). 2017. http://www.adalah.org/en/content/view/7771. Accessed November 26, 2019.

Adetiba, Elizabeth, and Tarana Burke. 2018. "Tarana Burke Says #MeToo Should Center Marginalized Communities." In *Where Freedom Starts: Sex Power Violence #MeToo*, edited by Verso Books, 24–31. London: Verso.

Agamben, Giorgio. 2014. "Thought Is the Courage of Hopelessness: An Interview with Philosopher Giorgio Agamben." Interview by Jordan Skinner. *Verso Books*, June 17. https://www.versobooks.com/blogs/1612-thought-is-the-courage-of-hopelessness-an-interview-with-philosopher-giorgio-agamben.

Agamben, Giorgio. 2020a. "Clarifications." Translated by Adam Kotsko. March 17. https://itself.blog/2020/03/17/giorgio-agamben-clarifications/?fbclid=IwAR0ILFuLGompYdf7cY1WJowe_Jag00pu3azcEQw6R8jUdGaWiyk-RyTDq5M.

Agamben, Giorgio. 2020b. "The Invention of an Epidemic." *European Journal of Psychoanalysis*, February 2. https://www.journal-psychoanalysis.eu/coronavirus-and-philosophers/.

Agamben, Giorgio. 2020c. "New Reflections." April 22. https://medium.com/@ddean3000/new-reflections-giorgio-agamben-c5534e192a5e.

Ahmed, Sara. 2000. *Strange Encounters: Embodied Others in Post-coloniality*. London: Routledge.

Ahmed, Sara. 2008. "'Liberal Multiculturalism Is the Hegemony—It's an Empirical Fact'—a Response to Slavoj Žižek." *Darkmatter: In the Ruins of Imperial Culture*, February 19. http://www.darkmatter101.org/site/2008/02/19/%E2%80%98liberal-multiculturalism-is-the-hegemony-%E2%80%93-its-an-empirical-fact%E2%80%99-a-response-to-slavoj-zizek/.

Ahmed, Sara. 2014a. *The Cultural Politics of Emotion*. 2nd ed. Edinburgh: University of Edinburgh Press.

Ahmed, Sara. 2014b. *Willful Subjects*. Durham, NC: Duke University Press.

Ahmed, Sara. 2014c. "Those Who Tend to Cause Trouble." *VisAvis*, April 7. http://www.visavis.dk/2014/04/those-who-tend-to-cause-trouble/.

Alcoff, Linda Martín. 2007. "Mignolo's Epistemology of Coloniality." *CR: The New Centennial Review* 7, no. 3: 79–101.

American-Israeli Cooperative Enterprise. N.d. "U.S.-Israel Strategic Cooperation: Joint Police & Law Enforcement Training." https://www.jewishvirtuallibrary.org/joint-us-israel-police-and-law-enforcement-training. Accessed April 22, 2021.

Amin, Samir. 1976. *Unequal Development: An Essay on the Social Formations of Peripheral Capitalism*. New York: Monthly Review Press.

Amin, Samir. 1990. *Delinking: Towards a Polycentric World*. London: Zed.

Anzaldúa, Gloria. 1987. *Borderlands / La Frontera: The New Mestiza*. San Francisco: Spinsters / Aunt Lute.

Arendt, Hannah. 1958. *The Origins of Totalitarianism*. New York: Meridian Books.

Aronoff, Kate, Alyssa Battistoni, Daniel Cohen, and Thea Riofrancos. 2019. *A Planet to Win: Why We Need a Green New Deal*. London: Verso.

Asad, Talal. 2003. *Formations of the Secular: Christianity, Islam, Modernity*. Stanford, CA: Stanford University Press.

Asher, Kiran. 2013. "Latin American Decolonial Thought, or Making the Subaltern Speak." *Geography Compass* 7, no. 12: 832–42.

Badiou, Alain. 2006. *Polemics*. Translated by Steve Corcoran. London: Verso.

Badiou, Alain. 2010. *The Communist Hypothesis*. Translated by Steve Corcoran and David Macey. London: Verso.

Badiou, Alain, and Alain Finkielkraut. 2014. *Confrontation*. Translated by Susan Spitzer. Cambridge: Polity Press.

Badran, Margot. 2009. *Feminism in Islam: Secular and Religious Convergences*. Oxford: Oneworld.

Balibar, Étienne. 1991. "Citizen Subject." In *Who Comes after the Subject?*, edited by Eduardo Cadava, Peter Connor, and Jean-Luc Nancy, 33–57. New York: Routledge.

Balibar, Etienne. 2002. *Politics and the Other Scene*. London: Verso.

Balibar, Étienne. 2004. "A Complex Urgent Universal Political Cause." Address before the conference of Faculty for Israeli-Palestinian Peace (FFIPP). Université Libre de Bruxelles, July 3–4.

Balibar, Étienne. 2011. "Toward a Diasporic Citizen? From Internationalism to Cosmopolitics." In *The Creolization of Theory*, edited by Françoise Lionnet and Shu-mei Shih, 207–25. Durham, NC: Duke University Press.

Balibar, Étienne. 2014. *Equaliberty: Political Essays*. Translated by James Ingram. Durham, NC: Duke University Press.

Balibar, Étienne. 2015. *Violence and Civility: On the Limits of Political Philosophy*. Translated by G. M. Goshgarian. New York: Columbia University Press.

Balibar, Étienne. 2017a. "A New Querelle of Universals." *Philosophy Today* 61, no. 4: 929–45.

Balibar, Étienne. 2017b. "Translation and Conflict: The Violence of the Universal— a Conversation with Étienne Balibar." Interview by Jean Birnbaum. *Verso Books*, February 16. https://www.versobooks.com/blogs/3100-translation-and-conflict-the-violence-of-the-universal-a-conversation-with-etienne-balibar.

Balibar, Étienne. 2020. *On Universals: Constructing and Deconstructing Community*. Translated by Joshua David Jordan. New York: Fordham University Press.

Balibar, Étienne, and Jean-Marc Lévy-Leblond. 2006. "A Mediterranean Way for Peace in Israel-Palestine?" *Radical Philosophy* 140: 2–8.

Barr, Caelainn. 2017. "Inequality Index: Where Are the World's Most Unequal Countries?" *The Guardian*, April 26. https://www.theguardian.com/inequality/datablog/2017/apr/26/inequality-index-where-are-the-worlds-most-unequal-countries.

Baviskar, Amita. 2007. "Indian Indigeneities: Adivasi Engagements with Hindu Nationalism in India." In *Indigenous Experience Today*, edited by Marisol de la Cadena and Orin Starn, 275–304. Oxford: Berg.

BBC. 2016a. "Migrant Crisis: Migration to Europe Explained in Seven Charts." *BBC*, March 4. https://www.bbc.com/news/world-europe-34131911.

BBC. 2016b. "Wealth of Top 1% 'Equal to Other 99%.'" January 18. https://www.bbc.com/ news/business-35339475.

Beauvoir, Simone de. 2010. *The Second Sex*. Translated by Constance Borde and Sheila Malovany-Chevallier. New York: Alfred Knopf.

Bee, Vanessa A. 2020. "Would We Have Already Had a COVID-19 Vaccine under Socialism?" *In These Times*, April 20. https://inthesetimes.com/features/covid-19- coronavirus-vaccine-capitalism-socialism-innovation.html.

Beinart, Peter. 2020. "I No Longer Believe in a Jewish State." *New York Times*, July 8. https://www.nytimes.com/2020/07/08/opinion/israel-annexation-two-state- solution.html.

Benhabib, Seyla. 1984. "Epistemologies of Postmodernism: A Rejoinder to Jean-François Lyotard." *New German Critique* 33: 103–26.

Benhabib, Seyla. 1992. *Situating the Self: Gender, Community, and Postmodern Contemporary Ethics*. New York: Routledge.

Benhabib, Seyla. 2001. *Transformations of Citizenship: Dilemmas of the Nation-State in the Era of Globalization*. Amsterdam: Van Gorcum.

Benhabib, Seyla. 2004. "On Culture, Public Reason, and Deliberation: Response to Pensky and Peritz." *Constellations* 11, no. 2: 291–99.

Benhabib, Seyla. 2006. *Another Cosmopolitanism*. Oxford: Oxford University Press.

Benhabib, Seyla. 2011. *Dignity in Adversity: Human Rights in Troubled* Times. Cambridge: Polity Press.

Benhabib, Seyla. 2017. "Rethinking Questions of Belonging: An Interview with Seyla Benhabib." Interview by Matt Landes. *The Current*, Spring. http://www.columbia- current.org/rethinking-questions-of-belonging.html.

Benhabib, Seyla. 2018a. *Exile, Statelessness and Migration: Playing Chess with History from Hannah Arendt to Isaiah Berlin*. Princeton, NJ: Princeton University Press.

Benhabib, Seyla. 2018b. "Painting the Others: Law, Ethics and 'the Right to Have Rights' between Cosmopolitan Identities and Cultural Claims." Interview by David Ragazzoni. *Cosmopolis* 15: 1–2. https://www.cosmopolisonline.it/articolo. php?numero=IV12009&id=14.

Bennett, Jane. 2004. "The Force of Things: Steps toward an Ecology of Matter." *Political Theory* 32, no. 3: 347–72.

Bennett, Jane. 2010. *Vibrant Matter: A Political Ecology of Things*. Durham, NC: Duke University Press.

Bennett, Jane. 2015. "Systems and Things: On Vital Materialism and Object- Oriented Philosophy." In *The Nonhuman Turn*, edited by Richard Grusin, 223–39. Minneapolis: University of Minnesota Press.

Berlant, Lauren. 2011. *Cruel Optimism*. Durham, NC: Duke University Press.

Bhabha, Homi. 2003. "Statement for the Critical Inquiry Board Symposium." *Critical Inquiry* 30, no. 2: 342–49.

Bloch, Nadine. 2015. "The Art of #BlackLivesMatter." *OpenDemocracy*, February 3. https:// www.opendemocracy.net/transformation/nadine-bloch/art-of-blacklivesmatter.

Bowen, John R. 2007. *Why the French Don't Like Headscarves: Islam, the State, and Public Space*. Princeton, NJ: Princeton University Press.

Brockelman, Thomas. 2003. "The Failure of the Radical Democratic Imaginary: Žižek versus Laclau and Mouffe on Vestigial Utopia." *Philosophy & Social Criticism* 29, no. 2: 183–208.

Brody, Richard. 2019. "*Joker* Is a Viewing Experience of Rare, Numbing Emptiness." *New Yorker*, October 3. https://www.newyorker.com/culture/the-front-row/joker-is-a-viewing-experience-of-rare-numbing-emptiness.

Bronfenbrenner, Kate, ed. 2007. *Global Unions: Challenging Transnational Capital through Cross-Border Campaigns*. Ithaca, NY: Cornell University Press.

Brown, Wendy. 1995. *States of Injury: Power and Freedom in Late Modernity*. Princeton, NJ: Princeton University Press.

Brown, Wendy. 2005. *Edgework: Critical Essays on Knowledge and Politics*. Princeton, NJ: Princeton University Press.

Bruckner, Pascal. 1986. *The Tears of the White Man: Compassion as Contempt*. Translated by William R. Beer. New York: Free Press.

Bryant, Levi R. 2011a. *The Democracy of Objects*. Ann Arbor: Open Humanities Press.

Bryant, Levi R. 2011b. "Of Parts and Politics: Onticology and Queer Politics." *Identities* 8, no. 1: 13–28.

Butler, Judith. 1993. *Bodies That Matter: On the Discursive Limits of "Sex"*. New York: Routledge.

Butler, Judith. 2012. *Parting Ways: Jewishness and the Critique of Zionism*. New York: Columbia University Press.

Butler, Judith. 2020. "Capitalism Has Its Limits." *Verso Books*, March 30. https://www.versobooks.com/blogs/4603-capitalism-has-its-limits.

Butler, Judith, and Athena Athanasiou. 2013. *Dispossession: The Performative in the Political*. Cambridge: Polity Press.

Butler, Judith, Ernesto Laclau, and Slavoj Žižek. 2000. *Contingency, Hegemony, Universality: Contemporary Dialogues on the Left*. London: Verso.

Cadena, Marisol de la, and Orin Starn. 2007. "Introduction." In *Indigenous Experience Today*, edited by Marisol de la Cadena and Orin Starn, 1–32. Oxford: Berg.

Cardoso, Fernando Henrique, and Enzo Faletto. 1979. *Dependency and Development in Latin America*. Berkeley: University of California Press.

Castro-Gomez, Santiago. 2008. "(Post)coloniality for Dummies: Latin American Perspectives on Modernity, Coloniality, and the Geopolitics of Knowledge." In *Coloniality at Large: Latin America and the Postcolonial Debate*, edited by Mabel Moraña, Enrique D. Dussel, and Carlos A. Jáuregui, 259–85. Durham, NC: Duke University Press.

Césaire, Aimé. 2000. *Discourse on Colonialism*. Translated by Joan Pinkham. New York: Monthly Review Press.

Clarno, Andy. 2017. *Neoliberal Apartheid: Palestine/Israel and South Africa after 1994*. Chicago: University of Chicago Press.

Coates, Ta-Nehisi. 2015. *Between the World and Me*. New York: Spiegel and Grau.

Collins, Jon. 2012. "Minn. Police Learn from Israeli Counter-Terrorism Conference." *MPR News*, June 26. https://www.mprnews.org/story/2012/06/25/minn-police-learn-from-israeli-counter-terrorism-conference?fbclid=IwAR0-nzeeD1v7XzIPaobpROPHpYae4 3lJhgECZRU3OgwK2_bJhSfwY5ic2AQ.

Collyns, Dan. 2019. "Bolivia President's Initial Indigenous-Free Cabinet Heightens Polarization." *The Guardian*, November 14. https://www.theguardian.com/world/ 2019/nov/14/bolivia-president-jeanine-anez-cabinet-indigenous.

Copjec, Joan. 1994. *Read My Desire: Lacan against the Historicists*. London: Verso.

Coronil, Fernando. 2008. "Elephants in the Americas? Latin American Postcoﾠﾠﾠ Studies and Global Decolonization." In *Coloniality at Large: Latin America and the Postcolonial Debate*, edited by Mabel Moraña, Enrique D. Dussel, and Carlos A. Jáuregui. Durham, NC: Duke University Press.

Cowley, Chris. 2014. "Economics." In *The Žižek Dictionary*, edited by Rex Butler, 75–79. Durham, NC: Acumen Publishing.

Crenshaw, Kimberlé. 1991. "Mapping the Margins: Intersectionality, Identity Politics and Violence against Women of Color." *Stanford Law Review* 43: 1241–99.

Cwikowski, Anne-Marie. 2021. "Negotiating the Secular and the Sacred in the Struggle for Democracy in Islam." Doctoral thesis. Toronto: Department of Political Science, University of Toronto.

D'Alisa, Giacomo, Federico Demaria, and Giorgos Kallis, eds. 2015. *Degrowth: A Vocabulary for a New Era*. London: Routledge.

Dabashi, Hamid. 2015. *Can Non-Europeans Think?* London: Zed Books.

Daly, Herman E. 1992. *Steady-State Economics*. London: Earthscan.

Davies, James, and Anthony Shorrocks. 2018. "Comparing Global Inequality of Income and Wealth." United Nations University World Institute for Development Economics Research (WIDER), Working Paper 160. https://www.wider.unu.edu/sites/default/files/Publications/Working-paper/PDF/wp2018-160.pdf.

Davis, Angela Y. 2016. *Freedom Is a Constant Struggle: Ferguson, Palestine, and the Foundations of a* Movement. Chicago: Haymarket Books.

de Sousa Santos, Boaventura. 2016. "Epistemologies of the South and the Future." *From the European South* 1: 17–29.

Dean, Jodi. 2006. *Žižek's Politics*. New York: Routledge.

Deleuze, Gilles. 1990. *The Logic of Sense*. Translated by Mark Lester with Charles Stivale. New York: Columbia University Press.

Derbyshire, Jonathan. 2009. "Interview with Slavoj Zizek." *New Statesman*, October 29. https://www.newstatesman.com/ideas/2009/10/today-interview-capitalism.

Derrida, Jacques. 1992. *The Other Heading: Reflections on Today's Europe*. Bloomington: Indiana University Press.

Dershowitz, Alan. 2016. "Black Lives Matter Must Rescind Anti-Israel Declaration." *Boston Globe*, August 12. https://www.bostonglobe.com/opinion/columns/2016/08/12/black-lives-matter-must-rescind-anti-israel-declaration/EHDYV3gNLwrTTwfp0JA8QN/story.html.

Devji, Faisal. 2008. *The Terrorist in Search of Humanity: Militant Islam and Global Politics*. New York: Oxford University Press.

Douzinas, Costas, and Slavoj Žižek. 2010. *The Idea of Communism*. London: Verso.

Edelman, Lee. 2004. *No Future: Queer Theory and the Death Drive*. Durham, NC: Duke University Press.

Eisenstein, Paul, and Todd McGowan. 2012. *Rupture: On the Emergence of the Political*. Evanston, IL: Northwestern University Press.

Elliott, Larry. 2019. "World's 26 Richest People Own as Much as Poorest 50%, Says Oxfam." *The Guardian*, January 21. https://www.theguardian.com/business/2019/jan/21/world-26-richest-people-own-as-much-as-poorest-50-per-cent-oxfam-report.

Else, Liz. 2010. "Slavoj Zizek: Wake Up and Smell the Apocalypse." *New Scientist*, August 28: 28–29.

Enns, Diane. 2005. "A Conversation with Etienne Balibar." *Symposium* 9, no. 2: 375–99.

Erakat, Noura. 2019. *Justice for Some: Law and the Question of* Palestine. Stanford, CA: Stanford University Press.

Escobar, Arturo. 2008. *Territories of Difference: Place, Movements, Life, Redes*. Durham, NC: Duke University Press.

Escobar, Arturo. 2018. "Transition Discourses and the Politics of Relationality: Towards Designs for the Pluriverse." In *Constructing the Pluriverse: The Geopolitics of Knowledge*, edited by Bernd Reiter, 90–116. Durham, NC: Duke University Press.

Faludi, Susan. 2020. "'Believe All Women' Is a Right-Wing Trap." *New York Times*, May 18. https://www.nytimes.com/2020/05/18/opinion/tara-reade-believe-all-women.html?smid=em-share&login=email&auth=login-email.

Fanon, Frantz. 1963. *The Wretched of the Earth*. Translated by Richard Philcox. New York: Grove Press.

Fanon, Frantz. 2008. *Black Skin, White Masks*. Translated by Richard Philcox. New York: Grove Press.

Fauci, Anthony. 2020. "Dr. Fauci Answers Trevor's Questions about Coronavirus." Interview by Trevor Noah. *Daily Social Distancing Show*, March 26. https://www.youtube.com/watch?v=8A3jiM2FNR8.

Finkielkraut, Alain. 1994. *The Imaginary Jew*. Translated by Kevin O'Neill and David Suchoff. Lincoln: University of Nebraska Press.

Finkielkraut, Alain. 1995. *The Defeat of the Mind*. Translated by Judith Friedlander. New York: Columbia University Press.

Finkielkraut, Alain. 2005. "The Religion of Humanity and the Sin of the Jews." *Azure* 21: 23–32.

Finkielkraut, Alain. 2010. "Remembrance and Resentment." Seventh International Conference on Holocaust Education: "Shoah Education and Remembrance in Hindsight and in Foresight: Text and Context," June 12–13. https://www.yadvashem.org/education/intl-conferences/2010.html.

Finkielkraut, Alain. 2013a. *L'identité malheureuse*. Paris: Stock.

Finkielkraut, Alain. 2013b. "'There Is a Clash of Civilizations': Interview with Alain Finkielkraut." Interview by Mathieu von Rohr and Romain Leick. *Spiegel Online*, December 6. https://www.spiegel.de/international/world/interview-french-philosopher-finkielkraut-on-muslims-and-integration-a-937404-2.html.

Foucault, Michel. 1970. *The Order of Things: An Archaeology of the Human Sciences*. London: Tavistock.

Foucault, Michel. 1972. *Archaeology of Knowledge*. New York: Pantheon.

Foucault, Michel. 1978. *The History of Sexuality*. Vol. 1: *An Introduction*. New York: Pantheon.

Foucault, Michel. 1980. *Power/Knowledge: Selected Interviews and Other Writings, 1972–1977*. Edited by Colin Gordon. New York: Pantheon Books.

Foucault, Michel. 1983. "On the Genealogy of Ethics: A Work in Progress." In *Michel Foucault: Beyond Structuralism and Hermeneutics*, edited by Hubert L. Dreyfus and Paul Rabinow, 229–52. Chicago: University of Chicago Press.

Foucault, Michel. 1985. *The History of Sexuality*. Vol. 2: *The Use of Pleasure*. New York: Pantheon.

Foucault, Michel. 1986. *The History of Sexuality*. Vol. 3: *The Care of the Self*. New York: Pantheon.

Foucault, Michel. 2008. *The Birth of Biopolitics: Lectures at the Collège de France, 1978–79*. Basingstoke: Palgrave Macmillan.

Frank, Andre Gunder. 1967. *Capitalism and Underdevelopment in Latin America*. New York: Monthly Review Press.

Fraser, Nancy. 1981. "Foucault on Modern Power: Empirical Insights and Normative Confusions." *Praxis International* 1, no. 3: 272–87.

Fraser, Nancy, and Linda Nicholson. 1988. "Social Criticism without Philosophy: An Encounter between Feminism and Postmodernism." In *Universal Abandon? The Politics of Postmodernism*, edited by Andrew Ross, 83–104. Minneapolis: University of Minnesota Press.

Freud, Sigmund. 1953–74. *The Interpretation of Dreams*. In *The Standard Edition of the Complete Psychological Works of Sigmund Freud*, vol. 4, edited by James Strachey, ix–627. London: Hogwarth.

Garcia, Sandra E. 2017. "The Woman Who Created #MeToo Long before Hashtags." *New York Times*, October 20. https://www.nytimes.com/2017/10/20/us/me-too-movement-tarana-burke.html.

Garwood, Edith. 2016. "With Whom Are Many U.S. Police Departments Training? With a Chronic Human Rights Violator—Israel." *Amnesty International*, August 25. https://www.amnestyusa.org/with-whom-are-many-u-s-police-departments-training-with-a-chronic-human-rights-violator-israel/.

Geraghty, Jim. 2019. "Burning It All Down, Nihilism, and the Joker." *National Review*, September 4. https://www.nationalreview.com/corner/burning-it-all-down-nihilism-and-the-joker/.

Ghosh, Bobby. 2015. "Talking Politics, Diabetes, and Socks with Iran's Most Liberal Grand Ayatollah." *Quartz*, December 9. https://qz.com/569314/talking-politics-diabetes-and-socks-with-irans-most-liberal-grand-ayatollah/.

Gill, Rosalind, and Shani Orgad. 2018. "The Shifting Terrain of Sex and Power: From the 'Sexualization of Culture' to #MeToo." *Sexualities* 21, no. 8: 1313–24.

Glynos, Jason. 2002. "Psychoanalysis Operates upon the Subject of Science: Lacan between Science and Ethics." In *Lacan and Science*, edited by Jason Glynos and Yannis Stavrakakis, 51–88. New York: Karnac Books.

Goldberg, David Theo. 2015. "Why 'Black Lives Matter' Because All Lives Don't Matter in America." *Huffington Post*, September 25. https://www.huffingtonpost.com/david-theo-goldberg/why-black-lives-matter_b_8191424.html.

Gramsci, Antonio. 2000. *The Gramsci Reader: Selected Writings, 1916–1935*. Edited by David Forgacs. New York: New York University Press.

Habermas, Jürgen. 1987. *The Philosophical Discourse of Modernity: Twelve Lectures*. Cambridge: Polity Press.

Habermas, Jürgen. 2012. *The Crisis of the European Union: A Response*. Cambridge: Polity Press.

Haddad, Toufic. 2016. *Palestine Ltd.: Neoliberalism and Nationalism in the Occupied Territories*. London: I.B. Tauris.

Haider, Asad. 2018. *Mistaken Identity: Race and Class in the Age of Trump*. London: Verso.

Halberstam, Jack. 2013. "The Wild Beyond: With and for the Undercommons." In *The Undercommons: Fugitive Planning & Black Study*, by Fred Moten and Stefano Harney, 2–12. New York: Minor Compositions.

Hall, Stuart. 1986. "Gramsci's Relevance for the Study of Race and Ethnicity." *Journal of Communication Inquiry* 10, no. 5: 5–27.

Hallward, Peter. 1997. "Deleuze and the 'World without Others.'" *Philosophy Today* 41, no. 4: 530–44.

Harb, Ali. 2021. "Covid-19: Why Oslo Doesn't Absolve Israel of Duty to Vaccinate Palestinians." *Middle East Eye*, January 29. https://www.middleeasteye.net/news/covid-israel-palestine-vaccine-oslo-not-absolve-duty.

Hardt, Michael, and Antonio Negri. 2000. *Empire*. Cambridge, MA: Harvard University Press.

Hardt, Michael, and Antonio Negri. 2004. *Multitude: War and Democracy in the Age of Empire*. New York: Penguin.

Hardt, Michael, and Antonio Negri. 2009. *Commonwealth*. Cambridge, MA: Belknap Press of Harvard University Press.

Hardt, Michael, and Antonio Negri. 2017. *Assembly*. Oxford: Oxford University Press.

Harney, Stefano, and Fred Moten. 2013. *The Undercommons: Fugitive Planning & Black Study*. New York: Minor Compositions.

Harten, Sven. 2011. *The Rise of Evo Morales and the MAS*. London: Zed Books.

Harvey, David. 2003. *The New Imperialism*. Oxford: Oxford University Press.

Harvey, David. 2005. *A Brief History of Neoliberalism*. Oxford: Oxford University Press.

Harvey, David. 2014. *Seventeen Contradictions and the End of Capitalism*. New York: Oxford University Press.

Heatherton, Christina. 2016. "#BlackLivesMatter and Global Visions of Abolition: An Interview with Patrisse Cullors." In *Policing the Planet: Why the Policing Crisis Led to Black Lives Matter*, edited by Jordan T. Camp and Christina Heatherton, 35–40. London: Verso.

Heer, Jeet. 2020. "Dr. Anthony Fauci Has a Target on His Back." *The Nation*, April 6. https://www.thenation.com/article/politics/fauci-target-coronavirus-trump/.

Hegel, Georg Wilhelm Friedrich. 1977. *Phenomenology of Spirit*. Translated by John Niemeyer Findlay. Oxford: Clarendon Press.

Hegel, Georg Wilhelm Friedrich. 2010. *The Science of Logic*. Translated by George Di Giovanni. Cambridge University Press.

Hélie-Lucas, Marie-Aimeé. 1994. "The Preferential Symbol for Islamic Identity: Women in Muslim Personal Laws." In *Identity Politics and Women: Cultural Reassertions and Feminisms in International Perspective*, edited by Valentine M. Moghadam, 391–407. Boulder, CO: Westview Press.

Hickel, Jason. 2017. "Is Global Inequality Getting Better or Worse? A Critique of the World Bank's Convergence Narrative." *Third World Quarterly* 38, no. 10: 2208–22.

Huntington, Samuel P. 1997. *The Clash of Civilizations and the Remaking of World Order*. London: Penguin.

Hutchings, Kimberly. 2019. "Decolonizing Global Ethics: Thinking with the Pluriverse." *Ethics & International Affairs* 33, no. 2: 115–25.

Iqbal, Muhammad. 1964. "Muhammad Iqbal: Poet and Philosopher of the Islamic Revival." In *Sources of Indian Tradition*, edited by William Theodore De Bary, 197–217. New York: Columbia University Press.

Iqbal, Muhammad. 1986. *The Reconstruction of Religious Thought in Islam*. Lahore: Iqbal Academy.

Iqtidar, Humeira, and Tanika Sarkar, eds. 2018. *Tolerance, Secularization and Democratic Politics in South Asia*. Cambridge: Cambridge University Press.

Jameson, Fredric. 1991. *Postmodernism, or The Cultural Logic of Late Capitalism*. London: Verso.

Jameson, Fredric. 2003. "Future City." *New Left Review* 21: 65–79.

Jameson, Fredric. 2011. *Representing "Capital": A Reading of Volume One*. London: Verso.

Kanbur, Ravi. 2019. "Inequality in a Global Perspective." *Oxford Review of Economic Policy* 35, no. 3: 431–44.

Kant, Immanuel. 1996. "An Answer to the Question: What Is Enlightenment?" In *What Is Enlightenment? Eighteenth-Century Answers and Twentieth-Century Questions*, edited by James Schmidt, 58–64. Berkeley: University of California Press.

Kapoor, Ilan. 2004. "Hyper-Self-Reflexive Development? Spivak on Representing the Third World 'Other.'" *Third World Quarterly* 25, no. 4: 627–647.

Kapoor, Ilan. 2008. *The Postcolonial Politics of Development*. London: Routledge.

Kapoor, Ilan. 2018. "Introduction: Psychoanalysis and the Global." In *Psychoanalysis and the Global*, edited by Ilan Kapoor, xix–xxiv. Lincoln: University of Nebraska Press.

Kapoor, Ilan. 2020. *Confronting Desire: Psychoanalysis and International Development*. Ithaca, NY: Cornell University Press.

Kelley, Robin D. G. 2019. "From the River to the Sea to Every Mountain Top: Solidarity as Worldmaking." *Journal of Palestine Studies* 48, no. 4: 69–91.

Khader, Jamil. 2013. *Cartographies of Transnationalism in Postcolonial Feminisms: Geography, Culture, Identity, Politics*. Lanham, MD: Lexington Books.

Khader, Jamil. 2015. "Why Zizek's Critics Are Wrong—and Where They Could Have Gotten It Right." *In These Times*, December 11. https://inthesetimes.com/article/18683/why-zizeks-critics-are-wrong-and-where-they-could-have-gotten-it-right.

Khalel, Sheren. 2020. "US Police Departments under Pressure to End Training Programmes with Israel." *Middle East Eye*, June 22. https://www.middleeasteye.net/news/israel-us-police-training-end-knee-neck-protests.

Khomami, Nadia. 2017. "#MeToo: How a Hashtag Became a Rallying Cry against Sexual Harassment." *The Guardian*, October 20. https://www.theguardian.com/world/2017/oct/20/women-worldwide-use-hashtag-metoo-against-sexual-harassment.

Kiely, Ray. 1999. "The Last Refuge of the Noble Savage? A Critical Assessment of Post-development Theory." *European Journal of Development Research* 11, no. 1: 30–55.

Kindig, Jessie. 2018. "Introduction." In *Where Freedom Starts: Sex Power Violence #MeToo*, edited by Verso Books, 15–23. London: Verso.

Klausen, Jimmy Casas. 2019. "Review of 'On Decoloniality: Concepts, Analytics, Praxis' (Mignolo, Walsh)." *Perspectives on Politics* 17, no. 3: 866–69.

Klein, Naomi. 2009. *The Shock Doctrine: The Rise of Disaster Capitalism*. Toronto: Alfred A. Knopf Canada.

Klein, Naomi. 2014. *This Changes Everything: Capitalism vs. the Climate*. Toronto: Alfred A. Knopf Canada.

Klein, Naomi. 2019. *On Fire: The Burning Case for a Green New Deal*. Toronto: Alfred A. Knopf Canada.

Kurmanaev, Anatoly, and Maria Silvia Trigo. 2020. "A Bitter Election. Accusations of Fraud. And Now Second Thoughts." *New York Times*, June 7. https://www.nytimes.com/2020/06/07/world/americas/bolivia-election-evo-morales.html.

Kurzman, Charles, ed. 1998. *Liberal Islam: A Source Book*. New York: Oxford University Press.

Lacan, Jacques. 1977. *The Seminar. Book XI. The Four Fundamental Concepts of Psychoanalysis*. Translated by Alan Sheridan. London: Hogarth Press and Institute of Psycho-Analysis.

Lacan, Jacques. 1998a. *The Four Fundamental Concepts of Psychoanalysis, The Seminar of Jacques Lacan, Book XI*. Edited by Jacques-Alain Miller. Translated by Alan Sheridan. New York: Norton.

Lacan, Jacques. 1998b. *On Feminine Sexuality, The Limits of Love and Knowledge, 1972–1973: Encore, The Seminar of Jacques Lacan, Book XX.* Translated by Bruce Fink. New York: Norton.

Lacan, Jacques. 2007. *The Seminar of Jacques Lacan, Book XVII: Other Side of Psychoanalysis.* Edited by Jacques-Alain Miller. Translated by Russell Grigg. New York, NY: Norton.

Laclau, Ernesto. 1990. *New Reflections on the Revolution of Our Time.* London: Routledge, Chapman & Hall.

Laclau, Ernesto. 1996. *Emancipation(s).* London: Verso.

Laclau, Ernesto. 2004. "Can Immanence Explain Social Struggles?" In *Empire's New Clothes: Reading Hardt and Negri,* edited by Paul A. Passavant and Jodi Dean, 21–30. New York: Routledge.

Laclau, Ernesto, and Chantal Mouffe. 1985. *Hegemony and Socialist Strategy: Towards a Radical Democratic Politics.* Verso.

Laclau, Ernesto, and Chantal Mouffe. 1990. "Post-Marxism without Apologies." In *New Reflections on the Revolution of Our Time,* by Ernesto Laclau, 97–132. London: Verso.

Latour, Bruno. 1993. *We Have Never Been Modern.* Translated by Catherine Porter. Cambridge, MA: Harvard University Press.

Latour, Bruno. 2004a. *Politics of Nature: How to Bring the Sciences into Democracy.* Translated by Catherine Porter. Cambridge, MA: Harvard University Press.

Latour, Bruno. 2004b. "Why Has Critique Run Out of Steam? From Matters of Fact to Matters of Concern." *Critical Inquiry* 30: 225–48.

Latour, Bruno. 2005. *Reassembling the Social: An Introduction to Actor-Network-Theory.* Oxford: Oxford University Press.

Latour, Bruno. 2020. "Is This a Dress Rehearsal?" *Critical Inquiry: Posts from the Pandemic,* March 26. https://critinq.wordpress.com/2020/03/26/is-this-a-dress-rehearsal/.

Latour, Bruno, and Nikolaj Schultz. 2019. "A Conversation with Bruno Latour and Nikolaj Schultz: Reassembling the Geo-social." *Theory, Culture & Society* 36, nos. 7–8: 215–30.

Lazar, Sian, ed. 2017. *Where Are the Unions? Workers and Social Movements in Latin America, the Middle East and Europe.* London: Zed.

Lemke, Thomas. 2016. *Foucault, Governmentality, and Critique.* New York: Routledge.

Lentin, Ronit. 2018. *Traces of Racial Exception: Racializing Israeli Settler Colonialism.* New York: Bloomsbury.

Li, Darryl. 2019. *The Universal Enemy: Jihad, Empire, and the Challenge of Solidarity.* Stanford, CA: Stanford University Press.

Lorde, Andre. 1984. "'The Master's Tools Will Never Dismantle the Master's House." In *Sister Outsider: Essays and Speeches,* 110–13. Berkeley, CA: Crossing Press.

Lyotard, Jean-François. 1984. *The Postmodern Condition: A Report on Knowledge.* Translated by Geoff Bennington and Brian Massumi. Manchester: Manchester University Press.

Lyotard, Jean-François. 1988. *The Differend: Phrases in Dispute.* Translated by Georges Van Den Abbeele. Minneapolis: University of Minnesota Press.

Maggiori, Robert, and Anastasia Vécrin. 2015. "Slavoj Žižek: Tout le monde peut être socialiste, même Bill Gates." *Libération,* June 5. https://next.liberation.fr/culture/2015/06/05/slavoj-zizek-je-reste-communiste-car-tout-le-monde-peut-etre-socialiste-meme-bill-gates_1323864.

Malabou, Catherine. 2011. *Changing Difference.* Translated by Carolyn Shread. Cambridge: Polity Press.

Manoharan, Karthick. 2019. "'We Are All Clowns'—a Defense of Joke." *Philosophical Salon*, October 14. https://thephilosophicalsalon.com/we-are-all-clowns-a-defense-of-joker/.

Marchart, Oliver. 2007. *Post-foundational Political Thought*. Edinburgh: Edinburgh University Press.

Martel, James R. 2017. *The Misinterpellated Subject*. Durham, NC: Duke University Press.

Martínez-Alier, Joan. 2012. "Environmental Justice and Economic Degrowth: An Alliance between Two Movements." *Capitalism Nature Socialism* 23, no. 1: 51–73.

Marx, Karl. 1887. *Capital: A Critique of Political Economy*. Vol. 1. Edited by Friedrich Engels. Translated by Samuel Moore and Edward Aveling. Moscow: Progress Publishers. https://www.marxists.org/archive/marx/works/1867-c1/index.htm.

Marx, Karl. 1973. *Grundrisse: Foundations of the Critique of Political Economy*. Translated by Martin Nicolaus. New York: Vintage.

Marx, Karl. 1975. "Letters from the *Deutsch-Französische Jahrbucher*." In *Collected Works of Marx and Engels*, vol. 3, 133–45. New York: International Publishers.

Marx, Karl. 1992. *Early Writings*. Harmondsworth: Penguin.

Massad, Joseph. 2013. "The Last of the Semites." *Al Jazeera*, May 21. https://www.aljazeera.com/opinions/2013/5/21/the-last-of-the-semites.

Mbembe, Achille. 2003. "Necropolitics." *Public Culture* 15: 11–40.

Mbembe, Achille. 2017. *Critique of Black Reason*. Translated by Laurent Dubois. Durham, NC: Duke University Press.

McGowan, Todd. 2013. "Hegel as Marxist: Žižek's Revision of German Idealism." In *Žižek Now: Current Perspectives in Žižek Studies*, edited by Jamil Khader and Molly Anne Rothenberg, 31–53. Cambridge: Polity Press.

McGowan, Todd. 2018. "The Absent Universal: From the Master Signifier to the Missing Signifier." *Problemi International* 2, no. 2: 195–214.

McGowan, Todd. 2019. *Emancipation after Hegel: Achieving a Contradictory Revolution*. New York: Columbia University Press.

McGowan, Todd. 2020. *Universality and Identity Politics*. New York: Columbia University Press.

McNay, Lois. 2000. *Gender and Agency: Reconfiguring the Subject in Feminist and Social Theory*. Cambridge: Polity Press.

Meillassoux, Quentin. 2008. *After Finitude: An Essay on the Necessity of Contingency*. Translated by Ray Brassier. New York: Continuum.

Menon, Madhavi. 2015. *Indifference to Difference: On Queer Universalism*. Minneapolis: University of Minnesota Press.

Merino, Roger. 2016. "An Alternative to 'Alternative Development'? Buen Vivir and Human Development in Andean Countries." *Oxford Development Studies* 44, no. 3: 271–86.

Michaelsen, Scott, and Scott Cutler Shershow. 2007. "Rethinking Border Thinking." *South Atlantic Quarterly* 106, no. 1: 39–60.

Mignolo, Walter D. 2002. "The Geopolitics of Knowledge and the Colonial Difference." *South Atlantic Quarterly* 101, no. 1: 57–96.

Mignolo, Walter D. 2003. *The Darker Side of the Renaissance: Literacy, Territoriality, and Colonization*. Ann Arbor: University of Michigan Press.

Mignolo, Walter D. 2007. "Delinking." *Cultural Studies* 21, nos. 2–3: 449–514.

Mignolo, Walter D. 2010. "Delinking: The Rhetoric of Modernity, the Logic of Coloniality and the Grammar of De-coloniality." In *Globalization and the Decolonial Option*, edited by Walter D. Mignolo and Arturo Escobar, 303–68. London: Routledge.

Mignolo, Walter D. 2011. *The Darker Side of Western Modernity: Global Futures, Decolonial Options*. Durham, NC: Duke University Press.

Mignolo, Walter D. 2012. *Local Histories / Global Designs: Coloniality, Subaltern Knowledges, and Border Thinking*. Princeton, NJ: Princeton University Press.

Mignolo, Walter D. 2015. "On Pluriversality." http://convivialism.org/?p=199.

Mignolo, Walter D. 2018. "Foreword: On Pluriversality and Multipolarity." In *Constructing the Pluriverse: The Geopolitics of Knowledge*, edited by Bernd Reiter, ix–xvi. Durham, NC: Duke University Press.

Mignolo, Walter D., and Arturo Escobar, eds. 2010. *Globalization and the Decolonial Option*. London: Routledge.

Mignolo, Walter D., and Mónica González García. 2006. "Towards a Decolonial Horizon of Pluriversality: A Dialogue with Walter Mignolo on and around the Idea of Latin America." *Lucero* 17, no. 1: 38–55.

Miller, Sarah. 2019. "My So-Karen Life." *New York Times*, December 7. https://www.nytimes.com/2019/12/07/style/its-karentown.html.

Mohanty, Chandra Talpade. 2003. *Feminism without Borders: Decolonizing Theory, Practicing Solidarity*. Durham, NC: Duke University Press.

Moore, Michael. 2019. "Review of Joker Is Posted on Facebook." October 5. https://www.facebook.com/mmflint/posts/10156278766436857.

Morgan, Robin. 1984. *Sisterhood Is Global: The International Women's Movement Anthology*. New York: Anchor Press / Doubleday.

Mosley, Ray. 1995. "Islam Is Not the Threat NATO Makes It Out to Be." *Chicago Tribune*, February 12. https://www.chicagotribune.com/news/ct-xpm-1995-02-12-9502120298-story.html.

Mouffe, Chantal. 2005a. *On the Political*. London: Routledge.

Mouffe, Chantal. 2005b. *The Return of the Political*. London: Verso.

Munayyer, Yousef. 2019. "There Will Be a One-State Solution: But What Kind of State Will It Be?" *Foreign Affairs*, November–December. https://www.foreignaffairs.com/articles/israel/2019-10-15/there-will-be-one-state-solution.

Negri, Antonio. 2008. *Reflections on Empire*. Edited by Antonio Negri. Cambridge: Polity Press.

Negri, Antonio. 2017. *Marx and Foucault: Essays*. Vol. 1. Cambridge: Polity Press.

Nossiter, Adam. 2013. "Behind Those Fast Growth Rates, Rising Inequality." *New York Times*, November 5. http://www.nytimes.com/2013/11/06/world/africa/behind-those-fast-growth-rates-rising-inequality.html.

Olssen, Mark. 2006. *Michel Foucault: Materialism and Education*. New York: Routledge.

Patterson, Orlando. 1982. *Slavery and Social Death: A Comparative Study*. Cambridge, MA: Harvard University Press.

Pember, Mary Annette. 2019. "#MeToo in Indian Country; 'We Don't Talk about This Enough.'" *Indian Country Today*, May 28. https://indiancountrytoday.com/news/metoo-in-indian-country-we-don-t-talk-about-this-enough-oXkstdPmDk2-zSXoDXZSZQ.

Perkins, Patricia E., ed. 2020. *Local Activism for Global Climate Justice: The Great Lakes Watershed*. Abingdon, Oxon: Routledge.

Pieterse, Jan Nederveen. 2000. "After Post-development." *Third World Quarterly* 21, no. 2: 175–91.

Piketty, Thomas. 2014. *Capital in the Twenty-First Century*. Translated by Arthur Goldhammer. Cambridge, MA: Belknap Press of Harvard University Press.

Platt, Stephen R. 2012. "Is China Ripe for a Revolution?" *New York Times*, February 9. https://www.nytimes.com/2012/02/12/opinion/sunday/is-china-ripe-for-a-revolution.html.

Posner, Gerald. 2020. "Big Pharma May Pose an Obstacle to Vaccine Development." *New York Times*, March 2. https://www.nytimes.com/2020/03/02/opinion/contributors/pharma-vaccines.html.

Puar, Jasbir K. 2012. "'I Would Rather Be a Cyborg Than a Goddess': Becoming-Intersectional in Assemblage Theory." *philoSOPHIA* 2, no. 1: 49–66.

Quammen, David. 2020. "We Made the Coronavirus Epidemic." *New York Times*, January 28. https://www.nytimes.com/2020/01/28/opinion/coronavirus-china.html?smtyp=cur&smid=tw-nytopinion.

Quijano, Aníbal. 2000. "Coloniality of Power and Eurocentrism in Latin America." *International Sociology* 15, no. 2: 215–32.

Quijano, Aníbal. 2007. "Coloniality and Modernity/Rationality." *Cultural Studies* 21, nos. 2–3: 168–78.

Rabin-Havt, Ari. 2020. "COVID-19 Treatments Belong to the People, Not Price-Gouging Pharma Companies." *Jacobin*, July 2. https://www.jacobinmag.com/2020/07/remdesivir-gilead-science-coronavirus-covid-treatment-cost.

Rahnema, Saeed. 2009. "The Tragedy of the Left's Discourse on Iran." *Europe Solidaire sans Frontières*, July 9. http://europe-solidaire.org/spip.php?article14358.

Rancière, Jacques. 1999. *Disagreement: Politics and Philosophy*. Minneapolis: University of Minnesota Press.

Rancière, Jacques. 2010. *Dissensus: On Politics and Aesthetics*. Translated by Steve Corcoran. London: Continuum.

Ranta, Eija Maria. 2016. "Toward a Decolonial Alternative to Development? The Emergence and Shortcomings of Vivir Bien as State Policy in Bolivia in the Era of Globalization." *Globalizations* 13, no. 4: 425–39.

Renan, Ernest. 1883. *L'Islamisme et la science*. Paris: Ancienne Maison Michel Lévy Frères.

Reul, Sabine, and Thomas Deichmann. 2001. "The One Measure of True Love Is: You Can Insult the Other." *Spiked*, November 15. http://www.spiked-online.com/newsite/article/10816#.W0VMLxD3N54.

Rickford, Russell. 2019. "To Build a New World": Black American Internationalism and Palestine Solidarity." *Journal of Palestine Studies* 48, no. 4: 52–68.

Roberts, Sean R. 2020. *The War on the Uyghurs: China's Internal Campaign against a Muslim Minority*. Princeton, NJ: Princeton University Press.

Ronchi, Rocco. 2020. "The Virtues of the Virus." *European Journal of Psychoanalysis*, March 14. https://www.journal-psychoanalysis.eu/coronavirus-and-philosophers/.

Rose, Jacqueline. 2018. "I Am a Knife." *London Review of Books*, February 22.

Rottenberg, Catherine. 2017. "Can #MeToo Go Beyond White Neoliberal Feminism?" *Al Jazeera*, December 13. https://www.aljazeera.com/indepth/opinion/metoo-white-neoliberal-feminism-171213064156855.html.

Rottenberg, Catherine. 2018. *The Rise of Neoliberal Feminism*. Oxford: Oxford University Press.

Rozsa, Matthew. 2020. "How *Joker* Became a Victim of the White Male Rage It Depicts." *Salon*, February 8. https://www.salon.com/2020/02/08/joker-oscars-white-male-rage-win/.

Ruti, Mari. 2018. *Distillations: Theory, Ethics, Affect*. New York: Bloomsbury.

Safi, Omid, ed. 2003. *Progressive Muslims on Justice, Gender, and Pluralism*. New York: Oneworld Publications.

Said, Edward W. 1979. *Orientalism*. New York: Vintage Books.

Said, Edward W. 1983. *The World, the Text and the Critic*. Cambridge, MA: Harvard University Press.

Said, Edward W. 1994. *Culture and Imperialism*. New York: Vintage Books.

Said, Edward W. 1996. *Representations of the Intellectual: The 1993 Reith Lectures*. New York: Vintage Books.

Said, Edward W. 1999. "The One-State Solution." *New York Times*, January 10. https://www.nytimes.com/1999/01/10/magazine/the-one-state-solution.html.

Said, Edward W. 2000. *The Edward Said Reader*, edited by Moustafa Bayoumi and Andrew Rubi. New York: Vintage Books.

Said, Edward W. 2001. "My Right of Return." In *Power, Politics, and Culture: Interviews with Edward W. Said*, edited by Gauri Viswanathan, 443–58. New York: Vintage.

Said, Edward. W. 2003. *Orientalism*. 25th anniversary ed. New York: Vintage Books.

Said, Edward W. 2014. *Freud and the Non-European*. London: Verso.

Salhi, Zahia Smail. 2013. *Gender and Violence in Islamic Societies: Patriarchy, Islamism and Politics in the Middle East and North Africa*. London: Bloomsbury.

Sardar, Ziauddin. 1999. *Orientalism*. Buckingham: Open University Press.

Scott, Mark, and Steven Overly. 2020. "Conspiracy Theorists, Far-Right Extremists around the World Seize on the Pandemic." *Politico*, May 13. https://www.politico.com/news/2020/05/12/trans-atlantic-conspiracy-coronavirus-251325.

Sekyi-Otu, Ato. 1996. *Fanon's Dialectic of Experience*. Cambridge, MA: Harvard University Press. http://www.library.yorku.ca/e/resolver/id/1977527.

Sekyi-Otu, Ato. 2019. *Left Universalism: Africacentric Essays*. New York: Routledge.

Sexton, Jared. 2008. *Amalgamation Schemes: Antiblackness and the Critique of Multiracialism*. Minneapolis: University of Minnesota Press.

Sexton, Jared. 2010. "People-of-Color-Blindness: Notes on the Afterlife of Slavery." *Social Text* 28, no. 2 (issue 103): 31–56.

Sexton, Jared. 2011. "The Social Life of Social Death: On Afro-Pessimism and Black Optimism." *In*Tensions 5: 1–47.

Sexton, Jared. 2019. "Affirmation in the Dark: Racial Slavery and Philosophical Pessimism." *The Comparatist* 43: 90–111.

Shalhoub-Kevorkian, Nadera, Sarah Ihmoud, and Suhad Dahir-Nashif. 2014. "Sexual Violence, Women's Bodies, and Israeli Settler Colonialism." *Jadaliyya*, November 17. https://www.jadaliyya.com/Details/31481.

Shamir, Ronen. 2008. "The Age of Responsibilization: On Market-Embedded Morality." *Economy and Society* 37, no. 1: 1–19.

Sharma, Sanjay, and Ashwani Sharma. 2000. "'So Far So Good . . .': *La Haine* and the Poetics of the Everyday." *Theory Culture & Society* 17, no. 3: 103–16.

Sindayigaya, Aime Muligo. 2015. "Rwanda: Looking beyond Economic Growth Numbers (Part One)." *Insightful Quotient*, February 23. http://insightfulquotient.com/rwanda-looking-beyond-economic-growth-numbers-part-one/.

Smith, David Michael. 2017. "Counting the Dead: Estimating the Loss of Life in the Indigenous Holocaust, 1492–Present." University of Houston–Downtown. https://web.archive.org/web/20190702051019/http://www.se.edu/nas/files/2018/08/A-NAS-2017-Proceedings-Smith.pdf.

Stam, Robert, and Ella Shohat. 2012. *Race in Translation: Culture Wars around the Postcolonial Atlantic*. New York: New York University Press.

Storey, Andy. 2000. "Post-development Theory: Romanticism and Pontius Pilate Politics." *Development* 43, no. 4: 40–46.

Storm, Servaas. 2018. "Financial Markets Have Taken Over the Economy: To Prevent Another Crisis, They Must Be Brought to Heel." *Institute for New Economic Thinking*, February 13. https://www.ineteconomics.org/perspectives/blog/financial-markets-have-taken-over-the-economy-to-stop-the-next-crisis-they-must-be-brought-to-heel.

Strickland, Patrick. 2014. "Bombing of Gaza Children Gives Me 'Orgasm': Israelis Celebrate Slaughter on Facebook." *Electronic Intifada*, July 13. https://electronicintifada.net/blogs/patrick-strickland/bombing-gaza-children-gives-me-orgasm-israelis-celebrate-slaughter-facebook.

Swyngedouw, Erik. 2011. "Whose Environment? The End of Nature, Climate Change and the Process of Post-politicization." *Ambiente & Sociedade* 14, no. 2: 69–87.

Taguieff, Pierre-André. 2004. *Rising from the Muck: The New Anti-Semitism in Europe*. Chicago: Ivan R. Dee.

Tamari, Sandra. 2020. "The Problem with Israel's Annexation Is Its Brutality, Not Its Optics." *In These Times*, July 1. http://inthesetimes.com/article/22638/annexation-israel-palestine-apartheid-aipac-j-street-biden?link_id=5&can_id=839242f129 045dcf95563791cad9b53c&source=email-the-lefts-resurgence-is-for-real-first-you-bomb-and-starve-a-country-then-youre-praised-for-sending-in-aid&email_referrer=email_850963&email_subject=your-white-neighbors-black-lives-matter-yard-sign-is-not-enough-frederick-douglass-on-the-meaning-of-july-4th.

Tambe, Ashwini. 2018. "Reckoning with the Silences of #MeToo." *Feminist Studies* 44, no. 1: 197–203.

Tayeb, Sami. 2019. "The Palestinian McCity in the Neoliberal Era." *Middle East Report* 290: 24–28.

Taylor, Chloe. 2017. *The Routledge Guidebook to Foucault's "The History of Sexuality"*. New York: Routledge.

Taylor, Keeanga-Yamahtta. 2020. "Of Course There Are Protests. The State Is Failing Black People." *New York Times*, May 29. https://www.nytimes.com/2020/05/29/opinion/george-floyd-minneapolis.html.

Telesur. 2017. "Morales Declares 'Total Independence' from World Bank and IMF." July 22. https://www.telesurenglish.net/news/Morales-Declares-Total-Independence-from-World-Bank-and-IMF--20170722-0020.html.

Thunberg, Greta. 2019. "'You Did Not Act in Time': Greta Thunberg's Full Speech to MPs." *The Guardian*, April 23. https://www.theguardian.com/environment/2019/apr/23/greta-thunberg-full-speech-to-mps-you-did-not-act-in-time.

Tobin, Damian. 2011. "Inequality in China: Rural Poverty Persists as Urban Wealth Balloons." *BBC News*, June 29.

Tomba, Massimiliano. 2019. *Insurgent Universality: An Alternative Legacy of Modernity*. New York: Oxford University Press.

UNDP (United Nations Development Programme). 2016. *Human Development Report 2016: Human Development for Everyone*. New York.

USACBI (US Campaign for the Academic and Cultural Boycott of Israel). 2020. "Important Victory for the Campaign to Boycott Israeli Universities." July 8. https://usacbi.org/2020/07/important-victory-for-the-campaign-to-boycott-israeli-universities/.

Varoufakis, Yanis. 2019. "Interview: Yanis Varoufakis on Capitalism, Democracy and Europe." *DiEM25* (blog), November 4. https://diem25.org/interview-yanis-varoufakis-on-capitalism-democracy-and-europe/.

Varoufakis, Yanis, and David Adler. 2019. "It's Time for Nations to Unite around an International Green New Deal." *The Guardian*, April 23. https://www.theguardian.com/commentisfree/2019/apr/23/international-green-new-deal-climate-change-global-response.

Victor, Peter A. 2008. *Managing without Growth: Slower by Design, Not Disaster.* Cheltenham, UK: Edward Elgar.

Vighi, Fabio. 2020. "The Absent Cause: Time, Work and Value in the Age of Coronavirus." *Philosophical Salon*, June 4. https://thephilosophicalsalon.com/the-absent-cause-time-work-and-value-in-the-age-of-coronavirus/.

Vighi, Fabio, and Heiko Feldner. 2006. "United States of Europe or Free Trade Zone? No Thanks! Slavoj Žižek on the Future of Europe." *European Journal of Social Theory* 9, no. 3: 337–54.

Vighi, Fabio, and Heiko Feldner. 2007. *Žižek: Beyond Foucault.* Basingstoke: Palgrave-Macmillan.

Visweswaran, Kamala. 1994. *Fictions of Feminist Ethnography.* Minneapolis: University of Minnesota Press.

Wallerstein, Immanuel Maurice. 2004. *World-Systems Analysis: An Introduction.* Durham, NC: Duke University Press.

Warren, Calvin. 2018. *Ontological Terror: Blackness, Nihilism, and Emancipation.* Durham, NC: Duke University Press.

Webber, Jeffery R. 2017a. "Evo Morales, Transformismo, and the Consolidation of Agrarian Capitalism in Bolivia." *Journal of Agrarian Change* 17, no. 2: 330–47.

Webber, Jeffery R. 2017b. *The Last Day of Oppression, and the First Day of the Same: The Politics and Economics of the New Latin American Left.* Chicago: Haymarket Books.

Weiss, Philip. 2020. "George Floyd Killing Highlights Issue of US Police Training In Israel." *Mondoweiss*, June 4. https://mondoweiss.net/2020/06/george-floyd-killing-highlights-issue-of-us-police-training-in-israel/.

West, Cornel. 2016. "Black America's Neo-liberal Sleepwalking Is Coming to an End." Interview by George Souvlis. *OpenDemocracy*, June 13. https://www.opendemocracy.net/en/cornel-west-black-america-s-neo-liberal-sleepwalking-is-coming-to-end/.

Weston, Burns H., and David Bollier. 2013. *Green Governance: Ecological Survival, Human Rights, and the Law of the Commons.* Cambridge: Cambridge University Press.

"When I See Them I See Us." 2015. *Washington Post*, October 14. https://www.washingtonpost.com/video/world/when-i-see-them-i-see-us/2015/10/15/c8f8aa40-72c2-11e5-ba14-318f8e87a2fc_video.html.

WID (World Inequality Database). 2019. "Income Inequality, Rwanda, 2019." https://wid.world/country/rwanda/.

Wilderson, Frank B., III. 2003. "Gramsci's Black Marx: Whither the Slave in Civil Society?" *Social Identities* 9, no. 2: 225–40.

Wilderson, Frank B., III. 2010. *Red, White & Black: Cinema and the Structure of U.S. Antagonisms.* Durham, NC: Duke University Press.

Wilderson, Frank B., III. 2016. "'The Inside-Outside of Civil Society': An Interview with Frank B. Wilderson, III." Interview by Samira Spatzek, and Paula von Gleich. *Black Studies Papers* 2, no. 1: 4–22.

Wilderson, Frank B., III. 2018. "'We're Trying to Destroy the World': Anti-blackness and Police Violence after Ferguson Pages." In *Shifting Corporealities in Contemporary Performance: Danger, Im/mobility and Politics*, edited by Marina Gržinić and Aneta Stojnić, 45–59. New York: Palgrave.

Wilderson, Frank B., III. 2020. *Afropessimism*. New York: Liveright.

Wilderson, Frank B., III, Saidya Hartman, Steve Martinot, Jared Sexton, and Hortense J. Spillers. 2017. "Editors' Introduction." In *Afro-Pessimism: An Introduction*, edited by Frank B. Wilderson III, Saidya Hartman, Steve Martinot, Jared Sexton, and Hortense J. Spillers, 7–13. Minneapolis: Racked & Dispatched.

Wilson, Japhy, and Erik Swyngedouw. 2014. "Seeds of Dystopia: Post-politics and the Return of the Political." In *The Post-political and Its Discontents: Spaces of Depoliticisation, Spectres of Radical Politics*, edited by Japhy Wilson and Erik Swyngedouw, 1–22. Edinburgh: Edinburgh University Press.

Wolfe, Patrick. 2013. "Recuperating Binarism: A Heretical Introduction." *Settler Colonial Studies* 3, nos. 3–4: 257–79.

Wolff, Jonas. 2019. "The Political Economy of Post-neoliberalism in Bolivia: Policies, Elites, and the MAS Government." *European Review of Latin American and Caribbean Studies* 108 (December): 109–29.

Yancy, George, and Seyla Benhabib. 2015. "Whom Does Philosophy Speak For?" *New York Times*, October 29. http://opinionator.blogs.nytimes.com/2015/10/29/who-does-philosophy-speak-for/.

Yang, Yuan, and Nian Liu. 2020. "Inside China's Race to Beat Poverty." *Financial Times*, June 25.

Zalloua, Zahi. 2017. *Continental Philosophy and the Palestinian Question: Beyond the Jew and the Greek*. New York: Bloomsbury.

Zalloua, Zahi. 2020. *Žižek on Race: Toward an Anti-racist Future*. New York: Bloomsbury.

Zamora, Daniel, and Michael C. Behrent, eds. 2016. *Foucault and Neoliberalism*. Cambridge: Polity Press.

Zegada, María Teresa. 2011. *La democracia desde los márgenes: Transformaciones en el campo político boliviano*. Buenos Aires: CLASCO. https://searchworks.stanford.edu/view/9544976.

Zerilli, Linda M. G. 1998. "This Universalism Which Is Not One." *Diacritics* 28, no. 2: 3–20.

Zimeri, Sead. 2015. "Islam: How Could It Have Emerged after Christianity?" In *Repeating Žižek*. Durham, NC: Duke University Press.

Žižek, Slavoj. 1989. *The Sublime Object of Ideology*. London: Verso.

Žižek, Slavoj. 1990. "Beyond Discourse Analysis." In *New Reflections on the Revolution of Our Time*, edited by Ernesto Laclau, 249–60. London: Verso.

Žižek, Slavoj. 1991. *For They Know Not What They Do: Enjoyment as a Political Factor*. London: Verso.

Žižek, Slavoj. 1992. *Enjoy Your Symptom! Jacques Lacan in Hollywood and Out*. New York: Routledge.

Žižek, Slavoj. 1993. *Tarrying with the Negative: Kant, Hegel, and the Critique of Ideology*. Durham, NC: Duke University Press.

Žižek, Slavoj. 1997a. "Multiculturalism, or, the Cultural Logic of Multinational Capitalism." *New Left Review* 225, no. 1: 28–51.

Žižek, Slavoj. 1997b. *The Plague of Fantasies*. London: Verso.

Žižek, Slavoj. 1998. "A Leftist Plea for 'Eurocentrism.'" *Critical Inquiry* 24, no. 4: 988–1009.

Žižek, Slavoj. 1999. *The Ticklish Subject: The Absent Center of Political Ontology.* London: Verso.

Žižek, Slavoj. 2000a. *The Fragile Absolute; or, Why Is the Christian Legacy Worth Fighting For?* London: Verso.

Žižek, Slavoj. 2000b. "Holding the Place." In *Contingency, Hegemony, Universality: Contemporary Dialogues on the Left,* edited by Judith Butler, Ernesto Laclau, and Slavoj Žižek, 308–29. London: Verso.

Žižek, Slavoj. 2002a. "Afterword: Lenin's Choice." In V. I. Lenin, *Revolution at the Gates: Selected Writings of Lenin from 1917,* edited by Slavoj Žižek, 165–336. London: Verso.

Žižek, Slavoj. 2002b. *Welcome to the Desert of the Real.* London: Verso.

Žižek, Slavoj. 2002c. "I Plead Guilty—but Where Is the Judgment?" *Nepantla: Views from South* 3, no. 3: 579–83.

Žižek, Slavoj, ed. 2002d. *Revolution at the Gates: Selected Writings of Lenin from 1917.* London: Verso.

Žižek, Slavoj. 2003. *The Puppet and the Dwarf: The Perverse Core of Christianity.* Cambridge, MA: MIT Press.

Žižek, Slavoj. 2004a. "Ethical Socialism? No, Thanks! Reply to Boucher." *Telos* 129: 173–89.

Žižek, Slavoj. 2004b. *Iraq: The Borrowed Kettle.* London: Verso.

Žižek, Slavoj. 2004c. *Organs without Bodies: On Deleuze and Consequences.* New York: Routledge.

Žižek, Slavoj. 2005a. "Against Human Rights." *New Left Review* 34: 115–31.

Žižek, Slavoj. 2005b. *The Metastases of Enjoyment: Six Essays on Women and Causality.* London: Verso.

Žižek, Slavoj. 2006a. *How to Read Lacan.* New York: Norton.

Žižek, Slavoj. 2006b. "Neighbors and Other Monsters." In *The Neighbor: Three Inquiries in Political Theology,* edited by Slavoj Žižek, Eric L. Santner, and Kenneth Reinhard, 134–90. Chicago: University of Chicago Press.

Žižek, Slavoj. 2006c. *The Parallax View.* Cambridge: MIT Press.

Žižek, Slavoj. 2006d. "Against the Populist Temptation." *Critical Inquiry* 32, no. 3: 551–74. https://doi.org/10.1086/505378.

Žižek, Slavoj. 2007. "Afterword: With Defenders Like These, Who Needs Attackers?" In *The Truth of Žižek,* edited by Paul Bowman and Richard Stamp, 197–255. New York: Continuum.

Žižek, Slavoj. 2008a. *In Defense of Lost Causes.* London: Verso.

Žižek, Slavoj. 2008b. "Nature and Its Discontents." *SubStance* 37, no. 3: 37–72.

Žižek, Slavoj. 2008c. *Violence: Six Sideways Reflections.* New York: Picador.

Žižek, Slavoj. 2009a. *First as Tragedy, Then as Farce.* London: Verso.

Žižek, Slavoj. 2009b. "Berlusconi in Tehran." *London Review of Books,* July 23. https://www.lrb.co.uk/the-paper/v31/n14/slavoj-zizek/berlusconi-in-tehran.

Žižek, Slavoj. 2009c. "The Fear of Four Words: A Modest Plea for the Hegelian Reading of Christianity." In Slavoj Žižek and John Milbank, *The Monstrosity of Christ: Paradox or Dialectic?,* edited by Creston Davis, 24–109. Cambridge: MIT Press.

Žižek, Slavoj. 2009d. *Philosophy in the Present.* Cambridge: Polity Press.

Žižek, Slavoj. 2009e. "How to Begin from the Beginning." *New Left Review* 57: 43–56.

Žižek, Slavoj. 2010a. "Neighbors and Other Monsters: A Plea for Ethical Violence." In *The Neighbor: Three Inquiries in Political Theology,* edited by Slavoj Žižek, Eric L. Santner, and Kenneth Reinhard, 134–90. Chicago: University of Chicago Press.

Žižek, Slavoj. 2010b. *Living in the End of Times*. London: Verso.

Žižek, Slavoj. 2011. "From Democracy to Divine Violence." In *Democracy in What State?* Edited by Giorgio Agamben et al., 100–120. New York: Columbia University Press.

Žižek, Slavoj. 2012a. *Organs without Bodies: On Deleuze and Consequences*. London: Routledge.

Žižek, Slavoj. 2012b. *The Year of Dreaming Dangerously*. London: Verso.

Žižek, Slavoj. 2012c. "The Revolt of the Salaried Bourgeoisie." *London Review of Books*, January 26. https://www.lrb.co.uk/v34/n02/slavoj-zizek/the-revolt-of-the-salaried-bourgeoisie.

Žižek, Slavoj. 2012d. *Less Than Nothing: Hegel and the Shadow of Dialectical Materialism*. London: Verso.

Žižek, Slavoj. 2013a. *Demanding the Impossible*. Edited by Yong-June Park. Cambridge: Polity Press.

Žižek, Slavoj. 2013b. *A Reply to My Critics*. London: Birbeck Institute for the Humanities, University of London. https://backdoorbroadcasting.net/2013/02/slavoj-zizek-a-reply-to-my-critics/.

Žižek, Slavoj. 2013c. "King, Rabble, Sex, and War in Hegel." In *Žižek Now: Current Perspectives in Žižek Studies*, edited by Jamil Khader and Molly Anne Rothenberg, 177–206. Cambridge: Polity Press.

Žižek, Slavoj. 2013d. "Anti-Semitism and Its Transformations." In *Deconstructing Zionism: A Critique of Political Metaphysics*, edited by Gianni Vattimo and Michael Marder, 1–13. New York: Bloomsbury.

Žižek, Slavoj. 2014a. *Absolute Recoil: Towards a New Foundation of Dialectical Materialism*. London: Verso.

Žižek, Slavoj. 2014b. *Event: Philosophy in Transit*. London: Penguin.

Žižek, Slavoj. 2014c. *Trouble in Paradise: From the End of History to the End of Capitalism*. London: Allen Lane.

Žižek, Slavoj. 2014d. "Rotherham Child Sex Abuse: It Is Our Duty to Ask Difficult Questions." *The Guardian*, September 1. https://www.theguardian.com/commentisfree/2014/sep/01/rotherham-child-sex-abuse-difficult-questions.

Žižek, Slavoj. 2015a. "The Charlie Hebdo Massacre: Are the Worst Really Full of Passionate Intensity?" *New Statesman*, January 10. https://www.newstatesman.com/world-affairs/2015/01/slavoj-i-ek-charlie-hebdo-massacre-are-worst-really-full-passionate-intensity.

Žižek, Slavoj. 2015b. "Slavoj Žižek on Greece: This Is a Chance for Europe to Awaken." *New Statesman*, July 6. https://www.newstatesman.com/politics/2015/07/Slavoj-Zizek-greece-chance-europe-awaken.

Žižek, Slavoj. 2015c. "Capitalism Has Broken Free of the Shackles of Democracy." *Financial Times*, February 1. https://www.ft.com/content/088ee78e-7597-11e4-a1a9-00144feabdc0.

Žižek, Slavoj. 2015d. "The Need to Traverse the Fantasy." *In These Times*, December 28. http://inthesetimes.com/article/18722/Slavoj-Zizek-on-Syria-refugees-Eurocentrism-Western-Values-Lacan-Islam.

Žižek, Slavoj. 2016a. *Against the Double Blackmail*. https://www.youtube.com/watch?v=TnGG5xW9_9Y. Accessed 22 June, 2017.

Žižek, Slavoj. 2016b. "Dear Britain: Elena Ferrante, Slavoj Žižek and Other European Writers on Brexit." *The Guardian*, June 4. https://www.theguardian.com/books/2016/jun/04/dear-britain-letters-from-europe-referendum.

Žižek, Slavoj. 2016c. "Disorder under the Heaven." *DiEM25* (blog), June 26. https://diem25.org/disorder-under-the-heaven/.

Žižek, Slavoj. 2016d. *Refugees, Terror and Other Troubles with the Neighbors: Against the Double Blackmail*. London: Penguin Random House.

Žižek, Slavoj. 2016e. "Slavoj Žižek on Brexit, the Crisis of the Left, and the Future of Europe." *OpenDemocracy*, June 30. https://www.opendemocracy.net/en/can-europe-make-it/slavoj-i-ek-on-brexit-crisis-of-left-and-future-of-eur/.

Žižek, Slavoj. 2016f. *Disparities*. New York: Bloomsbury.

Žižek, Slavoj. 2016g. "No Way Out? Communism in the New Century." In *The Idea of Communism 3: The Seoul Conference*, edited by Alex Taek-Gwang Lee and Slavoj Žižek, 240–57. London: Verso.

Žižek, Slavoj. 2016h. "The Seeds of Imagination." In *An American Utopia: Dual Power and the Universal Army*, by Fredric Jameson, edited by Slavoj Žižek, 267–308. London: Verso.

Žižek, Slavoj. 2017a. *The Courage of Hopelessness: Chronicles of a Year of Acting Dangerously*. New York: Allen Lane.

Žižek, Slavoj. 2017b. "Lessons from the 'Airpocalypse.'" *In These Times*, January 10. http://inthesetimes.com/article/19787/spaceship-earth-lessons-of-airpocalypse-slavoj-zizek-climate-ecology-smog.

Žižek, Slavoj. 2017c. *The Incontinence of the Void: Economico-Philosophical Spandrels*. Cambridge: MIT Press.

Žižek, Slavoj. 2017d. "An Interview with Slavoj Žižek: The Belated Actuality of Lenin." Interview by Agon Hamza and Frank Ruda. *Crisis & Critique* 4, no. 2: 429–48.

Žižek, Slavoj. 2018a. "The Yellow Vest Protesters Revolting against Centrism Mean Well—but Their Left Wing Populism Won't Change French Politics." *The Independent*, December 17. https://www.independent.co.uk/voices/yellow-vest-protests-france-paris-gilets-jaunes-macron-fuel-tax-minimum-wage-populism-a8686586.html.

Žižek, Slavoj. 2018b. *Like a Thief in Broad Daylight: Power in the Era of Post-humanity*. London: Penguin.

Žižek, Slavoj. 2018c. "Marx Reads Object-Oriented Ontology." In *Reading Marx*, edited by Slavoj Žižek, Frank Ruda, and Agon Hamza, 17–61. Cambridge: Polity Press.

Žižek, Slavoj. 2019a. "More on *Joker*: From Apolitical Nihilism to a New Left, or Why Trump Is No Joker." *Philosophical Salon*, November 11. https://thephilosophicalsalon.com/more-on-joker-from-apolitical-nihilism-to-a-new-left-or-why-trump-is-no-joker/.

Žižek, Slavoj. 2019b. "Yes, It Is a Climate Crisis. And Your Tiny Human Efforts Have Never Seemed So Meagre." *The Independent*, September 4. https://www.independent.co.uk/voices/amazon-fires-rainforest-capitalism-bolsonaro-climate-crisis-zizek-a9091966.html.

Žižek, Slavoj. 2019c. "Greta Thunberg Is No Genius—She's an Apostle." *The Spectator*, October 4. https://spectator.us/greta-thunberg-genius-apostle/.

Žižek, Slavoj. 2019d. "Morales Proved in Bolivia That Democratic Socialism Can Work – but the People Cannot Be Ignored." *The Independent*, November 19. https://www.independent.co.uk/voices/bolivia-protests-coup-evo-morales-socialism-election-religion-a9208871.html.

Žižek, Slavoj. 2019e. "The 'Planetary Health Diet'—or Communism through the Backdoor?" *Spectator Life*, March 12. https://life.spectator.co.uk/articles/the-planetary-health-diet-or-communism-through-the-backdoor/.

Žižek, Slavoj. 2019f. "'System Deadlock': Joker Artistically Diagnoses Modern World's Ills." *RT*, November 3. https://www.rt.com/news/472541-joker-movie-horror-violence-Žižek/.

Žižek, Slavoj. 2020a. "Both the Hard Right and Liberal Left Are Steeped In Racism and Its Legacy. The Hope for Change Comes from Elsewhere." *The Independent*, June 9.

Žižek, Slavoj. 2020b. *Pandemic! COVID-19 Shakes the* World. New York: OR Books.

Žižek, Slavoj. 2020c. "May 1 in the Viral World Is a Holiday for the New Working Class." *RT News*, May 1. https://www.rt.com/op-ed/487517-slavoj-zizek-new-working-class/.

Žižek, Slavoj. 2020d. "Greta and Bernie Should Be Leading in These Troubled Times, but They Are Not Radical Enough." *RT International*, June 15. https://www.rt.com/op-ed/491881-bernie-sanders-greta-thunberg/.

Žižek, Slavoj. 2020e. "The Simple Things That Are Hard to Do." *Philosophical Salon*, July 20. https://thephilosophicalsalon.com/the-simple-things-that-are-hard-to-do/.

Žižek, Slavoj. 2020f. "Power, Appearance, and Obscenity: Five Reflections." *Philosophical Salon*, June 22. https://thephilosophicalsalon.com/power-appearance-and-obscenity-five-reflections/.

Žižek, Slavoj. 2020g. *A Left That Dares to Speak Its Name*. Cambridge: Polity Press.

Žižek, Slavoj. 2020h. *Sex and the Failed Absolute*. New York: Bloomsbury.

Žižek, Slavoj, and Glyn Daly. 2004. *Conversations with Žižek*. Cambridge: Polity Press.

Žižek, Slavoj, and Boris Gunjević. 2012. *God in Pain: Inversions of Apocalypse*. New York: Seven Stories Press.

Žižek, Slavoj, and Srećko Horvat. 2015. *What Does Europe Want? The Union and Its Discontents*. New York: Columbia University Press.

Žižek, Slavoj, and John Milbank. 2009. *The Monstrosity of Christ: Paradox or Dialectic?* Edited by Creston Davis. Cambridge, MA: MIT Press.

Žižek, Slavoj, Eric L. Santner, and Kenneth Reinhard. 2006. "Introduction." In *The Neighbor: Three Inquiries in Political Theology*, edited by Slavoj Žižek, Eric L. Santner, and Kenneth Reinhard, 1–10. Chicago: University of Chicago Press.

Index